LAND SCAPING YOUR HOME

WM. R. NELSON JR.

UNIVERSITY OF ILLINOIS COLLEGE OF AGRICULTURE COOPERATIVE EXTENSION SERVICE   CIRCULAR 858

Chapters

Issued in furtherance of Cooperative Extension Work, Acts of May 8 and June 30, 1914, in co-operation with the U.S. Department of Agriculture. John B. Claar, *Director*, Cooperative Extension Service, University of Illinois at Urbana-Champaign. Urbana, Illinois, January, 1963. Reprinted with revisions in Chapter 14, November, 1971.

This book is a part of the Landscape Extension Project of the University of Illinois College of Agriculture Cooperative Extension Service

The author wishes to express his sincere thanks to Richard Moores for editing and designing the book, to K. E. Cessna and Carmen Mowry Gilman for the many valuable illustrations, and to Robert Jarnagin for reviewing the original manuscript.

1: YOUR LANDSCAPE NEEDS

Your home deserves the most attractive setting you can give it. When you bought your home, you provided for your family's comfort and convenience by choosing a house with adequate sleeping areas, living areas, and storage space.

It is important to give equal consideration to the space surrounding your home. If you develop this space properly, you can actually extend your living activities into the landscape.

Many homes are either "overlandscaped" or not landscaped at all. You have seen attractive houses without plants or hidden behind a forest of plantings. Many people surround their lot with a fence, and then plant an unrelated collection of trees and shrubs without considering what their final effect will be. This "shotgun" approach demands as much money and effort as an orderly, well-designed landscape.

Merely planting trees and shrubs is not landscaping. Designing a landscape is an art — the growing of plants is a craft. Landscaping means creating a plan to make the best use of the space available in the most attractive way. It means shaping the land to make the most of the site's natural advantages. It means building such necessary structures as fences, walls, and patios. Finally, it means selecting and growing the plants that best fit the design.

The smaller the home grounds, the greater the need for proper planning. Every square foot of space and every dollar must be made to produce maximum results. A skilled landscape architect can help you solve problems too involved for you to handle. He is trained in art and design, and has a sound understanding of ground forms and related engineering and site-development principles. He knows about the use and culture of plant materials. He also has the ability to design needed structures so that they will be in harmony with the other elements of the landscape plan.

The function of landscape architecture is to create and preserve beauty and make the surroundings useful at the same time. A landscape architect does not sell plants or actually execute the plan. His sole responsibility is to design a plan within the terms of agreement with his client. This plan may contain detailed construction and planting designs that will be carried out by the nurseryman or contractor. Either the landscape architect or the client may supervise the job.

A nurseryman is also important in home-landscape development. Reputable nurserymen are licensed by the state, and are usually members of their state and national professional organizations. A nurseryman will supply plant materials, and will plant according to the landscape architect's plan. He can advise and assist in the culture and maintenance of your plantings, and sell you vigorous, high-quality stock.

Successful landscape planning involves three considerations. First, you should consider your lot or site as a cube of space, very much like a room. The ground is its floor and your property lines are its walls. The ceiling is the canopy created by structures, tree plantings, or the sky. A good landscaping plan is developed in terms of these three dimensions.

Next, study the floor plan, window locations, and primary living areas of your house so that there is a relationship between living and service areas in the house and similar areas out of doors. Finally, consider the design from outside the house as viewed by yourself and by others.

Your final landscape plan will depend upon your lot and its orientation to wind and sun, your house

Attractive homes are often hidden because of overlandscaping. Planning your landscape design before buying plants will save you money in the initial cost of plants, and you will not need to remove overgrown material in 10 to 15 years.

plan, the amount of money, time, and effort you want to spend on maintenance, your family's interests and activities, and even the neighborhood itself.

Try to preserve all of the best natural resources of the site, such as trees, brooks or streams, good soil, rock outcroppings, and turf. Carefully study good as well as bad views. Keep attractive views open and framed for greatest value. Screen out unattractive and objectionable views either by structures or by proper plantings. Develop pleasing lawn and planting areas in relation to the views from the main rooms in the house.

Sunshine, rain, snow, wind, heat, and cold will influence your landscape design. Consider plantings that give protection from the summer sun and also allow warmth from the winter sun, wind barriers (fences or plantings) to reduce winds in the outdoor living areas, and grades to carry rain and melted snow away from the house and garden structures.

The main rooms of the house should benefit from both winter sun and summer breezes. When you plan what shade you will need to modify the extremes of the sun, consider possible shade from your neighbors' trees and houses as well as shade from your own trees and house. Carefully plot future shade patterns

from trees to keep sunny areas for gardens and shady areas for house and patio.

An inventory of your family activities will help you in planning the overall layout and use of your land. Allow space for outdoor living needs, the children's play area, and the service area. If your family does not want to spend much time puttering around the yard, keep the design simple and the plantings of the type that do not need much care. Base your planning efforts on how much time you can give to your garden and how much money you can spend to develop your property.

It is certainly not necessary for you to complete your total design all at once. Your first job is to put on paper what your development will include when it is completed. Then, as money is available to finish different sections, these sections will fit into the total picture. Completing the entire plan could take five years or more.

Many families have found it helpful to include a set amount each year in their regular budgets for landscaping purposes. Whether this amount is 50 or 500 dollars, it can be made to go a long way when you know exactly what is to be done, how much you can buy, and how much you can do yourself.

You will also need to consider the vegetation already on your property. If you have heavy woods, you are fortunate. But it may take courage to remove unnecessary or undesirable plants. Trees growing in a heavy woods usually become tall, spindly, and poorly shaped because of competition with other trees for light, food, and moisture. Removal of the poorer trees will allow the better ones to develop their natural form and become handsome additions to the total picture. If you have only a few trees on your property, you should protect them against damage during construction.

Geographical location and climate largely determine the plants you can use. For example, people living in southern Illinois or Indiana are able to use many plant materials that will not grow successfully in northern Illinois or Indiana. Place plants that will grow successfully in shade on the north and east sides of your house. Locate shade trees where they will best shade the house, terrace, and outdoor living areas.

Decide how much privacy you will need to make your outdoor living areas useful for family life. Study total lot area and its relationship to the neighborhood to determine whether you should screen or frame a view. Consider the proximity of your neighbors, the height of the surrounding land, and views of your property from other yards.

Soil type will affect your choice of design and plants. It is easiest to work with those plants best suited to your particular type of soil. You also need to know whether your soil is wet or dry. Poorly drained, wet soil is difficult for any home gardener to work with, and very dry soils limit the kinds of materials that will grow successfully. You must also consider the ability of your soil to support structures. Will subsurface preparations for drainage and footings be extensive?

Your family is probably the most important consideration in planning your landscape garden. An inventory of your family's needs will tell you which basic elements will make a livable, useful, and attractive setting for your home.

For example, if you have small children, you will probably want to locate their play equipment (sandbox, teeter-totter, etc.) so that you can supervise the children from the kitchen. If your family likes lawn games, then you should certainly leave an open area for favorite games.

You might want to develop the total landscape picture to encourage such hobbies as bird watching,

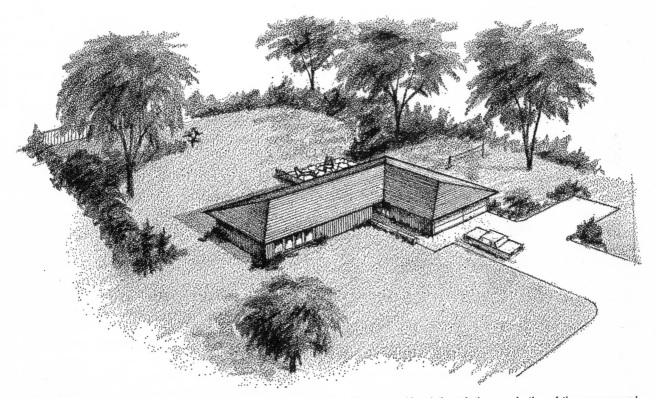

Function and beauty are the two requirements of landscape architecture. These are achieved through the organization of the space around the house into "use" areas. If possible, there should be close communication between living and service areas within the house and living and service areas out-of-doors. Make the best use of available space to create a landscape into which you can extend your living.

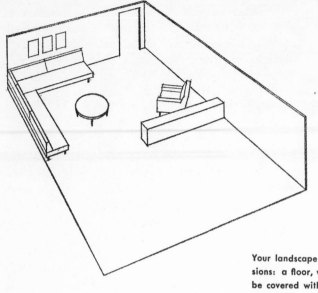

If protection from insects at night is important to you, you will want to consider some kind of screening for your terrace or patio. How often does the family want to live outdoors for family cookouts, entertaining, or simple relaxation? If your main interest is entertaining, then the terrace or patio should be large enough to accommodate more than the family itself. A smaller paved area would be enough for your own relaxation and enjoyment.

Do you want to grow vegetables? It is usually best to locate a vegetable garden near the service area. Do you want a garden to grow cut flowers? This special type of garden is difficult to incorporate into a landscape development. Perhaps you should also

Your landscape can be compared to a room in your house. Each has three dimensions: a floor, walls, and a ceiling. The floor of your landscape is the earth. It may be covered with lawn, ground cover, or hard surfacing materials. The walls of your landscape are structures, shrub borders, etc., and the ceiling is formed by the horizontal plane of an overhead structure and the canopy of tree branches, as well as by the sky itself.

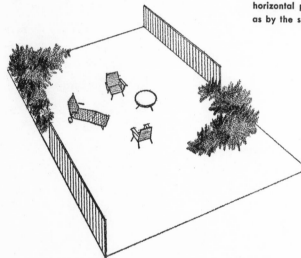

locate a cutting-flower garden in the service area where the plants can be put in rows especially for cutting.

Will you need to store equipment? Many new homes are built on a slab with only a small utility room in which to store gardening equipment. If your garage or utility room is not large enough to hold all of your yard equipment, you may want to consider building a garden and storage shelter.

This partial inventory of family interests will help you organize your thinking. A list of your wants and needs will be very helpful in fashioning your final

collecting butterflies, or growing specimen flowers for arrangements or garden club competitions.

If gardening is a family hobby, you might consider a greenhouse for raising plants during the winter or starting seedlings early in the spring. If your family has little interest in gardening or yard work, you will want to plan for minimum maintenance time.

The frequency with which you entertain is also a consideration. For example, a socially active family might give special attention to parking needs. If your property is large enough, or if you are located in a rural area, you might want to set aside a special area for guest cars so that they will not block traffic in your drive or lane. If you plan to entertain outdoors during the warm months, you should plan a place for this entertainment.

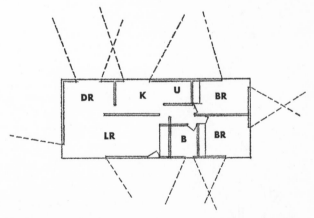

A drawing of the floor plan of your house will help you decide upon the views from each room that should be screened and the views that should be featured. If you do not have interesting views from the living areas of the house, you will want to create them. A floor plan will also help you establish a correlation between living areas in the house and "use" areas out-of-doors.

landscaping plan. It will tell you how to spend your time, money, and effort most wisely, and will certainly help you to develop a well-integrated living environment, both inside and outside the home.

You should also inventory your liabilities. An unsightly view on neighboring property demands a planting that will screen it out, and create an interesting scene on your own property at the same time. You will also need to consider screening for privacy from your neighbors. One consideration is the height of surrounding land and houses. You can screen by fencing and by skillful placement of shrubs and trees.

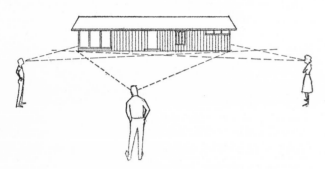

To determine the most effective means of blending your house to its site, study the views outside your house from the street and the views from the rear of your house. Note on your plan those areas that require attention.

Another possible liability is the orientation of your lot and house. Do you need to modify the climate and temperature? A house built on a high elevation may catch winds that need to be modified by barrier plantings, windbreaks, or fences. Carefully placed trees will shade and protect outdoor areas as well as living areas within the house.

Flat or sloping ground can be an asset or a liability. Grade changes are not necessarily a liability. They offer many chances to create an interesting design. A very steep slope is a liability, however, because it tends to erode under heavy rains. It needs a heavy ground cover for protection, or terraces and retaining walls to get additional level area and to eliminate erosion.

Completely flat ground can also cause gardening problems because it lacks surface drainage. Flat ground often demands special grading to help move excess water to underground sumps or lower areas on the property.

The relative acidity or alkalinity, texture, humus content, and drainage of the soil need to be investigated. Soils that are extremely acid or alkaline restrict plant growth. A very heavy clay soil will drain poorly and keep needed air from the plant roots. For easy maintenance, it is best to choose plants that will tolerate your particular soil condition.

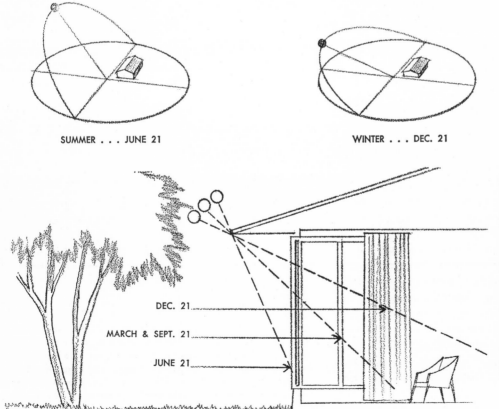

SUMMER . . . JUNE 21

WINTER . . . DEC. 21

DEC. 21

MARCH & SEPT. 21

JUNE 21

Trees and shrubs can serve dual functions in a landscape. They add beauty and interest in line, form, color, and texture, and they provide screening and enclosure for climate control. Notice the angle of the summer sun as compared with that of the winter sun. The placement of the tree not only gives background to the house but also protects the house from the summer sun, while allowing the winter sun to reach the house for important solar heat.

The family inventory can be broken down into three divisions: quiet living, active living, and working activities. The primary basis for your design should be your family's interests.

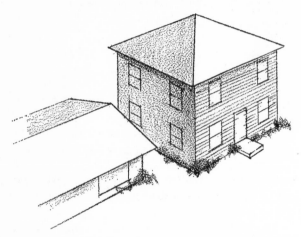

The height of surrounding land and neighbors' houses are important considerations in obtaining privacy from above as well as on a level. Also study the shade patterns cast by nearby structures. These shade areas are important in selecting plants.

Trees and other vegetation already growing on the property can be considered assets. Don't be afraid to take out excess trees so that the remaining specimens will develop their most beautiful form. You may want to leave some native vegetation, but be sure that it fits the overall plan. If it doesn't, take it out and add more suitable ornamental plantings.

A distant view can create an interesting focal point in the landscape. Special treatment is usually necessary to frame this view. If the view is made up primarily of vertical elements (groves of trees, mountains, buildings, etc.), the framing material should also have dominant vertical lines. A view composed mostly of horizontal elements (low, rolling hills, lakes, cultivated land, etc.) should be framed with low shrub borders that project at right angles from the side planting to repeat the horizontal character of the view. You may want to screen part of a nearby view to focus attention on a distant view.

Such water features as a stream or brook, or rock outcroppings are natural objects that will modify the design of your landscape plan. Feature and accent these objects. Their potential design qualities are most desirable in developing any landscape picture.

Don't overlook the chance to use a pleasant adjoining environment. For example, if your house borders a golf course, a large park area, or any other landscape development, you have an opportunity to use all of this extra lawn area to give a feeling of space.

Look at your inventory often as you work out your landscaping plan. It will help you to organize your thinking and give you an orderly approach to the greatest enjoyment and use of your indoor-outdoor living area.

Each family's needs are different. Include in your plan only those family interests that will make the living space, both inside and out, most livable and useful for your family. This plan will tell you what you have to work with. You can then determine the space needed for lawn, patio or terrace, game or play area, and planting area.

Your final plan will take the guesswork out of landscaping. It will tell you which landscape elements should be added to those already established by the family inventory. Although you may have to complete the plan in stages, you will be working toward a final, well-organized design.

2: STARTING YOUR PLAN

Any good landscaping design is planned on the basis of three major areas: the public area, the living area, and the service area.

Working out the design on paper is very helpful. It is amazing how ideas will develop and mistakes show up on a plan. The more accurate you are, the more effectively your plan will serve its basic function: to control the physical forms (structures, slopes, grades, plants, etc.) and the actual arrangements of these forms on the ground according to basic design principles. Careful measurement insures that, when you execute the design later, specific areas will be in scale and in proper proportion to the actual space on the ground. You may need to use a tape. Be sure that the tape is held tight without a sag.

For outdoor measurements, draw a rough sketch of the property and of the shape of the house on a sheet of paper. Allow enough space to jot down the measurements as you make them. Some of the features that should be measured include the setback distance of the house, the walk and drive locations, and locations of such other permanent features as sewer lines, septic tank, trees, and other plantings. In measuring from the building, always measure straight out at a right angle from the corner of the building. You can sight down the side of the house to make sure you are measuring at right angles.

Put the floor plan of the house on graph paper. You can buy graph paper with various scales at most stationery or book stores. A scale of ⅛-, ¼-, or 1/16-inch equal to 1 foot will allow you to use a standard ruler.

Draw bedrooms, living room, kitchen, and other rooms to scale on your plan. Mark all windows and doors. Add the outdoor measurements of the walks, drive, and plantings. This helps you to visualize the relationship between the house and the lot. You will want to try to locate certain service activities near the kitchen and utility areas. You will also want a pleasing picture from the family room and the living areas. Fasten a sheet of tracing paper over your basic house and lot plan. This "overlay" will allow you to try out various arrangements.

The public area lies between the road and the house. It is exposed to the full view of the public. The first impression of your house is the street-side design. Each house on your block adds to or detracts from the appearance of the street. Elements that make up the public area, or the front yard, include the walks to the front door, the drive and possible parking areas, tree plantings, shrub plantings, and lawn areas.

The most important item in the public area is the front door. This is the focal point of the design for the area, and the spot you will want to feature and make attractive. The walk that leads your guests to the front door is an important design element. Its location, scale, and form deserve serious study.

Walk location greatly affects the appearance of the public area. For example, an uninterrupted front lawn creates an illusion of depth in the foreground between the street and the house. A walk leading from the road to the front entrance cuts the lawn in two, and gives a strong, harsh line that divides the front-lawn area into sections or panels. This division is often repeated by the driveway. A broad, expansive lawn area undivided by these elements gives a more spacious and pleasing setting for your home. The best walk location is parallel to the front of the house connecting the front porch or entrance with the driveway.

With this walk location, the driveway should be wide enough to serve as the walk from the street, and should always run into the street at right angles so that the driver can see traffic clearly in both directions before he enters the street. Plantings at this point are not necessary to call attention to the entrance, and often obstruct the driver's view of the street.

If you want to outline the drive when snow has drifted across it, drive lengths of scrap pipe into the ground 15 to 20 feet apart flush with the turf. Then fit metal rods or wooden dowels into these ground pipes. Paint the tips of the rods or dowels with black, red, or fluorescent paint. Take them out in summer. Since you want the driveway to be as inconspicuous as possible in the total design, *do not* outline it with painted rocks, plantings, hedges, or flowers.

Driveway width will vary according to your needs and the total area available. Usually 10 feet is wide enough when the drive is surfaced with a permanent material. If you want a circular drive, you will need a width of 14 to 18 feet in the curved section so that moving cars can pass those parked on the curve.

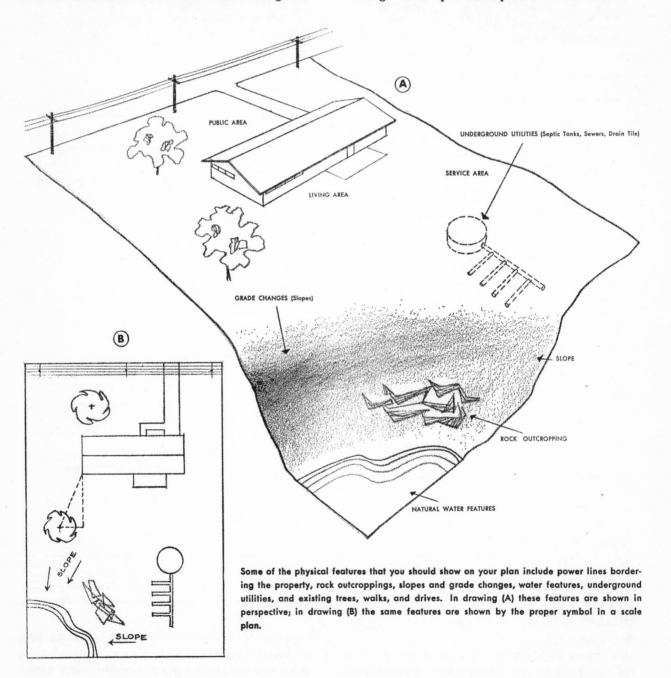

Some of the physical features that you should show on your plan include power lines bordering the property, rock outcroppings, slopes and grade changes, water features, underground utilities, and existing trees, walks, and drives. In drawing (A) these features are shown in perspective; in drawing (B) the same features are shown by the proper symbol in a scale plan.

The Landscape Architect's Sign Language

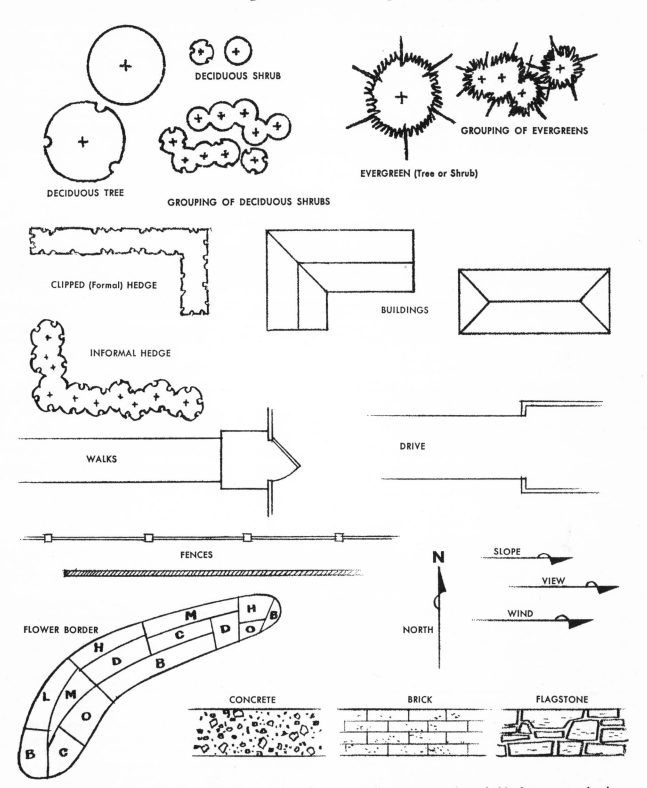

Each symbol represents a physical feature, and is used as a graphic representation of this feature on the base plan. These symbols (especially plants, structures, walks, and drives) should be drawn to scale on the plan. Show the mature size for plants; for example, the symbol for a deciduous tree should represent its mature spread. Letters such as shown for the "flower border" are often used as a key for a flower planting plan.

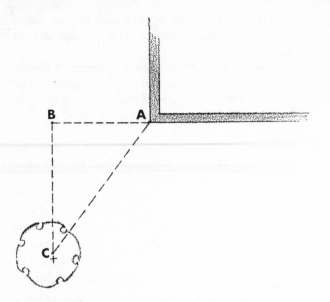

Locate physical features accurately for plotting to scale on your plan. For objects beyond the corners of the house, take a measurement from the corner of the house (A) to a point (B), which is at right angles to the object. Take another right-angle measurement from (B) to locate the object (C). To check your accuracy, take a third measurement from (C) to (A).

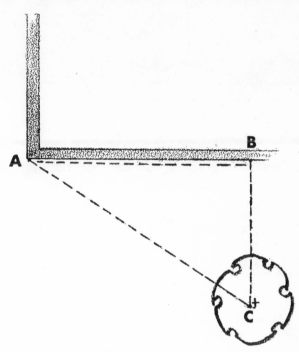

To locate objects between the corners of the house, measure from point (A) along the house to point (B), where a right-angle line intersects the object (C). Then measure the distance from (B) to (C). To check your accuracy, measure from (C) to the corner of the house (A).

For a two-car garage on a city lot, you may have to hold the width of the drive to a minimum of 8 to 10 feet and then flare to the width of the door openings. This leaves an area between door and corner for planting.

Tree plantings make up the third design element in the composition of the public area. Trees in the front-yard area serve to frame the front view of the house.

Always use a large lawn shade tree to frame a two-story house — a small flowering tree makes the house look taller. Select only those trees that branch high enough so that you can still see the house from the street below the canopy of foliage. Houses facing the south or west may need more than one large shade tree for adequate protection from the afternoon sun. In this case, you will need several large, high-headed trees at the front. Hold them to the sides of the house as much as possible to avoid hiding the front of the house from the road or sidewalk.

Foundation planting or the planting across the front of the house is the fourth design element. This planting serves to complement the house design and to tie the house to the site or ground. Since the house is the most important part of the public-area design, the foundation plantings should not compete with it.

The final design element of the public area is the lawn. The lawn serves as the connecting link between all the other elements. It ties these elements into a single composition and gives a broad, expansive setting to the house. A lawn unbroken by planting, walks, or special features will do this best. Island flower beds, gazing balls, bird baths, painted tractor tires with petunias, flamingo birds, and other novelties have no place in the front lawn. The next time you drive past a house with any of these novelties in front, notice that the novelty, not the house and its complementary foundation planting, catches your eye. The novelty breaks the cardinal rule that the house is the most important part of the design.

Next, locate the private or outdoor living area on your tracing-paper overlay. Recent urban and suburban developments provide so little indoor space that it is desirable to use the space around the home for additional living area and as an extension of the house into the landscape. The trend toward outdoor living has increased interest in this area.

The outdoor area must be easy to get to if it is to be used. For this reason, the best location is usually at the place where the door leads from the house. However, the shape of the property may not allow enough room at the door location, or another side of the house may be better suited climatically for outdoor living.

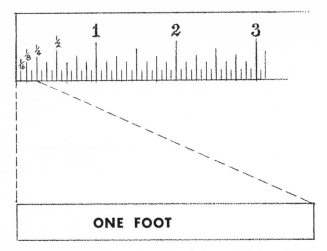

In a scale drawing, a fraction of an inch equals 1 foot. In the sketch above, ¼-inch equals 1 foot.

If possible, locate the living area where you can see it from the living room, family room, or d ng room. Since the living area will be the most highly developed landscape picture in the yard, it should be located so that it can be enjoyed as fully from inside as from outside.

Many design ements go into the de pment of the living area. t all of them can e included in any one landscape. You will want to select those that best meet your family's needs and desires. Some of these design elements are as follows:

1. Enclosure (fences, walls, or screen plantings)
2. Plantings (shrubs, hedges, flower borders, ground cover, trees)
3. Surface areas (patio, terrace, walk, paths, sitting areas, steps)
4. Garden embellishments (barbecue pits, seats, water features, garden furniture, portable planters, sculpture, lighting, objects of art, rocks, raised beds).

Enclosure forms the sides of your outside room. It provides privacy and screens the view from the property. It controls the movement of people and dogs both within and without, and serves as a partial climate control and noise baffle. The enclosure is extremely flexible. It can be high and solid to screen out neighbors or unsightly views, or it can be low and solid, or high and of open design when you want the garden to be seen.

Plantings are important, although they are not the only unit of design in the landscape. All plants — annuals, perennials, woody shrubs, and trees — are important elements used to create interest as individual plants or as a mass of material. They provide a pleasing, refreshing, and soul-satisfying setting around a home. The number of plants you use de-

pends upon your interest in gardening or your desire for a garden that needs as little maintenance as possible.

Surfaced areas have become prominent design units in an outdoor living area. If you consider the ground surface as the floor of the outdoor room, you will want material that prevents weeds, dust, heat reflection, mud, and dirt.

The basic surfacing types are (1) paving for heavy traffic; (2) lawn for medium traffic; (3) sawdust, tanbark, sand, and gravel materials for little-used areas; (4) ground covers where no one will walk; and (5) flower- and shrub-bed areas. Patterns formed by each of these surfacing elements add greatly to the total composition. To avoid too busy a picture, consider surfaces along with detailing and design of the enclosure and shelter elements. Simple forms and patterns are best.

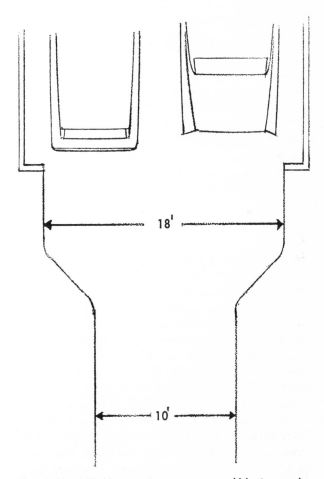

If a double-width drive to a two-car garage would be too massive in the public area, the drive could be held to an 8- to 10-foot width and flared to the width of the door openings close to the garage. Always hold the paved drive to the width of the door openings to allow for garage corner plantings.

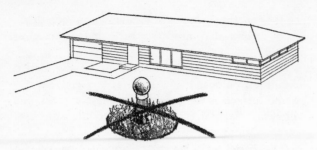

A broad expanse of lawn uninterrupted by bird baths, island flower beds, flamingos, and other novelties is the best possible setting for your house. Banish all novelties from your public area. They detract from the thing you want to emphasize most — your house.

Garden embellishments are comparable to home furnishings and accessories. For example, pictures, lamps, and decorator items are used to complement, accent, and contrast with the basic furnishings of the home. Rather than adding superfluous beauty to an already well-designed area, you will want to select, design, and detail each item to be a part of the total landscape. Use only those items important to the types of activity in which your family will take part.

The third landscape area is the service or utility area. All of the utilities that can be screened by a fence should be assigned to this area. It may not be practicable to group everything together, since each presents a separate problem.

Garbage cans should be located close to the house for convenience, but far enough away to avoid odors and to allow for adequate structural screening.

Most homes need clotheslines, even with a drier. Lines that are not used much can be placed some distance from the house. Many types of lines allow the center post standard to be removed. The surface beneath the lines should be of material that will not soil the clothes if they should fall.

The clothes-drying area can be combined with a vegetable or cut-flower garden. You can also work storage space into the area for the odds and ends needed for garden work. Compost piles and garden work benches can also be provided in the area.

The amount of available space will determine to a great extent the screening for this particular area. A fence is superior to plants as a visual barrier when space is limited. The line of the fence depends upon the design of the rest of the area. It can be in straight lines, angled, serpentine, or curved. Overall landscape layout best determines the actual lines of the fence. The fence is a basic part of the landscape, and its placement, function, and design serve to emphasize a line, create space, or define an area.

In later chapters, you will be working out your landscape design in detail, but at this point it may be well to think more specifically about those items that will go into the living and service areas.

You will use the living area for a variety of activities, depending upon your family's interests. You may use it for reading, sitting, sunbathing, entertaining (dancing, cookouts), or for lawn sports, such as badminton and croquet. You may want to locate the children's sandbox, swings, and teeter-totter in this area; or you may want to use part of it for hobby gardening.

The following check list will help you decide what landscaping elements or garden embellishments will be located in the living area. Since you may change your mind later, check the items lightly with a pencil so that the marks can be erased easily.

Shrubs . . . . ———

Trees . . . . ———

Ground cover . . . . ———

Hedges . . . . ———

Flowers . . . . ———

Patio or terrace . . . . ———

Lawn . . . . ———

Walks . . . . ———

Paths . . . . ———

Steps . . . . ———

Trailer parking area . . . . ———

Water features . . . . ———

Barbecue pit . . . . ———

Garden furniture . . . . ———

Portable planters . . . . ———

Sculpture or objects of art . . . . . . ———

Rocks or boulders............. ____

Lighting .... ____

Raised planting beds.......... ____

Fences .... ____

Walls................... ____

Screen plantings .... ____

The service or utility area will contain several items that are not landscaping elements, but which you will need to consider in making your plan. The check list below will help you determine which of these items you may want in the service area.

Place to hang laundry........ ____

Vegetable or small-fruit garden.. ____

Garbage pail .... ____

Incinerator................ ____

Cold frame or greenhouse...... ____

Potting bench .... ____

Compost pile .... ____

Cut-flower garden .... ____

Storage for garden tools....... ____

The following check list contains items that may be located in either the living or service areas.

Portable wading pool......... ____

Sandbox .... ____

Swings..................... ____

Teeter-totter................ ____

Slide .... ____

Other play equipment........ ____

Badminton area .... ____

Croquet area .... ____

Volleyball area .... ____

Basketball area .... ____

These check lists are designed to clarify your thinking as to the items that will go into the living and service areas. As you develop your plan in detail, you may discover that you will want to move certain items from one area to the other. For example, you may plan to locate the children's play equipment in the living area, and later decide to move this equipment to the service area so that the children can be supervised from the kitchen. It is a good idea to refer to these check lists frequently while working out your landscape design.

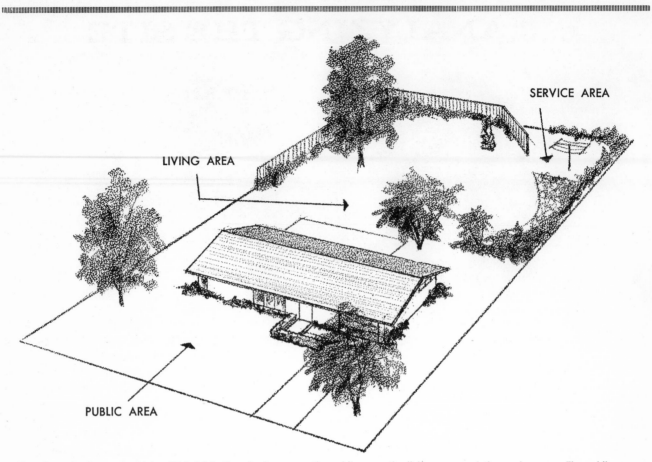

Your home landscape should be divided into three basic areas — the public area, the living area, and the service area. The public area is located from the street to the house. The living area is located at the rear of the property. It should provide privacy and enclosure, and may include a patio, plantings, and sculpture. The service area can be located to the side or rear of the property, depending upon the elements to be included and the frequency with which it will be used.

3: ANALYZING THE SITE

The character of your land — its slopes and plains or hills and valleys — will determine the basic landscape design.

Do not start your landscape design without first considering the original shape of the surface on which it will be worked out. Before moving into the details of the three major landscaping areas and proposed plantings, you will need to study the natural ground forms. Look for their inherent beauty and decide how you can adapt existing grades so that they will be beautiful as well as usable for family living.

Consider the ground forms on your property as a part of similar ground formations in your locality. One of the first requirements in site development is to keep enough of present elevations, forms, and shapes of the land so that your overall design stays in harmony with other nearby land forms. Think of your land as one unit of the area, not as an "island" unrelated to the surrounding areas.

Try to preserve the natural features of the land. But don't try to condense on your small area all the patterns that nature has exhibited around you. Instead, try to make the best use of the topography that presently exists on your property.

Grading can change or emphasize these natural features. Your family inventory will tell you whether you want a patio, a children's play area, areas for lawn games or passive recreation, or areas for special garden hobbies. In some cases, you may want to change the ground form in order to have certain activities. In other cases, you may want to locate an activity on a part of the site already adapted for maximum usefulness and beauty.

Your site does not end with the property boundaries. Consider the areas beyond your property boundaries as the extensional site and landscape. As you study the natural ground forms on the site, draw on your plan the main elements of the surrounding area, as well as the features on your own site. These observations and notes will help you to understand the relationships of your land to neighboring property and to decide which elements to preserve and which elements to remove, screen, or in some way de-emphasize.

The check list below will help you analyze your site. Go through the list and check "yes" or "no" for each question. A "no" indicates that nothing needs to be done about that item. A "yes" means that the condition needs improving or that it will be an important consideration in designing your plan. Then write down on a separate sheet of paper what needs to be done for each "yes" answer. For example, if you checked "yes" for numbers 1, 2, and 5 (among others) your notes might read:

1. *Straighten driveway, so that it will come into the street at a right angle.*

2. *Make sidewalk wider so that two people can walk side by side.*

5. *Shrubs are too close to rear door. Move them to a different place or discard them.*

The following list includes most of the things you will need to consider about your site. You will probably want to add others. For your convenience, those chapters in which the items are discussed are listed beside the various categories.

WALKS AND DRIVES (Chapters 2, 4, 5, 10)

1. Does the walk or drive need to be relocated for greater convenience or attractiveness? Yes_____ No_____

2. Does either need to be made wider? Yes_____ No_____

3. Does water drain onto them? Yes_____ No_____

STRUCTURES, existing or proposed (Chapters 4, 5)
(shelter, patio, terrace, fences or walls)

4. Can the locations be improved? Yes_____ No_____

5. Can access to the structures be improved? Yes_____ No_____

6. Does the location of the structures affect plantings? Yes_____ No_____

7. Is more protection needed against sun and wind? Yes_____ No_____

8. Are any of the structures too large or too small in relation to the lot? Yes_____ No_____

9. Can the construction materials be made to blend with the surroundings? Yes_____ No_____

DRAINAGE (Chapter 3)

10. Is drainage poor from the house or from other structures and areas? Yes_____ No_____

11. Is there a natural slope that can be used for septic-tank drainage? Yes_____ No_____

12. Is there drainage from a neighbor's property? Yes_____ No_____

13. Is there drainage onto a neighbor's property? Yes_____ No_____

EXISTING VEGETATION (Chapters 1, 3)

14. Do some trees need to be removed or changed? Yes_____ No_____

15. Do some shrubs need to be removed or changed? Yes_____ No_____

16. Is there a need for ground cover? Yes_____ No_____

17. Does the lawn need to be improved? Yes_____ No_____

SOIL (Chapters 3, 6)

18. Does topsoil need to be added? Yes_____ No_____

19. Is your soil too acid or alkaline? (See the county extension office about a soil test.) Yes_____ No_____

20. Does the structure of the soil present a problem (either too much clay or too much sand)? Yes_____ No_____

21. Does drainage need improvement? Yes_____ No_____

22. Should humus be added? Yes_____ No_____

23. Does your soil need fertilizers? (See the county extension office about a soil test.) Yes_____ No_____

EXTENSIONAL LANDSCAPE (Chapters 1, 2, 3)

24. Do you want to change your neighbor's view of your property? Yes_____ No_____

25. Do you need to frame a good view or to screen a bad one? Yes_____ No_____

26. Are noises from a nearby boundary road a problem? Yes_____ No_____

27. Are there adjoining pleasant areas (golf course, park, grove of trees, etc.) that you can take advantage of in your plan? Yes_____ No_____

28. Do you need more protection and privacy in the public area? Yes_____ No_____

29. Do you need more protection and privacy in the living area? Yes_____ No_____

NATURAL FEATURES (Chapters 1, 3)

30. Are there bodies of water or rock outcroppings on your land that you may want to feature? Yes_____ No_____

31. Are there sunken areas that you may need to grade and fill? Yes_____ No_____

32. Are there eroded areas that need attention? Yes_____ No_____

33. Do you have steep slopes that require retaining walls or special plantings? Yes_____ No_____

34. Do you have a slope that prevents using the yard for lawn games? Yes_____ No_____

35. Does your neighbors' ground elevation affect your landscaping? Yes_____ No_____

CLIMATE (Chapters 1, 2, 3, 6)

36. Does the pattern of the sun indicate a need for more shaded areas? Yes_____ No_____

37. Does the prevailing wind (write down the direction of it) mean that you will need protection in certain areas?   Yes_____ No_____

38. Will the temperature extremes in your area (write down the usual maximum and minimum) affect your choice of plantings?   Yes_____ No_____

MICROCLIMATES AROUND BUILDINGS (Chapter 6)

Since these are situations that cannot ordinarily be changed, you cannot answer the following questions with a simple yes or no. Your notes should describe the location and extent of these microclimates so that you can take them into consideration when selecting plantings.

39. What areas are in the shade of buildings?

40. Where are the sunny areas near buildings?

41. Where are the wet areas and the dry areas?

42. What wind patterns caused by the buildings do you need to consider?

43. Where are the frost areas?

Use this check list along with your base plan when you study the site. Attach a sheet of tracing paper firmly over the base plan with masking tape. Put down information on this overlay that relates to your design. Include any changes or modifications that might be made by grading. Sketch in diagrams and measurements of areas that you want to keep "as is."

Other information to put on your overlay might include trees to be removed or retained, low spots that need drainage, off-property nuisances, high and low points, such natural features as shrubs, depth of topsoil, eroded areas, and water features, and any other items that might be important in your proposed project. Use this check list and your tracing-paper notations for adapting, modifying, or eliminating some of the conditions as the design goes along.

The next step is "goose-egg" planning. Put another sheet of tracing paper over the first sheet to sketch in the public, living, and service areas. Do not define the specific shape each area will finally take. Simply rough in the approximate locations of the patio, service area, children's play area, etc. This approach will help you determine the space required for each area, and what changes, if any, need to be made in ground forms.

The land can be altered or modified by grading. Nearly all landscape construction requires some re-shaping of existing ground forms to make the areas more useful. Grading moves earth and remolds, re-forms, and resculptures the land.

If land has less than 5 feet of vertical fall in each 100 feet measured along the ground, it is considered flat land. Although flat land needs least alteration for outdoor use, moving surface water across it may be difficult, and drainage will be poor if there is tight

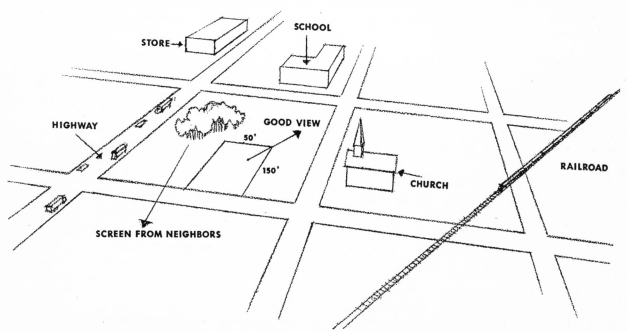

A sound approach to landscape planning is to consider the extensional landscape — those areas beyond your property boundaries. Don't rely on your memory. Make careful observations at the site itself of all features — good and bad — of the total extensional site.

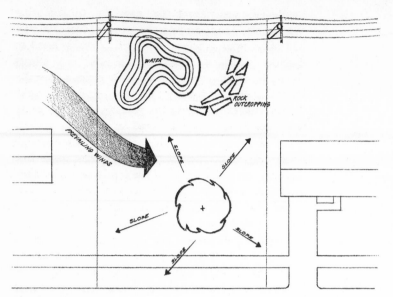

You can best study the site with a scale plan. A plan will help you understand the character of the site and its possibilities for development. Show all natural features (rock outcroppings, water, slope, vegetation, etc.) and man-made features (buildings, walks, drives, etc.) on your plan. If your property has extensive changes in grade, rock outcroppings, etc., a more detailed record of these features, as shown in a topographic survey, may be necessary.

soil beneath it. You may want to change the levels and grades of flat ground to add variety and interest to the landscape design. This might be done through the use of raised planting beds.

People can still move around comfortably on sloping or rolling ground with a fall of up to about 10 feet in 100. Rolling ground offers more opportunity for interesting development than flat ground, but controlling erosion on sloping ground often requires extra construction and grading.

Steep slopes fall more than 10 feet in 100, and are difficult to stand or move around on. Although their soil is likely to be thin and poor, these slopes offer opportunities for dramatic arrangements. The cost of developing steep slopes is considerably higher than the cost of developing rolling or flat ground.

Grading should shape the ground surface so that water will flow away from structures, walks, and surfaced areas. If you have very flat land and tight subsurface soil, you may have to grade so that water will flow into diversion ditches and on into a sump or natural outlet off your property. On the other hand, slopes may move water so fast that it has to be controlled to stop erosion. You can cover steep slopes with vegetation or terrace them with retaining walls.

Grading also fits various elements of the plan to the site. For example, you might have to grade enough level space for the house and for an outdoor living area such as a patio or terrace. You might also have to grade steep slopes to obtain more gentle slopes for walks or driveways.

Finally, grading may create a pleasing site appearance. Such land sculpture tries to take advantage of existing grade changes and build them into

prominent features of the total design. Long, monotonous, straight lines or level ground can be relieved by grading. Grading terraces can make steep slopes more pleasing and useful.

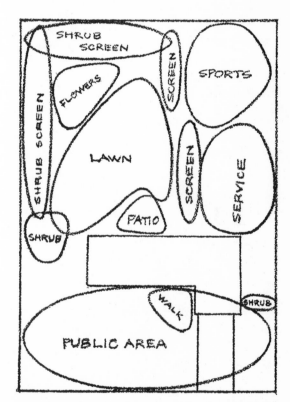

Goose-egg planning. Place an overlay sheet over your base plan. Draw rough shapes on this overlay to indicate assignment of services and activities to various areas on your lot. This assignment should be based generally upon your family's needs and the site analysis. Do not attempt to define the specific form or area each will assume.

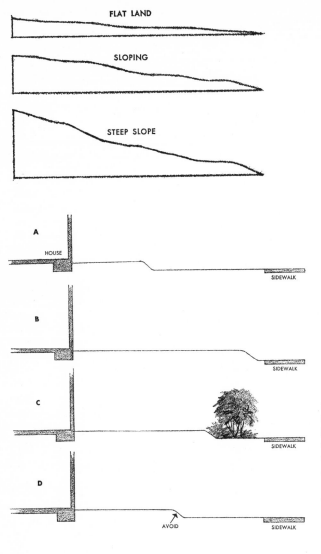

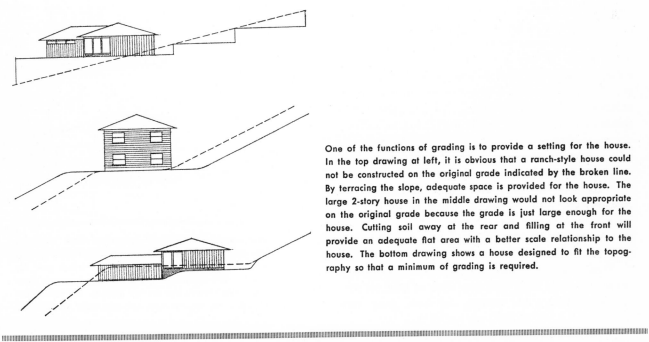

Review your check list carefully to see what changes you are going to make in your landscape that will affect your grading. You will probably need to consider which existing trees, shrubs, and plants should be saved or relocated; where roads and walks should be located for most efficient movement; what grades will be necessary to provide drainage away from new structures but blend in with the general shape of the land; and what utilities and subsurface structures will be needed. For example, a sewer line must fall from the house to the septic tank and then to a drain field, or from the house to the city sewer. Storm drains must carry water from the house to city storm sewers or to a sump for disposal.

When you "remold" your property, try to keep its elevations and forms in harmony with surrounding properties. Control surface drainage especially in relation to neighboring property. You don't want your neighbor's surface water running over your lawn, and your grading must not dump all of your water onto your neighbor's property.

Grading to the front of the house should allow for drainage away from the house and conform to certain standards of design and use. (A) Two level areas have been obtained — the 16-foot terrace area around the house, and the slope to the lower level extending to the sidewalk. If there is not enough space to make the slope gradual, a retaining wall may be required. (B) When the change in grade is made close to the sidewalk, leave a small, level area between the walk and the slope. (C) A 3- to 6-foot level area allows for a planting to screen and soften the abrupt change. (D) Do not divide a space into equal parts with the slope in the middle.

One of the functions of grading is to provide a setting for the house. In the top drawing at left, it is obvious that a ranch-style house could not be constructed on the original grade indicated by the broken line. By terracing the slope, adequate space is provided for the house. The large 2-story house in the middle drawing would not look appropriate on the original grade because the grade is just large enough for the house. Cutting soil away at the rear and filling at the front will provide an adequate flat area with a better scale relationship to the house. The bottom drawing shows a house designed to fit the topography so that a minimum of grading is required.

If your building site is very hilly and has many trees and other natural features, you may want a licensed surveyor to survey it for you. You may have to tell him what kind of survey you want. A property survey gives you the property lines, but a topographic survey also gives contour lines, indicating the relative heights of the land above a known elevation. You may not need this kind of survey if your land is level or nearly level.

A landscape architect, civil engineer, or contractor may use a few technical terms that you should understand. For instance, *rough grading* is done before construction work starts, *subgrade* is the top of the material on which surface construction (pavements, topsoil) rests, and *finished grade* is the final surface after all construction is completed. Excavated material and the resulting space is known as *cut,* and the process is known as *cutting.* When it is necessary to build up existing elevations, the material used and the result are known as *fill.*

Slope ratio is the rate at which a side slope slants from the vertical. In a 20 to 1 (20:1 or 20 in 1) slope ratio, the side slope slants at the rate of 20 units of length horizontally to each unit of height. The expression "the slope had such and such a grade" means the rate of slope between two points expressed as a percentage. A *contour line* is drawn at a constant elevation. Contour lines indicate the shape of the ground surface on a plan. A change in ground form requires changing the contour lines on your plan. Moving a contour line ½ inch on a plan may actually mean moving a ton of earth 50 feet on the site.

A steep slope may require the development of several levels with retaining walls. A series of low walls is more desirable than one large wall. The most pleasing picture and the best use of these level areas result when changes in grade are made below the house level rather than above it.

A topographic survey map consists of a number of lines called "contour lines." These lines indicate the elevation in feet measured from an established base point. The contour lines in the center of the map are evenly spaced, indicating an even slope. Contour lines curving toward you (top of the map) mean that the ground curves toward you, forming a ridge. Contour lines curving away from you (lower part of the map) mean that the ground curves away from you, forming a valley. The closer the contour lines, the steeper the slope or valley. Widely spaced contours indicate a gradual slope or level land.

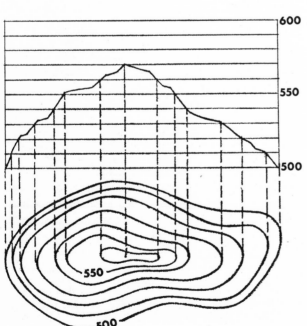

An elevation and plan of contour lines indicating a hilltop.

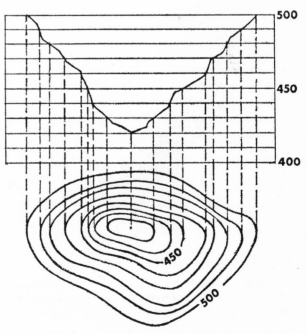

An elevation and plan of contour lines indicating a valley.

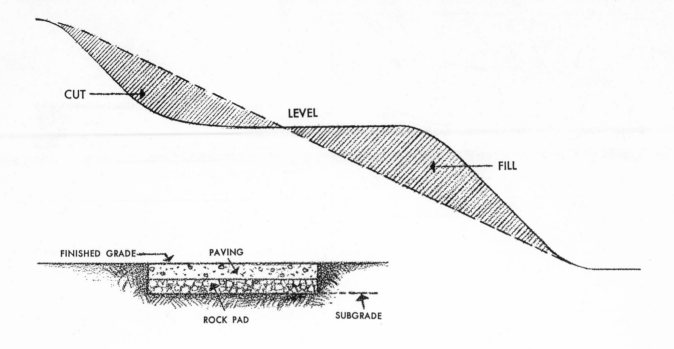

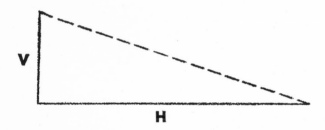

The degree of slope is expressed as a ratio between the horizontal units (H) and the vertical units (V). This is often shown as H:V or H to V.

Know what *contour interval* — the vertical distance between contour lines — was used on your plan. It makes a difference whether these lines are at intervals of 1 foot or 50 feet.

Material taken from a cut is ordinarily used to make a fill nearby. Balancing a cut and fill avoids excess hauling. But if the excavated material is of poor quality or more than you need for fill, have it hauled away.

Before any cuts or fills are made, remove all trees that are not to be left permanently on the site. Work carefully around trees so as not to disturb the existing grade. Leave access for water and air if you are filling around trees. Retaining walls can be built either to hold a grade around a tree or to keep a fill away.

When you have decided on the grade design, strip topsoil into a stockpile to be replaced later for planting and seeding. Grading over good topsoil covers valuable earth that you will need later for effective planting.

Fills are built up in compacted layers to form a stable section. Finish the surface as indicated on the grading plan. Compacting a fill is especially important if you plan to put a structure there later. Changing a natural grade by filling makes it a problem to provide solid footings for such structures. If the fill is not properly compacted, you may need to go down to undisturbed earth to find earth that is solid enough for footings.

Grading requires certain minimums to insure good surface drainage and practical relationships of elements in the site-development plan. Surfaces should not have less than a 100 to 1 slope. This is minimum for lawns and seeded areas; a more desirable slope is 100 to 2, and the maximum slope for lawns is 3 to 1. The maximum slope for plantings should be 2 to 1.

Providing good drainage is one important reason for grading. Surface drainage is the easiest problem to solve, but it requires a suitable outlet. You can't divert surface water onto your neighbor's yard, and you must grade so that surface water is carried off gently to avoid erosion.

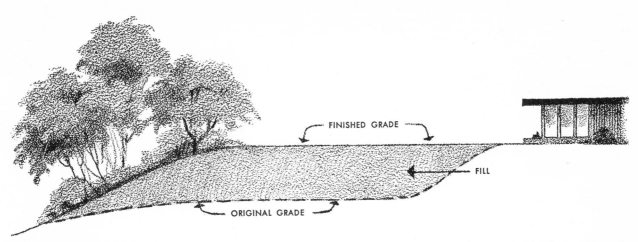

FINISHED GRADE

FILL

ORIGINAL GRADE

The broken line indicates the original grade — a short level area next to the house sloping rather steeply to a second level area. This grade was extended by filling. As a result, the house has a better setting, and the more gradual slope eliminates the need for a structural retaining wall.

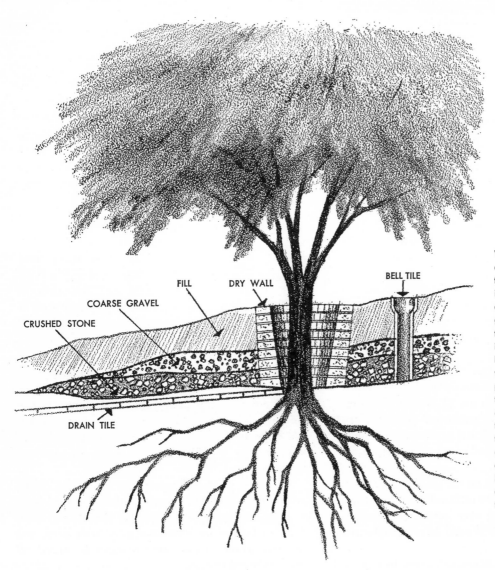

FILL   DRY WALL

BELL TILE

COARSE GRAVEL

CRUSHED STONE

DRAIN TILE

When the fill around a tree is deep, the soil is held from the trunk of the tree by constructing a dry wall around the trunk area. This exposes the original grade. On the side of deepest fill, dig several holes to original grade and place a 6-inch bell tile in each hole. In this way, water and fertilizer are placed as close as possible to the root zone. Place 4-inch drain tile leading from the tree to drain water away from the trunk. Add 8 to 10 inches of crushed stone over the tile and original grade. Place a 4-inch layer of coarse gravel over the crushed stone before adding the fill material.

Always grade around structures so that water flows away from them. To assure good drainage, allow at least 2 inches of fall in every 10 feet. If your surrounding ground slopes toward the house, you will need to grade a surface moat (indicated by broken line) at a distance of 14 to 16 feet from the house. This 16-foot area should be graded to near level with a fall of 4 inches.

Drain surface water into a sewer or onto areas where it will not be a bother. Rain gutters and downspouts discharging roof water directly on the ground create surface drainage problems. One solution is to collect water from each downspout in a catch basin at each corner of the house. Or you can run the water into drain tile laid around the house and discharge it into a large dry well or onto a street or roadside ditch.

You should also keep subsurface drainage in mind when you grade. Subsurface water, as well as surface water, will drain downhill toward the house and eventually seep into the basement unless it is diverted. One way to handle this problem is to lay footing tile around the foundation and run the water into a large dry well, sewer, or street. You can also connect a downspout discharge line with this system. If you do, be sure to have a drain tile large enough to carry both surface and subsurface drainage and a dry well big enough to handle all the water from a heavy rain.

Sometimes you can take care of subsurface drainage by grading a surface moat. If the ground slopes toward the house, you can start grading up toward the house from a spot about 16 feet away. Runoff water will then collect in this depression and will be diverted around the house.

If you have a high water table on your property, the only solution is to lay extensive drain tile for subsurface drainage. But it is wise not to build on a high water table if you can avoid it.

You can use a drain tile line to carry away downspout or surface water that stands on the property. Lay the line deep enough for water to flow to the sump or ditch. Lay drain tile in rows 8 feet apart. Two to 3 inches of drop in 10 feet is enough slope, but the tile must be laid in straight lines without any bends or twists, either up or down or sideways.

Drain tile lines work best if laid on 4 inches of gravel. Cover the joints with tar paper or roofing paper to prevent soil from seeping in. Then cover with gravel. If there is no natural place off the property where the tile can empty water, you may have to provide a sump at a low point on your property. A sump is merely an excavation filled with rocks so that water emptied into it can filter into the soil at a slow rate.

Before doing any grading on your site, consult your local city hall or courthouse about grading ordinances. Check through the requirements and limitations of these ordinances. They may set maximum cut and fill slopes and tell you what drainage controls are required.

You might also have a landscape architect prepare a complete grading plan. Such a plan may save you a great deal of trouble and pay off handsomely in the long run. Many problems and serious consequences can result from moving large amounts of earth without having studied the effect of these changes, not only on your property but on the property around you. The importance of a grading design cannot be stressed too highly. Once the landscaping is in, you won't want to change any grades.

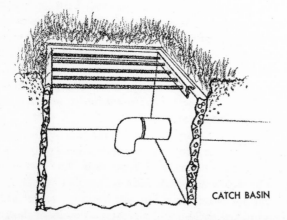

CATCH BASIN

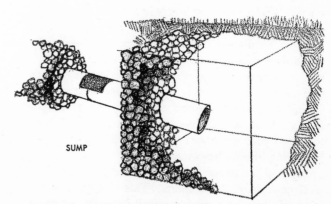

SUMP

Water collected by underground tile from rain-gutter downspouts can be carried to a catch basin or sump. Notice that the drain tile joints (right above) are covered with tar paper or roofing paper before the tile is covered with gravel.

4: CHOOSING LANDSCAPE STRUCTURES

Structures make your landscape design practical and functional. These structures include surfacing materials, steps to make movement between levels easier, and retaining walls, fences, baffles, or walls for privacy, usable space, and pattern.

Natural ground forms on your property, your property analysis, and your family inventory will help you decide which structures to use.

Size of the area largely determines the amount of construction. Both structures and plantings give privacy, organize space, serve as windbreaks, and hold slopes on a large area, but structures require the least amount of ground space to do these things. Only a few structures are necessary on a large property where there is ample room for plantings; you may need only to modify ground forms with grading and use ground covers and lawn for ramp-like connections between levels.

Landscape structures serve the same purpose on smaller city lots or farmstead areas as plantings do on large areas. You can use fences, baffles, and screens instead of shrubs and trees for privacy and as windbreaks. Walls can hold steep slopes and banks, and steps can provide easy access between levels.

Your family inventory might show that you want an outdoor eating area, a level space for lawn games, and some way to break the flow of prevailing winds over the patio. You may have 18 feet of level area behind the house. Beyond this area, the ground is rolling. Your site analysis shows that you will need to screen your neighbor's view and cut down on the prevailing breezes from the west.

Such a landscape will need some grading to be level enough for lawn sports. This change in earth form will require a retaining wall between the patio level and the lawn area. You will also need steps for easy movement between the two areas and a fence located along the west side to break the prevailing wind and provide the necessary screening from the neighbors. Several baffles located to the south will help create space for indoor-outdoor living and provide complete wind control.

On the other hand, a family living on a completely level lot may want to create interest and variety in the dominant horizontal line of the ground by building raised planting beds or low seat walls. A fence and baffles can still be used for wind protection and privacy.

Not all of the structures discussed in this chapter can be included on one piece of property. The key to building functional landscape structures is to blend them into a harmonious combination that will be practical and contribute to the overall design.

The term "enclosure" is used to describe the many types of barriers and screens that can be used in a home landscape. Enclosure in this sense does not necessarily mean a high barrier. In a landscape design, enclosure is an element that contributes to the development of space. Two or three spatial relationships may exist within one of the basic landscape areas. For example, in the outdoor living area you may create one cube of space in the patio area, another in the flower-shrub border area, and a third in the lawn sports area.

Since more than one spatial relationship may be created on one property, enclosures become important to the development of these areas. The enclosure may be as low as a seat. This is "implied" enclosure. It will not block vision but will interrupt movement. This implied enclosure also creates a dominant design pattern and line.

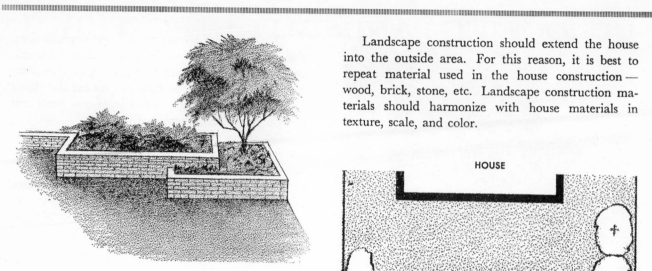

You can add interest and variety to level ground through the use of raised beds, seat walls, or a combination of the two.

The observer's eye stops at a low enclosure and his imagination continues a vertical effect to enclose a certain amount of space. This is space created by mental suggestion. The observer "reads" the landscape and organizes the area into space by enclosure placement. Tall enclosures block both movement and vision and define the space in terms that leave nothing to the imagination. They also provide privacy, a windbreak, screening, and a sense of protection.

Protection is important if you want to make full use of the outdoor living area. People do not feel comfortable in the open with nothing around them, but they can completely relax in the house where walls screen off outside eyes. The outside walls of the house create one large area of space, but the inside walls also define smaller areas of space. Outdoor enclosures should provide both effects.

Enclosures do not need to be continuous elements. For example, a fence need not run the full length of the area. Often the baffle effect of offset panels will create interesting spatial relationships as well as a feeling of enclosure and privacy.

Combining a solid enclosure along one side, a low, open enclosure along another, and baffles for another section will often result in a pleasing effect. All the enclosures for one area do not have to be the same, but the materials used should be related. Whatever material is used in a major enclosure should be harmonious in scale, texture, and color with that used in all other enclosures.

As a general rule, it is not desirable to use the same material for both paving and enclosure. For example, a brick patio should have a wooden enclosure rather than a brick one, although there are some exceptions to this rule.

Landscape construction should extend the house into the outside area. For this reason, it is best to repeat material used in the house construction — wood, brick, stone, etc. Landscape construction materials should harmonize with house materials in texture, scale, and color.

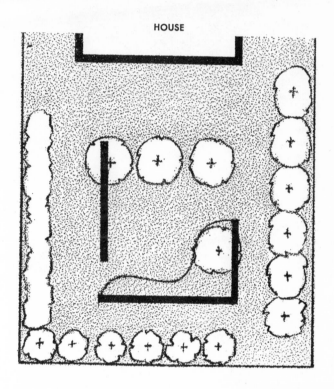

Trees, shrubs, fences, and walls contribute to the creation of space. The drawings above and below illustrate how these elements create two or three spatial relationships within a landscape.

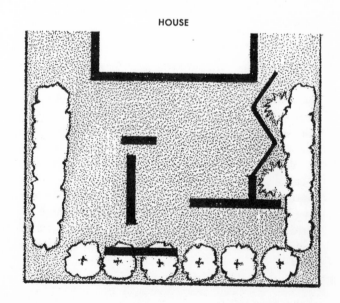

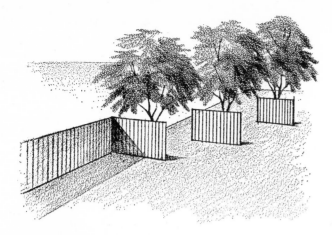

Enclosures need not run the full length of the property line. Offset panels provide interesting spatial relationships while retaining a sense of enclosure and privacy.

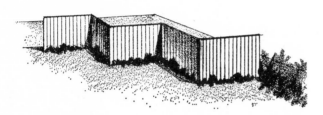

A stepped fence adds dominant pattern and line to a design.

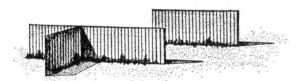

One panel placed at right angles creates a focal point that provides a setting for a piece of sculpture or specimen plant. Another panel is offset for additional enclosure and privacy.

Fences

Fences serve many purposes. They enclose and protect the garden, furnish a background for flowers and shrubs, screen out unsightly views, and shelter the sitting area, patio, or terrace from the wind. They also serve as barriers to keep children and pets within the yard and to prevent people from crossing the yard.

But usually the main reason for a fence is privacy. You can obtain privacy by outlining the area with a fence, but there are other ways. For example, you can build the fence as a series of baffles without regard to the property line. It may swing around an outdoor living area in a curve, or angle across at a slant.

The amount of privacy you will get depends upon the type of fence. Board fences, horizontal louvers, or close-set grape stakes give maximum screening. Vertical louver, board-on-board, or spaced-slat fences give medium screening. Lattice pickets or posts and rail give very little screening.

The size of the area to be enclosed will tell you whether to put a fence along your property lines, or whether to use sections and panels within the property. For example, fencing along a property line might be best for a small area, but fences, panels, and baffles built within the garden will do a better job of creating desired enclosure in a large area.

Walls

A wall can be a handsome addition to a landscape design. It can enclose an area within the property or be used along a property line. A wall does not have to be of the tall, screening type. Low walls are often used to mark boundaries between different parts of the garden and to tie together related elements in the garden plan. A wall can be built strong enough to hold soil, to be used as a seat, and to create raised beds.

Seat walls have become popular. A seat wall 16 to 18 inches high can be a useful and attractive garden addition. Often a low seat-wall can also serve as a curb or retainer around planting beds, a temporary table, a potting bench, or a potted-plant display shelf.

Taller walls are often used along property lines as well as within the property itself. A tall wall can be an attractive structure that will make a good screen. Masonry walls are probably the most effective way to reduce noises, but they must be located where they will not trap cold air and create a damp, humid area in the garden.

Retaining Walls

Sloping ground often requires a retaining wall to provide enough level space for a useful landscape, or to prevent erosion on steep slopes that will not support plant material, and that cannot easily be mowed or otherwise maintained.

A retaining wall may require the services of a landscape architect and civil engineer because it must hold its position against the pressure of water and earth. This is particularly true when the difference in height between the two ground levels is more than 3 feet.

From a design standpoint, it is better to use a series of close-set, low walls rather than one high

The basketweave fence has the advantage of providing an attractive pattern on both sides. Rough finish lumber is desirable for a softer texture.

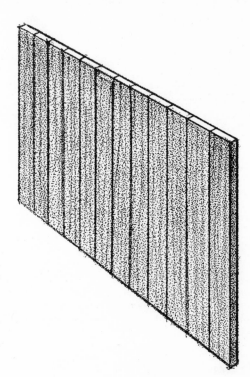

Although a solid board fence allows complete privacy, it is expensive to construct. It serves well as a wind barrier, screen, and background for plants, and also serves to extend the walls of the house into the yard.

Grape stakes are used to construct a popular rustic-type fence. Redwood stakes weather to a soft gray that complements plants, bricks, and stonework. Nail the stakes to your fence frame. Leave a small space between each stake to allow for expansion. For a two-sided effect, you may want to fit the stakes into a frame.

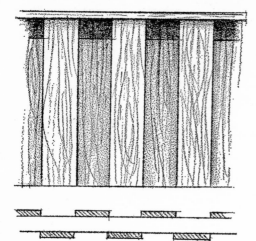

The board-on-board fence reduces strong wind currents while allowing air to circulate between the boards. This fence provides privacy, and the alternating boards form interesting shadow patterns.

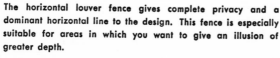

Top view of
board on board

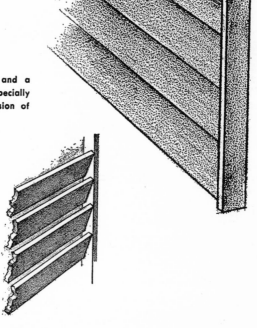

The horizontal louver fence gives complete privacy and a dominant horizontal line to the design. This fence is especially suitable for areas in which you want to give an illusion of greater depth.

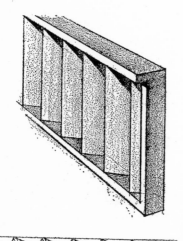

The louver fence is a strong design element. For this reason, it should be carefully integrated into the design and not concealed by plantings. The louvers not only allow air to flow through but also form attractive light and shadow patterns. These fences are expensive to build. They require a great deal of lumber and labor to make them structurally sound.

The vertical louver fence gives a partial view of the other side as you move along the fence. Because of its refined construction and airy effect, this fence is a good one to use close to the house.

Top view

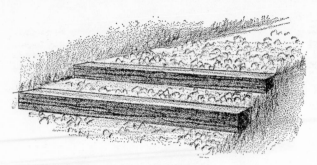

For steps in light traffic areas, railroad ties or redwood or cedar lumber can be used as risers. The treads can be gravel, tanbark, or turf. The same combination of materials can be used to construct a ramped step connection between levels.

wall for a steep slope or hillside. Low walls are more pleasing to the eye, easier to plant, and less likely to lean or topple downhill than high walls. Retaining walls offer a chance to add lines, patterns, and designs to the overall layout. You can build a retainer in any shape — curved, angled, or straight.

A dry wall can be used to hold a shallow slope. It has open joints that let water flow through, and is usually built of large stones or broken concrete with earth pockets between the stones. You can plant these pockets with small plants and vines. The face of a dry wall is always pitched in toward the hill or the thrust of a bank. Material used for this type of construction must be carefully placed, with a large amount of the material well anchored into the bank.

Steps

Steps or ramps are the best way to handle movement from one grade level to another, and they can serve as a soil-retaining wall at the same time. Steps offer a chance to develop interesting landscape arrangements. Unlike indoor steps, garden steps do not need to run in a straight flight. They can be irregular with various turns or angles, as long as they are scaled so that they do not look abrupt or pinched.

Even if the vertical rise of a series of steps is extremely steep, they should not be higher than they are wide. It is a good idea to break up a very long flight into smaller groups and separate these groups with landings. You can also change the direction of a set of steps at a landing.

Keep outdoor steps in scale with the outdoors. Outdoor steps should have a wide tread and a low riser. In other words, you should spread a flight of steps horizontally as much as possible. For outdoor steps, a 6-inch riser is the absolute maximum, and a 12-inch tread is the absolute minimum. Proper riser-

tread relationship is extremely important. Low, broad steps look better and are easier to climb and descend than steep ones. The recommended proportion for outdoor steps is a 5-inch riser to a 15-inch tread, or a 4-inch riser to an 18-inch tread, or a 3-inch riser to a 24-inch tread.

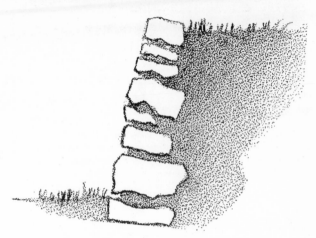

A dry wall can serve both as an effective retainer and as a distinctive design element. Notice that the stones are long enough to anchor into the soil, and that they are placed on a backward slant. The front end of the stone slants slightly upward, while the back end is tipped into the ground. The face of the wall should also slant into the slope for greater resistance against the pressures of the earth.

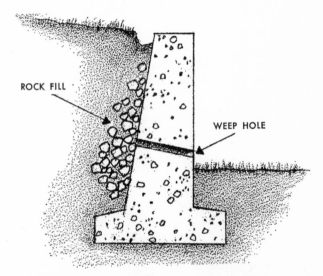

A concrete retaining wall should not be less than 12 inches thick at the top. The width of the base should be 48 to 50 percent of the height of the wall. The projecting foot at the front of the wall should be 1/12 of the height. The back of the wall should be sloped from the bottom and waterproofed with asphaltic compound. Weep holes should be set 6 feet apart and slanted to the front so that they will drain about 4 inches above ground. A rock fill should be tamped in behind the wall, although the top 12 or 18 inches can be filled with soil.

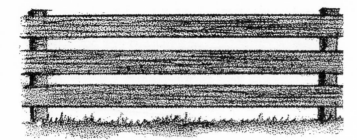

A rail fence is appropriate with low ranch-style houses and in the country. The strong horizontal lines of this fence blend with the topography of the Midwest, and the open design allows the viewer to see the landscape beyond the fence. A rail fence provides an efficient barrier, and is both inexpensive and easy to build.

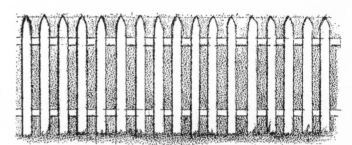

A picket fence is one of the most common types of fences. A wide variety of picket designs can be used. Varying the width of the pickets helps avoid monotony.

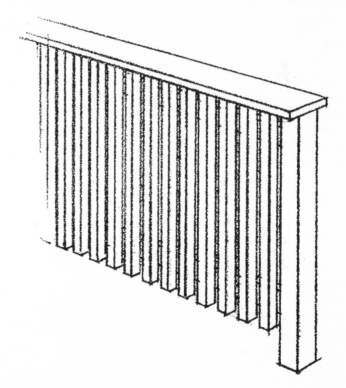

A slat fence, constructed of narrow lumber set vertically, defines an area with clean crisp lines and provides maximum privacy. The vertical lines offer a pleasing visual effect. The fence shown here is a typical slat fence, built of 1″ x 1″ or 1″ x 2″ milled lumber set close together.

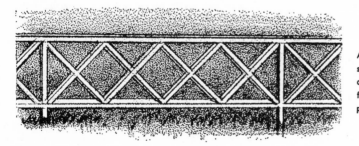

A tightly woven lattice fence gives privacy and serves as a screen. An open-lattice fence provides an open screen that creates space, line, and direction. If plants are grown on these fences, be sure that the fence will support the weight of the plants.

Ramps

Another way to connect two levels is by means of a ramp. Ramps are especially useful when you must roll a wheelbarrow or similar equipment up and down grade changes.

A desirable slope for a ramp is 15 feet in 100 feet. Ramped steps have risers 3 to 6 feet apart with some slope between. Be sure that the ramp treads are wide enough for people to take several steps on each tread. Typical ramp specifications would include risers between 4 and 6 inches high and treads 6 feet, 3 inches wide, with a maximum slope of 6 inches from the top of one riser to the top of the next.

Surfaces

The floor of our cube of space is the earth. You can modify the earth with certain materials — either hard or soft — to add patterns and forms to the design, and to make it more usable and comfortable.

Many landscape areas need some type of surfacing. Lawn is the most widely used surfacing material. A lawn is both practical and beautiful. It has the advantage of appearing cool, and of being pleasant to sit or lie on in hot weather.

But not all surfacing material needs to be lawn.

Ground covers can add green surfacing in areas with little foot traffic. You can combine ground covers with lawn in interesting patterns and shapes. Put a 2- by 4-inch wood divider between the ground cover and lawn to keep them apart.

Several loose surfacing materials can be used as secondary paving material. Pebbles, gravel, tanbark, brickchips, and crushed limestone are examples. These secondary materials are most usable in light traffic areas with no major family activity. An exception might be special areas where the design qualities — texture, color, and patterns — of loose surfacing materials offer striking contrasts and interest when combined with other surfacing material. This would include larger rocks not suitable for foot traffic.

The pattern may be a simple combination of paving and lawn or paving and loose surfacing. Or you can compose more complicated arrangements of all surfacings in a unified pattern.

There are unlimited possibilities for making patterns out of various surfacings. You can use straight, curved, or diagonal lines to form the shape that makes up the pattern. One shape may cut into another. Edgings used to divide the areas and hold the surfacing material in place emphasize dividing lines and the pattern being developed.

5: CHOOSING CONSTRUCTION MATERIALS

Keep landscape construction simple. Plants can furnish any patterns that you may want to soften the structural materials. Rely on the beauty of the materials, not on fancy dressing.

Landscape designs themselves often suggest what construction materials to use in terms of color, texture, and scale. But the key to proper selection lies in choosing those materials best adapted to carrying out the original design.

Choose materials that are appropriate to the needs and that are durable for the job, but be sure that they blend with each other and with the buildings on the property. Never select materials just because they are pretty or outstanding. You should also consider the maintenance that will be required over the years.

Surfacing Materials

Tanbark is a pleasantly soft surfacing material. Its natural color blends harmoniously with the landscape. Tanbark is made of oak-bark chips used in the leather tanning process. You can get it from a tannery. It scatters easily, but you can confine it by enclosing the area with 2- by 4-inch headers. One ton of tanbark will cover 175 square feet. Put it on top of 2 or 3 inches of gravel or sand for drainage.

Loose aggregates have not been commonly used as surfacing materials. Aggregates are usually gravel and small rocks that provide a rough and temporary surface. If you apply them directly to the soil in heavy traffic areas, they will sink into the earth over the years with heavy traffic. Small rocks will also kick out onto the lawn or planting areas and cause problems. Use aggregates only to supplement hard-surfaced areas or for secondary use in the private areas. Large rock aggregates may be used, for example, around the base of trees for contrast in texture or as patterned areas in combination with hard surfaces and ground cover.

Gravel is difficult to confine and uncomfortable to walk on. Weeds will grow through it, but these can be controlled by laying a double sheet of heavy-weight polyethylene plastic beneath the aggregate. Punch holes in the plastic at intervals to allow water to drain into the soil if needed. Gravel is available in four sizes, ranging from the smallest pea gravel to large rocks. Pea gravel is too small for walks because it sticks to shoes and is easily tracked into the house. The best gravel size is about ½ inch in diameter.

Mixed rock sizes are not good buys. Smaller rocks work to the bottom, leaving the larger rocks on the surface. Lay rocks about 1½ to 2 inches thick, and rake and roll them to make them firm. One cubic yard of rocks will cover about 200 square feet to a thickness of 1 inch.

Crushed limestone and granite are durable surfacing materials when properly applied. For best results, lay them in three 1-inch layers. Water and roll each layer thoroughly.

Some new types of *asphalt paving*, or *blacktop*, work very well for patios, paths, drives, and other surfaced areas. Many designers now use asphalt paving in combination with brick and concrete. And it costs much less than either of these materials.

Blacktop has some disadvantages as well as advantages. If it is not properly mixed or compacted, it will become soft in warm weather. But if properly laid over a solid bed of rock, it should form a durable, solid surface. Its black surface absorbs the sun's heat, and it will not reflect light and heat as concrete does.

You will also use less of it for specific jobs. For a drive, only ½- to ¾-inch topping on a good gravel or stone base will be enough. The recommended depth for a sidewalk or patio is 1½ to 2 inches. Asphalt needs a good foundation that has been carefully prepared to avoid cracks and sagging as a result of shifting soil. Weeds and plants will grow through asphalt unless the soil is sterilized beneath it.

You can apply asphalt either hot or cold. In the hot mixture, the asphalt binds the rock base together as it cools. One type of asphalt is called "cold mix." With this type, liquid asphalt is applied to the rock base. A carrier is used to hold the asphalt in solution, and as this carrier evaporates, the asphalt hardens and holds the rocks. The rate of evaporation depends upon the carrier used. A number of different types of carriers are available that offer a range of setting speeds.

Contractors with proper equipment can easily apply asphaltic concrete to large areas. The cost is reasonable, and you will probably get a more finished job than if you did the work yourself.

Bricks have proved to be one of the most handsome paving materials. They can be used in a great variety of patterns to achieve various textures. Their warm color provides a pleasant contrast with plant materials, ground covers, and soil.

Bricks also produce a solid and durable paving surface. When laid on sand, bricks give a rough or uneven surface. Frost action often results in heaving, but the bricks can easily be reset for the summer. A brick surface reduces glare. Since bricks are very porous, it is difficult to keep them clean. To prevent weeds and grass from growing beneath the bricks, use polyethylene plastic beneath the sand bed prepared for the bricks.

Visit your local building-materials dealer to see the wide variety of textures, colors, and sizes of bricks. Colors include red, orange, yellow, brown, gray, and blueblack.

Smooth-face brick or rough common brick is ordinarily used for garden surfaces. Face brick is used less often than smooth or common brick because it requires matching mortar joints in a professional manner, and it is more expensive. Wire-cut is a common brick. It is cut square, but it has a rough texture with a pitted surface. It is smoother laid on edge. Sand-mold brick is smooth and easier to clean than wire-cut brick, and is slightly larger. A third common type is clinker brick, which is oven-burned and has black spots and irregularities on the surface.

Hard-burned brick will outlast underburned brick. Well-burned brick has a dark red color, and under-burned brick is a salmon color. One test of hardness is to strike the brick with a hammer. Well-burned brick gives a metallic sound, while underburned brick gives a dull thud. Used brick is popular for home paving. Its weathered look, worn surfaces, and traces of old mortar create an attractive informal pavement.

Be sure that your dealer has enough bricks of the variety you need to finish your project so that you can avoid variations in color. In choosing your paving patterns, carefully consider the balance of the landscape. Avoid too busy a pattern that will dominate the design. There are several standard designs of paving patterns from which to choose — running bond, basket weave, or herringbone.

Flagstones cost more than any other paving material, but they give a solid pavement with a durable look and interesting texture. A flagstone pavement will last many years if properly built. The colors of buff, yellow, brownish red, or gray combine well with other elements in the garden, and the irregular shapes add pattern to the patio surface.

Flagstones must be used carefully to avoid an indiscriminate patchwork of colors or irregular stones put together in a busy pattern.

You can choose from among several types of flagstones. One readily available flagstone is crab orchard stone. The thickness of crab orchard slabs ranges from 1 to 2 inches. You will need the 2-inch thickness if you put it on a sand bed. Plastic can be used to prevent weed growth.

Concrete is inexpensive, wears well, and provides an excellent surface for games and dancing. Since concrete is a very plastic material, it can be used to develop many unusual patterns and shapes. But the use of concrete requires special equipment and fast work. Proper slope, subgrade preparation, and forming must be given careful attention before ordering concrete. The larger the area the more difficult it is to work, so consider taking small sections at a time.

One disadvantage of concrete is its surface glare, but you can pattern the surface to eliminate this glare. Staining, coloring, tapping in pebbles, brooming, and exposing the surface aggregates are also effective means of reducing glare.

Bricks or wood dividers forming 4- to 5-foot squares will relieve the monotony of a large concrete area. By brooming the surface of the concrete, you can obtain a textured pattern and reduce light reflection from the concrete at the same time. Tapping pebbles into newly poured concrete will also add texture, particularly to concrete panels framed in brick.

Paving Patterns

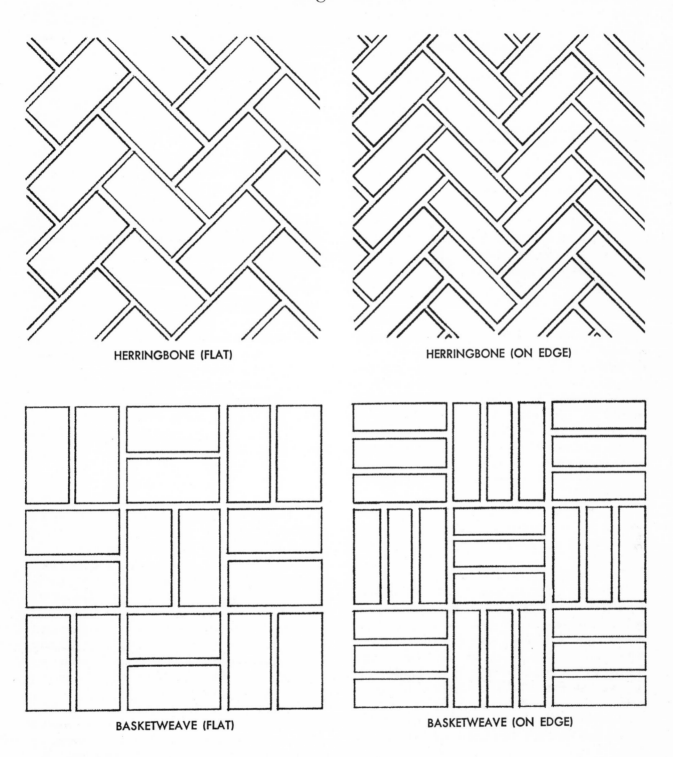

HERRINGBONE (FLAT)   HERRINGBONE (ON EDGE)

BASKETWEAVE (FLAT)   BASKETWEAVE (ON EDGE)

Paving Patterns

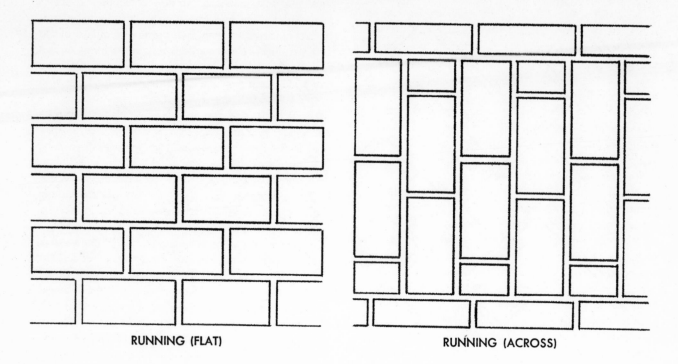

RUNNING (FLAT) RUNNING (ACROSS)

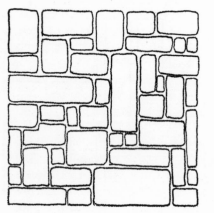

RANDOM
RECTANGULAR

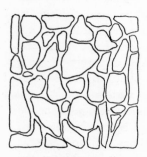

IRREGULAR

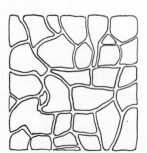

IRREGULAR (FITTED)

Wood blocks and rounds can be obtained in areas near sawmills. Wooden paving looks more natural in a garden setting than man-made elements. Its color and texture harmonize well with all other parts of the garden. Round disks cut straight through the trunk of a redwood, cedar, or cypress tree, or square blocks cut from railroad ties can be used. The pattern developed from the wood rounds will be a random one, but it should be carefully planned for a pleasant effect. The wood blocks from railroad ties should be laid in a more regular pattern. You may even adapt one of the brick paving patterns.

One disadvantage of wooden paving is that it is not permanent. Plan for eventual renewal or replacement when you put it in. The open grain of the wood soaks up moisture, accelerating decay and deterioration. You can slow decay by applying pentachlorophenol or other toxic wood preservative.

Steps

One way to make steps is to nail wood treads to 2- by 10-inch side pieces called stringers, leaving the risers open. Or you can use wood risers with different kinds of tread materials. For instance, you can fill the tread with dirt, gravel, tanbark, wood, or brick. You can use railroad ties for risers, with earth or grass providing a ramp-like change in levels. Such treads are often long enough for people to take several steps on each, depending upon the slope. Another possibility in light traffic areas is to use redwood or cedar-log risers treated with preservatives, with loose aggregates on the tread.

Brick treads and risers set in mortar offer almost unlimited design possibilities. Because of the alternate freezing and thawing in the Midwest, it is important to reinforce them with concrete. Another variation is to use brick treads with wood risers such as railroad ties or heavy milled lumber. Garden tile treads with brick or concrete risers is another pleasing combination. Broken concrete pieces stacked on top of one another may make a good tread and riser combination.

Pre-cast concrete slabs are often used, and plain concrete steps with reinforcing steel can be worked into an attractive arrangement. You can also use concrete blocks as risers and treads, or as risers in combination with paving brick, wood, or tile.

Walls

Walls have many different uses. They can be tall for screening, or low and sturdy to mark the edge of a flower bed. They can be used to hold soil in place, to support people, or simply to create a raised planting bed. Whenever a wall is used in a design, it can be planned to create space, to give line or pattern to the design, or to create a focal point.

A series of low walls is better than one high wall for holding a steep slope. Low walls are more pleasing to the eye, are easier to plant to vines or shrubs, and are less likely to lean or topple downhill.

Wood dry walls can serve as a retaining wall. Redwood makes a good wall material because it is naturally resistant to decay. Railroad ties are also a possibility. Or you can use precast reinforced concrete posts for a stepped dry wall.

Stone dry walls will successfully hold low banks. These walls are laid with stone pockets between them. A dry wall should always lean toward the slope. Stones used in a dry wall should be long enough to anchor well in the slope.

Concrete blocks make a good garden wall. Their porous texture and pleasant color can give interesting garden effects, and they can be put together in different combinations and sizes for variety. Regular foundation blocks are better than pumice or cinder blocks because they are more water-resistant. If you do not lay concrete building blocks too many rows high, you can hold them together by lining up the holes and filling them with pipe reinforcement and cement.

Brick walls are strong, have an elegant appearance, and weather well over the years. If a brick wall is not more than a foot or two high, it can be laid two bricks (8 inches) thick. A thickness of at least three bricks (12 inches) is recommended for brick walls higher than two feet. Special reinforcing must be considered. Bricks can make an interesting open grid wall or a seat wall with a redwood cap.

Stone walls can be strong elements in the garden, but be careful to design and construct them so that they look appropriate. They are not easy to build. The uneven surfaces of stone make it difficult to get a straight face on a wall. Cutting, shaping, and setting stone is a challenge to an amateur. Stone is not practicable unless you have a source of rock close by. You can build a stone wall with or without mortar.

Poured concrete can be curved, angled, or straight to fit the garden plan. Concrete walls can be finished smooth or rough. When properly designed, a concrete wall is the most durable wall for holding back a hillside or for enclosing a planter bed.

Since a poured concrete retaining wall more than 3 feet high requires special design features and construction methods, it should be designed by a qualified professional.

Probably the biggest mistake in building this kind of wall is in not providing ways to carry off water that collects behind it. During a wet season, much water flows downhill below the ground surface. When this water meets an obstruction, such as a retaining wall, it collects and builds up tremendous pressures that can either undermine the wall or burst through it. A wall should stand without any trouble if ways are provided to let this water flow through or around it. Ditches, gutters, drain tile, and proper planting can divert the flood. Weep holes, drain tile, and gravel backfill will help prevent undermining.

You can overcome the bleakness of a tall concrete wall by using brick capping, or by curving the wall and adding appropriate plantings. A wooden seat bench constructed along the wall also reduces the feeling of height by creating a strong, dominant, horizontal line.

Fences

Like walls, fences serve as enclosures, screens, baffles, and an occasional decoration.

Many people put up a fence the first weekend after moving into a new house. But after a few weeks, they often see that the fence was planned and constructed in too much haste. Fence planning is important. A fence must be an integral part of a landscape plan — it is actually an extension of the house into the landscape.

Privacy is often the main function of fencing. A solid board fence, horizontal louvers, or grape stakes give maximum screening, and vertical louvers, board-on-board, or spaced slat fences provide medium screening. Pickets, lattices, or rail and post fences give little privacy.

Another function of fences is to provide a barrier to keep both animals and children in or out. Wire fences are often used. They are not very attractive, but plantings can be used to screen them. If structural fences are used, a more solid design will be needed.

A properly designed fence can also help control sun, wind, and frost, as well as screen off property views. Fences do not have to be continuous. Panels or baffles may be all that is needed to create a feeling of privacy.

A *picket fence* is one of the few fences that can be used as a boundary in the public area. There are several patterns and widths available. The monotony of these fences can be relieved by varying the width or height of the pickets.

Picket fences are not good barriers, and they need painting often to keep a neat appearance. Since they do not provide much privacy, they are not suitable for the outdoor living area unless shielded by shrubs.

A *slat fence* is made of rough-finished wood sawed in 1-inch by 1-inch or 1-inch by 2-inch strips. The slats may be close together or far apart. When the slats are close together, leave a little space between them to allow for expansion. The fence can be almost any height. Since slats present a formal appearance, they are usually more appropriate in the city than in the country. Slats have regular edges to give a strong vertical pattern and privacy. Tests have shown that an open slat fence provides more effective wind protection than any other fence.

The split *grape stake fence* is a popular urban and rural fencing. Grape stakes are usually about 2 inches square and 3 to 6 feet high. Redwood grape stakes are decay-resistant and need little maintenance, but other types of woods can also be used to make grape stakes. Grape stakes are light, easy to handle, and simple to install. They can be used in many different ways to develop different designs. Grape stakes can be fitted inside a frame to provide a two-sided fence, and they can be attached either vertically or horizontally.

You can get attractive prefabricated rustic picket fencing either in panels or woven together in rows. One of these fences is referred to as stockade style. The typical snow fence seen along highways is another example. Woven pickets are easy to put up, make an effective fencing, may have interesting texture, and are built to last.

Although a high *board fence* is easily built, it is expensive because of the amount of lumber used in it. A solid board fence provides absolute privacy, but if it is not carefully designed, it can give a feeling of imprisonment and a monotonous view. Some basic design principles can add interest and pattern to board fences. One of the best tricks for a lighter feeling and a little view of the other side is to separate the boards in a tall board fence. Set boards slightly apart, slant them in a frame to form louvers, or offset them by mounting alternating boards on either side of the frame for a board-on-board effect.

Batten siding, tongue-and-groove boards, or alternate panels of vertical and horizontal boards can give pattern or texture to the fence. Using boards horizontally adds the effect of length to the fence and the area surrounding it. Designing the structural supports (vertical post and cross rails) to give strong lines and shadow patterns makes the fence interesting on either side. Or you can solve the problem by fitting the boards within the frame so that they appear the same on both sides.

Some interesting materials are available today for solid fences. *Plywood* is an old standby that can be attached straight or curved. Use only exterior plywood. Plywood edges need protection from moisture. A cap atop the upper edge will shield it from rain. Wide, solid surfaces put up a tremendous resistance to the wind, and must be installed on substantial framing.

Corrugated asbestos panels have a handsome appearance. Their muted natural color is satisfactory for garden use. They can also be painted. The corrugations result in interesting shadow patterns that give a continually changing effect when used close to the patio. This material combines well with plastics used as alternate panels. A fence constructed of corrugated asbestos panels makes an effective backdrop for plants. Since the panels are heavy, they should be attached to steel posts or to very heavy wood that has been well embedded in concrete.

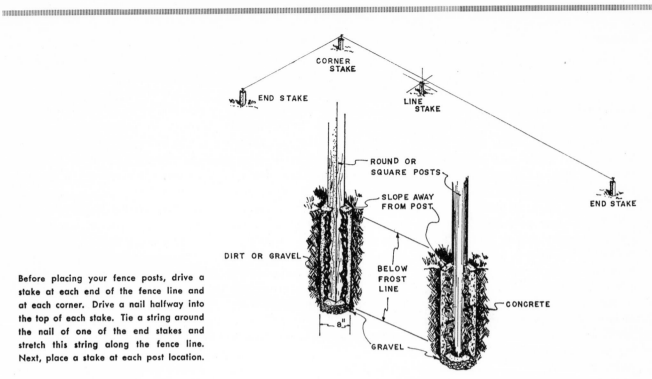

Before placing your fence posts, drive a stake at each end of the fence line and at each corner. Drive a nail halfway into the top of each stake. Tie a string around the nail of one of the end stakes and stretch this string along the fence line. Next, place a stake at each post location.

The depth at which you set your posts will depend upon the depth of frost penetration. Be sure to set them below frost level. You can secure your posts by any of the following three methods. (1) Backfill the hole with excavated soil. Be sure to add water at the same time. Continue adding water until the hole is filled with soupy mud. (2) Fill the hole with gravel. This method will give you a more permanent installation than the first method. (3) Fill the hole with concrete. This method is the most costly, but will give you the longest post life.

Check your work during and after backfilling to be sure that all posts are sticking out the same distance from the ground. Since accuracy is important, measure from the ground with a rule. For another check, stretch a string from each post top as you did with the stakes. By sighting down this line, you can quickly see which posts are out of line. The last step is to plumb your post with the aid of a level.

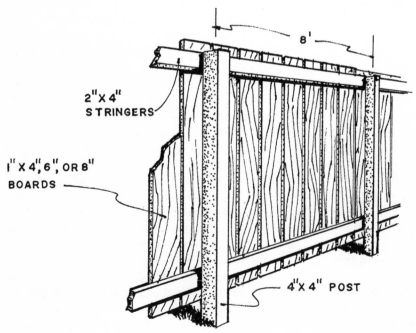

Plain Board Fence

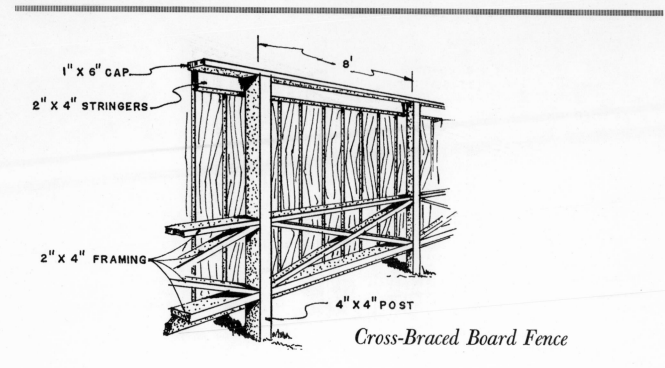

1" X 6" CAP

2" X 4" STRINGERS

8'

2" X 4" FRAMING

4" X 4" POST

Cross-Braced Board Fence

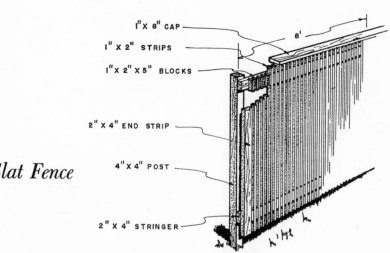

1" X 8" CAP

1" X 2" STRIPS

1" X 2" X 5" BLOCKS

8'

2" X 4" END STRIP

4" X 4" POST

2" X 4" STRINGER

Slat Fence

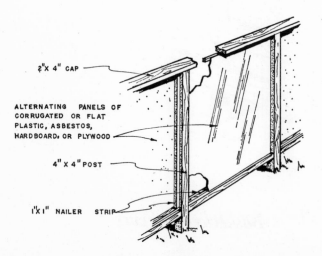

2" X 4" CAP

ALTERNATING PANELS OF CORRUGATED OR FLAT PLASTIC, ASBESTOS, HARDBOARD, OR PLYWOOD

4" X 4" POST

1" X 1" NAILER STRIP

Panel Fence

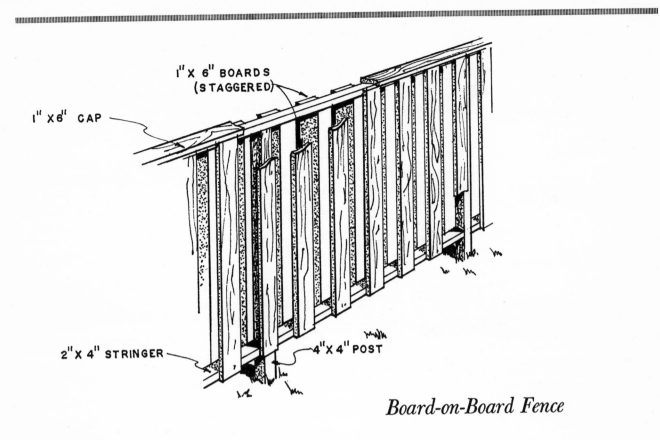

1" X 6" BOARDS (STAGGERED)

1" X 6" CAP

2" X 4" STRINGER

4" X 4" POST

Board-on-Board Fence

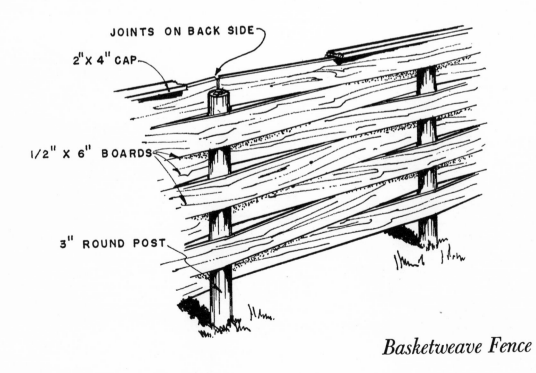

JOINTS ON BACK SIDE

2" X 4" CAP

1/2" X 6" BOARDS

3" ROUND POST

Basketweave Fence

Corrugated aluminum has a bright opaque surface. By contrast, *corrugated plastic* sheets give a soft, filtered glow of light to enclosed areas. These plastic sheets are available in various colors and sizes. Use the pastel shades for the best combination of plants and material.

Corrugated aluminum and plastic can be nailed, drilled, or sawed, and are easy to install. If you want a corrugated effect without the reflecting or translucent qualities of aluminum or plastic, you can paint either of these materials to harmonize with garden colors.

Another new type of fence consists of regular window screen sealed in clear plastic. This screen will block off a view without shutting out any sunlight. It diffuses sunlight in a soft radiance that looks cool, and the silhouette of plants behind the screen gives a very interesting effect.

A *louver fence* is handsome but expensive. Louvers give partial privacy, but also allow as much sunlight or shade as desired for plants on the inside. They can reduce air circulation in the garden and screen off views beyond. Vertical louvers give only partial privacy. For complete privacy, horizontal louvers are needed.

A louver fence should be matched to the house design. It can be painted or stained the house color or a complementary shade, but will need careful maintenance.

The popular *basketweave fence* provides complete privacy and interesting shadow patterns. The woven boards give the impression of a texture variation and are attractive on both sides.

A *lattice fence* can be used to screen out an objectionable view if the lattices are placed closely together. The lattice fence may also serve to create or divide space. Often vines are used on these fences. It is important to blend in a lattice fence as a part of the landscape. For example, do not paint it white when everything else is in more natural tones. Lattice does not have to be small lath-type structures. Larger posts and wider lumber for the lattice often give a better scale relationship.

A *rail fence* is ideally suited to a country scene, but it can also be designed to work well with an urban landscape. For most homes a rail fence would be a better means of defining the property line and discouraging "pathfinding" than the picket fence. A light rail fence goes best with a ranch-style home, but will look well with many other styles.

In planning for a fence, select materials adapted to carrying out your landscape design. It is to your advantage to use any easy or inexpensive source of materials.

Avoid design and texture that stands out alone. Choose both your design and materials for their simplicity. Some materials are more appropriate in certain localities than in others. For example, rocks are more appropriate in rocky areas than in cities.

The ways in which materials combine and blend with each other and with the buildings and site are as important as cost and availability. Don't select materials merely because they are pretty. Select them for their appropriateness, for their ability to blend together, and for their suitability to the materials and architecture of the house.

6: FITTING PLANTS TO YOUR ENVIRONMENT AND DESIGN

Plants are one of the major building materials in a landscape design. Good designing with plants is something more than merely putting bushes here and there. It requires understanding each plant's individual qualities and environmental needs.

Form, growth habits, texture, and color are important considerations in selecting plants to create a picture with lasting beauty. What is the mass effect of buildings in the area — the forms and lines that your plants must blend with, complement, or screen?

Choose specific plants for a planting composition only after you have considered the total environment in which they will have to live. Study the soil, temperatures, water, light, and wind exposures on your property. What is your soil type? Is the area shady, damp or dry, windy or protected? Each plant has certain conditions that best promote its growth and well-being, and you should choose your plants from those that "like" your conditions.

In this chapter, we will discuss the environmental needs and the design characteristics — color, form, texture, etc. — of plants, as well as some of the principles of art that apply to landscape design.

Soil is the loose surface material of the earth in which plants grow. It is continually moved about, carried away, and redeposited by wind, water, and ice. Plants add their decaying organic material to change the composition of the soil. But this organic material is almost entirely lacking in some areas. Clay, sand, silt, or gravel resulting from decomposition of rocks alone is not fertile.

Soils are classified into three major types according to the size of their mineral particles. These types are *sand, silt,* and *clay.* An ideal soil mixture contains all three types.

Soils are usually composed of five intermingled materials: (1) minerals; (2) humus, or the organic materials; (3) minute living organisms such as bacteria, protozoa, and fungi; (4) water, which holds dissolved mineral salts in solution; and (5) air.

Humus is the key to good soil. It readily absorbs the sun's rays in early spring that warm the soil and promote early plant growth. Humus helps prevent leaching of certain soluble plant foods, increases bacterial action in the soil, and makes it easier for plant roots to penetrate the soil in their search for food and water.

Humus also increases the water-holding capacity of the soil and modifies the arrangement of the soil particles. Mineral particles in the soil hold water only on their surface, but humus absorbs water like a sponge. Humus improves soil structure so that the soil is easily worked. For example, clay soils will compact and bake hard when dry, and will get lumpy and full of clods if worked when wet. But humus binds soil particles in larger aggregates to give a new texture that will not clod when worked.

Plants cannot grow without water. Even in the best soils artificial watering is often necessary to get water to plants. But too much water drives air from the soil and "drowns" the living plant cells by cutting off the air they need to live. Excess water may also remove nutrients too fast and leave the soil infertile. Too much water limits plant life to the bog types, and too little water limits plant life to desert types.

Plant growth and vigor depend in part upon the amount and circulation of air and water in the soil. Plowing and cultivation have important effects on both water and air content of the soil. Pore spaces filled with air mean too little water, and vice versa.

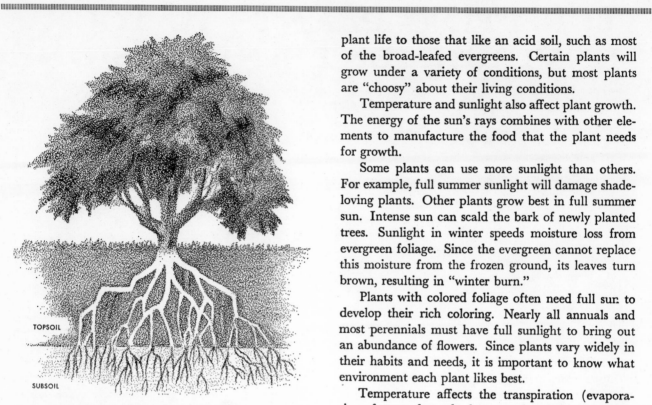

TOPSOIL

SUBSOIL

For proper plant growth, the soil should be porous enough to allow air, water, and roots to penetrate it, and yet have enough humus for bacterial activity and to hold water and nutrients. It must also have good subsoil drainage, and the mineral particles (sand, clay, and silt) must be in such proportions as to avoid the dryness of pure sand and the excessive moisture of pure clay.

Balances between the two determine the natural plant growth in various areas. Cultivation aids proper soil aeration. Working an overwet soil will cause compaction and interfere with air circulation.

The level of the natural water table helps determine the vegetation of a particular area. A high water table usually means a less fertile soil. Drainage is often needed to restore a proper balance between air and water so that desired plants may grow in the area. Air also affects soil temperature. A well-aerated soil is warmer than a wet soil. Good drainage means higher soil heat.

Air circulation over the earth's surface affects plants. Circulating air, breezes, and wind increase evaporation from both plants and the soil. Weak or brittle plants cannot grow in high wind regions because of breakage. General air circulation has a direct effect on plant growth. Cold air flows downhill to collect in low pockets and valleys. Frost occurs earlier in the autumn and persists later in the spring in these low areas, and plants must be able to withstand the still, cold air that collects.

Too much lime, or an alkaline soil, allows only alkaline-tolerant plants to grow. Too much acid limits

plant life to those that like an acid soil, such as most of the broad-leafed evergreens. Certain plants will grow under a variety of conditions, but most plants are "choosy" about their living conditions.

Temperature and sunlight also affect plant growth. The energy of the sun's rays combines with other elements to manufacture the food that the plant needs for growth.

Some plants can use more sunlight than others. For example, full summer sunlight will damage shade-loving plants. Other plants grow best in full summer sun. Intense sun can scald the bark of newly planted trees. Sunlight in winter speeds moisture loss from evergreen foliage. Since the evergreen cannot replace this moisture from the frozen ground, its leaves turn brown, resulting in "winter burn."

Plants with colored foliage often need full sun to develop their rich coloring. Nearly all annuals and most perennials must have full sunlight to bring out an abundance of flowers. Since plants vary widely in their habits and needs, it is important to know what environment each plant likes best.

Temperature affects the transpiration (evaporation of water from the leaves and stems) and aspiration (taking in carbon dioxide) of plants. The best temperature for most plant growth is between 50° and 65° F. Both air temperature and soil temperature have a great influence on plants.

Soil temperatures vary with different soils and in the shade of buildings or trees. Differences in soil temperature explain why some plants will grow better in one garden area than in another.

A plant reference book or the list of materials in Chapter 14 will help you select plants that are hardy for your area. The planting zones indicated in Chapter 14 have been determined on the basis of past experience with plants, but they are not entirely foolproof. Some plants will live where they are supposed to die and die where they apparently should live.

Microclimates exist within the limits of your own property, and must be considered when selecting your plants. For example, the corner of a building may have much higher winds than the sides of a building. Narrow spaces between houses and streets or driveways can act as wind tunnels. Wind patterns can be greatly altered by your plantings and fence locations and those of your neighbors. Your own prevailing wind may vary markedly from the prevailing southwest wind.

Plant growth is affected by various artificial conditions imposed by man. You cannot assume that soil in any city or suburb is in its natural condition. Housing developments nearly always change drainage patterns. Moving the soil changes its natural stability.

Loosening the soil might permit water and air to circulate too freely; compaction has the opposite effect.

Man also changes conditions above ground. Structures cast shadows, and their surfaces reflect heat and light to alter natural conditions. Your choice of plants should be influenced by local variations of heat and light in various parts of your garden.

If you ignore a plant's natural preference for certain living conditions, you will have to work harder to keep it healthy. Plants can live with minimum care under favorable conditions but you will have to watch and care for them constantly if conditions are unfavorable. And even with the best of care, they may not look as you want them to and may even die.

Choose plants that are relatively free from insect and disease problems. You will find that plants grown out of their natural habitat will be more subject to these problems than plants growing in an environment that they like.

Select each plant according to its mature size, growth rate, and life span. Other important qualities that need to be analyzed include the plant's natural form, structure and silhouette, texture and color of bark, foliage, flowers, and fruit.

Each plant has certain characteristics that hold true under a variety of conditions. The height and spread, texture, habits, and shape are usually fairly constant. But too much or not enough sunlight, competition from other plants, or improper soil conditions will affect a plant's growth rate and size, and even its ability to survive.

Many people select plants for their landscape design without considering the mature size, shape, texture, and growth habits of the plants. As a result, plantings often overpower the landscape itself. If you have ever had to cut out a man-made wilderness around a house, you know how important it is to choose plants on the basis of what they will look like when they are full-grown rather than on their appearance as small plants.

Overplanting is a big mistake. It is hard to visualize an 18- to 20-inch evergreen spreading 5 to 6 feet across at maturity. Learn the mature spread of plants, and then be sure to space each plant at least half the total spread of the two plants. For example, if a plant spreads 4 feet at maturity, set it at least 4 feet away from another plant of the same species. The spread of a deciduous shrub should be two-thirds the height of the shrub or equal to the height of the shrub.

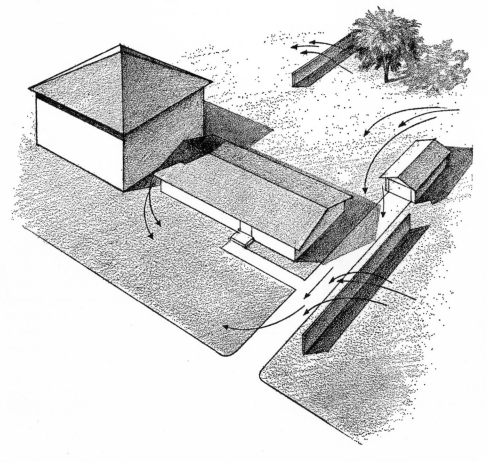

Microclimates are modifications of the general climate. They are a result of the structures and plantings on your property and those on your neighbor's property. Corners of buildings often have winds that are much higher than the winds along the sides of the buildings. Your house, garage, fences, and plantings, as well as those of your neighbors, direct and change wind patterns, create shade conditions, and increase light and heat by reflection. Corners of buildings and the narrow spaces between buildings and along drives can be wind tunnels.

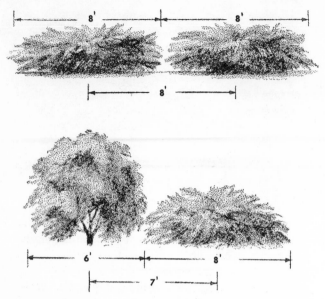

To space plants properly, be sure that the distance from the center of one plant to the center of the next plant is equal to ½ the mature spread of each plant. The spread of a deciduous shrub should be ⅔ the height or equal to the height of the plant.

You should also consider the plant's life span. Many plants grow fast but have short lives. If you choose a fast-growing tree because you are desperate for shade, you may solve the shade problem in a hurry, but be faced with replacement in 15 years or so. Such rapid-growing trees as Chinese elm, poplar, and willow are brittle. High winds, ice storms, and other natural events will damage them severely. Other fast-growing trees, such as hackberry, tulip tree, and sycamore, do not damage as easily, but long-lived plants will pay greater dividends over a period of time.

If you choose plants that will be natural-looking and graceful when they are full-grown, you won't have much trimming to do. Don't depend on pruning to get the shape you want. It is far more practical to choose a plant that will mature into that shape. Each shape has its own place in a landscape design. For example, deciduous shrubs are usually upright, round, or spreading. Deciduous trees are round, weeping, oval, vaselike, erect or columnar, and pyramidal. Evergreens are columnar, narrow pyramidal, broad pyramidal, round, spreading, or creeping. Conical-, pyramidal-, and columnar-shaped plants should always have foliage to the ground to look well in their surroundings. To reduce the striking accent of pyramidal plants, combine them with neutral (round or spreading) forms.

There is a definite relationship between the plant form and the topography in nature's landscape compositions. In a mountainous area, for instance, predominant plants are the conical or pyramidal evergreens. Plants are definitely horizontal in the Great Plains. On the rolling prairies, the dominant plants are rounded. Use this relationship in planning your own landscape design. Rounded plant forms will probably make up the majority of plants in midwestern gardens.

Using all plants of any one shape will be monotonous, of course. Different shapes provide variety and interest by accenting the major type with other forms. In the Midwest, for example, you can often create an interesting picture by adding conical or pyramidal evergreens with the dominant round types of plants. But the blend must be so skillful that the conical plants do not dominate the total picture. Scattering them throughout a shrub border will only result in a distracting composition.

Texture is another element in planting composition. It is a plant feature that is often overlooked or discounted as not being important, but it offers you another chance to add variety and interest to a planting picture. Texture can be defined as the relationship between the foliage and twig size to the rest of the

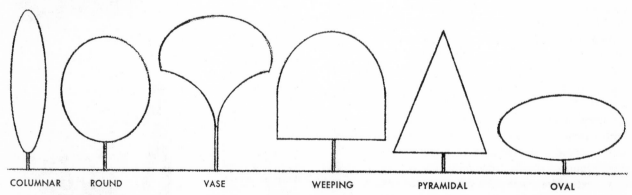

| COLUMNAR | ROUND | VASE | WEEPING | PYRAMIDAL | OVAL |

The form of a plant is one of its most important design qualities. Study the structure and silhouette of various plants. Do not try to include one plant of each shape. Limit your selection to several plant types that will serve as the dominant forms in the design.

MOUNTAINOUS   PLAINS   ROLLING PRAIRIE

There is a direct relationship between plant forms and topography. The basic form of the topography is repeated in the form of native plant materials. Since the rounded forms predominate in the Midwest (right), they should also predominate in your landscape plantings.

plant. But you must qualify this definition in terms of the distance from which the plant is to be seen. Close up, texture comes from the size, surface, and spacing of leaves and twigs at different seasons. At a distance, texture is the entire mass effect of plants and the effect of light and shadow.

Basically, texture is a plant's qualities of coarseness or fineness, roughness or smoothness, heaviness or lightness, thinness or denseness. Plants that are large when seen close up become smaller with distance, and may blend together or disappear at long range.

The texture of leaves depends upon the quality of the leaf surface, as well as upon the spacing and size of the leaves. For example, large leaves that are glossy and white on one side have a finer texture than other large leaves because of the effect of light and shadow. Leaves set on long slender petioles or with a long, tapering shape have a fine texture. Short leaves and petioles have an appearance of strength and coarseness. Density of foliage added to coarseness gives an effect of strength; sparse foliage gives a much weaker effect.

The patterns created by light and shade are also a part of texture. These patterns vary from season to season and even from hour to hour. The shadows cast by fine-textured plants are weak because of the spacing and size of the mass and because of light filtering through the foliage. The shadows cast by coarse-textured plants are strong and definite because the foliage is large or dense and light is reflected from the surface of it. This play of light and shadows emphasizes the fineness or coarseness of the plant's texture.

Good planting design usually strengthens corners with coarser texture and a more solid mass of plants. Use material of medium texture and density for the next group of shrubs, and more delicate plants with finer textures or more open masses in the center. Too much texture uniformity results in monotony. Use variations to get contrast and a play of light and

shadow, but avoid extremes. Never put the coarsest plant next to the finest one. Avoid putting coarse textures in small areas — they will appear harsh and cut down on apparent space.

Change textures in a graduated pattern. Move by steps from the plants with the coarsest texture in the composition to those with the finest texture. Each plant should have about one-half the leaf size of the plant that precedes it. As you move to plants of finer texture, use proportionately larger numbers. For example, you might move from one extremely coarse plant to 3 plants with one-half the leaf size of the first plant; then to 7 plants with the next finest texture; and finally, to 11 plants with the finest texture. Unless your area is extremely large, keep texture changes simple and gradual, and avoid too great a contrast. Your plantings should allow the viewer's eye to move smoothly from the coarsest to the finest textures.

Another plant characteristic is *habit*. This is similar to texture and may be considered part of it. Habit of growth refers to the looseness, density, or irregularity of the plant's branches. Loose, irregular plant types do not belong with those that have compact surfaces.

When viewed at a distance, the texture of a plant is the light and shadow effect of the entire mass. When viewed at close range, the texture of a plant is determined by the size, surface, and closeness of leaves and twigs during the various seasons.

The main purpose of plants in a garden is to provide a leafy, green setting that gives the garden an atmosphere of peace and restfulness. This background is more important than a shrub's flowers. Flowers are interesting for only a short time, but the tree and shrub foliage dominate the garden scene for the entire growing season. Neutral green plants in the garden should outnumber "showy" plants (those that are unusual in form or color) 9 to 1. When you use only a few, select plants for foliage, not for flowers.

Finally, you must consider *foliage color*. The greatest ornamental value of some deciduous trees and shrubs is the color of their leaves in the fall; others are interesting because of their many shades of green. Some ornamental trees and shrubs also have purple or yellow leaf colors in summer to contrast with the usual green. Foliage color must harmonize with the colors of existing or proposed buildings. The wrong choice can result in color clashes.

Color can either tie together or contrast various kinds of woody plants. For example, if you want to use a variety of forms and sizes of plants, it may be desirable to tie the planting together by selecting plants with similar foliage color. Variations of green can add contrast and interest to a planting. Use golden, purple, and variegated foliages cautiously as a strong accent. Remember, the ratio of brightly colored foliage plants to green foliage is 1 to 9.

Plants have color qualities in addition to foliage color that should be considered. Flowers blooming at the same time should harmonize with each other as well as with the color of nearby buildings. Clashing colors of plants blooming at the same time disrupt the beauty of the scene. Some plants, like redtwig dogwood or whitebark birch, have color in their bark and twigs. You can often get a harmonious blend of plant and background colors. An example would be an evergreen background for whitebark birch or redtwig dogwood. The foliage contrasts strikingly in summer, and the colored bark against the deep green evergreen foliage is attractive in the winter.

To develop your own plan, you should know the environmental requirements and design characteristics of plants, and understand how the principles of art apply to landscape design. Unity and harmony are achieved by means of the following: balance and sequence, simplicity and repetition with variety, and scale and proportion.

In a design, there must be a primary focal point or center of interest around which the various landscape elements (plants, structures, and open spaces) are grouped or balanced. The arrangement of these landscape elements should give a *sequence* leading to or away from the focal point.

Simplicity is gained through a repetition of landscape materials. To avoid monotony and add *variety* to your composition, introduce a few other types of plants (ground covers, vines, shrubs, or small trees) for contrast and interest. It is better to repeat a few well-arranged forms, colors, or textures in various areas than to use many different types of plants.

Scale relates to size of individual units and their relationship to other units, such as open space, structures, and plantings. If scale is kept in good balance, your design will have *proportion*. Proportion is a pleasing relationship of one part of the composition to another part and to the whole.

TEXTURE IS . . .

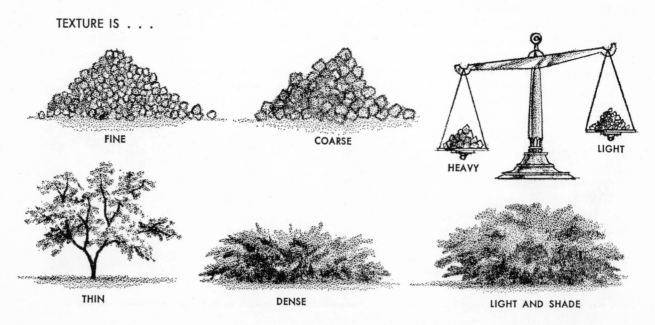

FINE   COARSE   HEAVY   LIGHT

THIN   DENSE   LIGHT AND SHADE

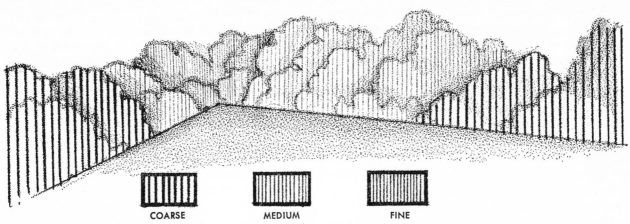

For an attractive border mass, start with the coarsest texture for the end plantings; then grade into medium texture for the next group of shrubs, and use a fine texture at the center of the mass.

DO NOT use coarse textures in a small area. They decrease the apparent size of the area and appear harsh.

To get the most harmonious arrangement, you will need a detailed plan showing the location of each planting. Before selecting specific plants, note on your plan the form (oval, horizontal, arching, etc.), height, spread, color, and texture of each planting. Your selection will also be determined by available space, exposure, and the need for structural enclosures.

Plants that repeat the lines and forms of the house and the texture of the house's construction materials give unity and harmony to a landscape design. Another way to achieve harmony is to select materials of contrasting or complementary colors. For example, dark-green Japanese yews offer a striking contrast against a white house. Or the gray-green leaves of such material as Russian olive or white fir complement a gray house with white trim.

Keep landscape arrangements simple and unified. To achieve unity, use one material several times to tie the design together. A landscape can have harmony when colors of the various plantings blend with one another and with their surroundings. *Balance* can come from the equalizing of masses rather than of forms around the focal point or center of interest.

The front door is the focal point of the public area around which all landscape elements are balanced. For example, a large tree on one side of the property will balance several small trees on the other side; or a medium-sized tree on one side will balance a group of shrubs on the other side.

Repetition is simply the reappearance of attractive materials at several places. You can tie your design together by using roof colors, exterior finishes, dominant building lines, and the same plants (or plants with similar qualities) in several locations. But too much repetition results in monotony.

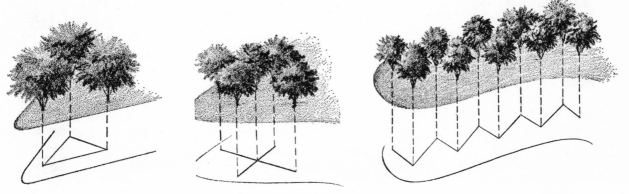

Plants may be set in a triangular staggered line (left), in a checkerboard pattern (middle), or in a staggered flowing line (right).

In a unified composition, you can recognize a similarity of forms throughout the picture. Unity is gained through repetition.

Each tree is a repetition of the other. Since the effect is monotonous, however, one or more different forms should be added for variety.

In this composition, the pyramidal evergreen form has been added to the predominant rounded form. Variety may also be achieved by varying form and color while keeping texture constant, by varying color and texture while keeping form constant, or by varying texture while keeping both form and color constant.

Try to make the best use of the cube of space that surrounds your home. Tall plants give a feeling of enclosure and add to the overall beauty of a landscape by serving as a special planting background. They can also be used to frame a house or a view. Low plants give line and pattern to the design, and, in a less obvious way, enclose and define space. Focus attention on plants with interesting branching habits by using them as specimens near walls, on a board fence, or as foreground.

Plants used in groups should be planted in cultivated beds to eliminate unnecessary maintenance, such as mowing grass between shrubs, etc. Plants placed in beds give a unified massing effect. The line formed between the lawn and the bed becomes a dominant element in the design that can be reinforced by the arrangement of the plants in the beds. Select the planting arrangement that best emphasizes the lines of your basic design.

Check your favorite plants to see if they meet your specifications. Plant selection works backward.

First determine the size and shape of the plants needed to carry out your design. Then look for plants that fit your requirements. Don't try to mold a garden to fit a plant.

Many types of plants are available. See if your local nurseryman can supply your needs. One of his services is to help you get the plants you want, even though he doesn't have the plants on hand.

You can get information about plants from reference materials in your local library or from your state university or college. Nursery catalogs or your nurseryman can also give you valuable information.

If you know exactly what plants you want, be firm in your demands and order only the plants you need. Do not allow substitutions to be made. If your nurseryman doesn't have what you want in stock, he will be able to order the plants for you. You can also order by mail, but be sure to order plants from a reliable nursery that grows its stock in a climate similar to yours. The plants may be hardy, but they will grow best if they are already acclimated.

7: FITTING TREES TO YOUR PLAN

In this chapter, we will discuss fitting trees to your plan. Chapter 8 deals with the selection of shrubs to fit your plan.

Locate trees in your planting plan first. Large trees are valuable for their shade. They also frame a big house when placed to the front, and provide a background for both one- and two-story houses when located at the rear of the property.

Plan tree placement carefully. Show a tree on the plan as a circle that is equal to the mature spread of the tree. Use tracing paper over the basic plan, and plot possible locations in relation to the house and its room arrangements so that you can get shade where you want it. You will want shade on the patio or terrace or the children's playground area, but don't overlook the possibility of using large trees to frame a good view off the rear of your property. A properly placed tree can shade the bedroom areas, provide a frame toward one side of your off-property view, and still serve as a background for the house.

A second large tree might be used to frame the other side of the view, and to shade the outdoor living area, children's play area, and the daytime living area of the house. The crown of the tree may also serve as a screen for an unwanted off-property view. You will need to keep all of these functions in mind to get the most out of any tree you use.

You must also consider underground utility locations when you place a tree. It is not advisable, for instance, to put trees over a septic tank, its drain field, or other underground tiles. Some trees with shallow root systems will interfere with underground utilities. In fact, any tree or plant not getting enough water will send its roots far to get water. These are the roots that clog drain tiles, sewers, and other underground tile lines.

Keep trees away from power and telephone lines running to the house and along the sides or rear of your property. Often large trees growing too close to utilities will engulf the wires. When the utility company trims out the trees to free its lines, you will find ugly holes in the crown disfiguring your landscape design.

When you use large trees for planting, consider the scale relationships between buildings and plant materials. A large tree will frame a large house, but it may overpower a small one. The house is the most important part of the landscape development in the public area. Don't put trees where they will compete with it or blot it out.

Large trees affect the entire planting scheme. For instance, a dense crown provides so much shade that any plants you put near the tree must be able to live under limited light conditions. It is difficult to grow plants or grass under a densely crowned tree. Often the only green mat you can get in such a situation is some kind of ground cover.

Trees also compete for soil nutrients and water. This competition can seriously affect the growth of grass, shrubs, flowers, and other nearby plantings. You will need to consider the rooting habits of trees as well as the shape and spread of their crowns. The surface roots of a tree affect what can grow beneath the tree. A tree whose roots are primarily near the surface should not be placed where it will overlap a planting area (see tree list in Chapter 14) because the tree roots will compete with other plantings. A rule of thumb is that the spread of the root system is roughly equal to the spread of the crown.

The number of trees you can use depends upon the size of the trees. The larger the trees, the fewer you can put on a given lot. Often only one large tree can be placed in the rear yard of a small property.

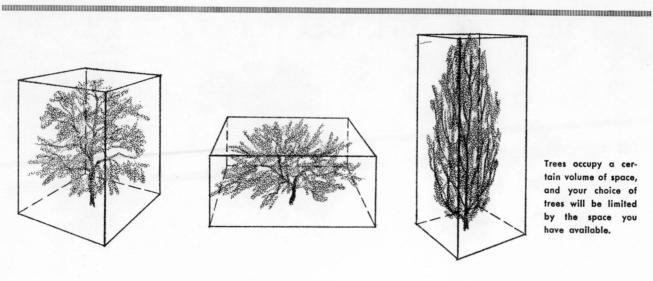

Trees occupy a certain volume of space, and your choice of trees will be limited by the space you have available.

Trees are used to frame a house from the street and provide a background for the house (above); to give variety to the silhouette of a shrub border (right); and to serve as specimen plants (below).

Choose trees that have a deep-descending root system that will not interfere with underground water, drain, and sewer lines, and that will not break curbs or sidewalks. The mature height of trees is also an important consideration. Be sure that the crowns of the mature trees will not engulf overhead power lines.

Consider soil condition, tree hardiness, maintenance needs, exposure, and rate of growth when you select a tree. Be sure that the tree will be adaptable to your yard situation.

The shape and branching habits of a tree are important. Upright or columnar trees have vertical ascending branches, vertically deflected branches, or horizontal branches. Other trees have oval forms, round forms with horizontal or ascending branches, or irregular branching.

If you plant young shade trees in your lawn, you will probably have to grow sun-loving plants in surrounding areas for the first several years. As the trees mature and their crowns grow more dense, you can shift to more shade-tolerant plants. Shade trees can be selected to provide either dense or light shade. Many trees give a light filtered shade; others give dense shade, depending upon their foliage and branching habits.

Trees lining a street provide a delicate canopy of foliage overhead, relieve the monotonous lines of houses, and give a feeling of character to the street and community. Choose a street tree carefully. An ideal street tree is easy to maintain, does not cause damage to curbs, sidewalks, and sewers, will not block street lights or interfere with overhead utilities, and does not have branches so close to the ground that people can't walk under them.

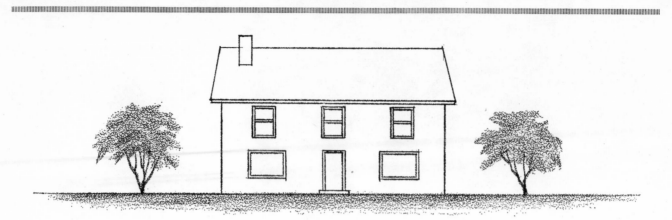

Trees to frame the house must be in scale with the building. A large house framed with small trees (above) appears even larger than it actually is, and a small house framed with large trees (below) appears smaller than it actually is.

The density of the crown is important. The shade may be so heavy that grass won't grow beneath the tree. As the tree matures and casts longer shadows, you must consider whether shrub and flower plantings close to the tree will tolerate the shade or partial shade.

Trees can be planted close together to form a screen (above) or a windbreak if foliage goes all the way to the ground. When their foliage is high, trees can also be planted close together to create a tracery that divides space and provides a partial screen (right). The spreading branches of a single tree (below) create a canopy that forms a part of the ceiling of our outside room.

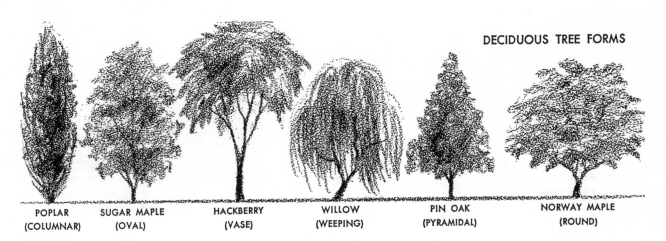

DECIDUOUS TREE FORMS

POPLAR (COLUMNAR)   SUGAR MAPLE (OVAL)   HACKBERRY (VASE)   WILLOW (WEEPING)   PIN OAK (PYRAMIDAL)   NORWAY MAPLE (ROUND)

Small trees planted near a fence soften the harsh lines and monotony created by the fence. The added height of the crown of the tree also results in more privacy.

The effects of land forms can be modified by plantings. An abrupt change in grade can be given a more pleasing transition by locating plants at the base of the slope.

The dominance of a higher piece of ground, such as a knoll or hill, can be reduced by planting at the base — not the top — of the rise.

If you want evergreens without supporting plantings, use at least three evergreens in a group to reduce their vertical effect and to conform to the rule that a planting should be wider than it is high.

The following recommendations will prove helpful in selecting a street tree:

1. If parking strips are 4 feet to 8 feet wide, plant the smaller growing trees, such as redbud or European mountain ash.

2. If parking strips are over 8 feet wide, seed to lawn and plant the larger growing trees, such as maples and oaks.

3. If the sidewalk is next to the curb, plant trees on the inside of the sidewalk. Locate the tree a minimum of 5 feet from the edge of the sidewalk.

4. Do not plant trees closer together than one-half of their total spread.

5. Avoid plantings that will interfere with motorists' vision at intersections and with the effectiveness of street lights. A tree should be planted a minimum of 25 feet from the corner of a block.

6. If there are overhead utility lines, *be sure* to select a tree whose ultimate height will be less than the height of the lowest line.

7. Restrict the planting of wide-spreading trees to wide streets and boulevards. For most residential streets, use trees whose crowns are compact and dense.

Small trees are among the most valuable garden plants, and should be used even more than they are now. In addition to giving shade, small trees interrupt the monotonous straight lines of a building or the top of a fence. Because of their height and form, they can screen objectionable views, provide more privacy by adding height to a fence, and give interest and variety to shrub plantings. Often their attractive flowers, foliage, fall coloring, or bark add seasonal beauty.

Most properties need both small and large trees. Small trees may be used to frame a house if they are planted close to the point from which the house will be viewed.

When planting around your house, do not plant directly in front of a door or window, near cesspools or underground pipe lines, close to walks and drives,

under overhead wires, or where the mature tree will overhang the house.

The forms of evergreens are related to the mountainous regions to which these trees are native. Their striking appearance tends to dominate the landscape here in the Midwest, and for this reason, evergreens should be used sparingly. They are well suited to provide an accent or an interesting silhouette in a shrub border. Most tall evergreen trees gradually narrow at the top. This pyramidal form creates a "saw-toothed" effect that does not fit harmoniously with the dominant round forms found in the Midwest. When tall, narrow evergreens are used, they should be grouped together in clumps of three or four to form a single wide mass.

Because of their strong vertical form, evergreens make striking accent plants in border masses. Since evergreens do not harmonize easily with the topography and plant forms of the Midwest, however, they should not be overused. In the drawing below, an accent is achieved by using evergreen forms, but their dominance is neutralized by the heavy, rounded forms of the background plants.

Remember the following points when selecting your trees:

1. Select trees that are hardy for your area.

2. Do not select trees that have "nuisance" litter, such as messy fruit, seed pods, and broken twigs. This is especially important when trees are near walks or drives.

3. Do not select trees with roots that are heavy surface feeders. Such trees will interfere with the growth of lawn and nearby plantings or will cause surrounding pavement to heave.

4. Do not select rapid-growing trees, such as black locust or Siberian elm (commonly called the Chinese elm). Although these trees will give shade quickly, they are shortlived and are prone to breakage from ice, snow, and wind.

5. Select trees that are longlived and resistant to ice and wind as well as to insects and disease.

6. Select trees that, when full-grown, will fit into the available overhead space.

When a tree is used in a shrub border, the border should be 1½ times as deep as the tree is tall. This rule applies only to the area where the tree is located.

8: FITTING SHRUBS TO YOUR PLAN

The word "shrub" usually refers to a woody perennial that flowers during the growing season. Since shrubs bloom for only a short time, choose them for their foliage, fruit, branching habits, and suitability for a specific location, as well as for their flowers. There is a wide range of shrubs to choose from, and with a little searching, you can find a plant that will exactly fit your plan.

People too often continue to use the same standard materials. Using something new to the neighborhood can bring you personal pleasure and still do its job well. You may not be able to find what you want at your local nursery because most nurserymen carry stock that is in greatest demand. But a nurseryman will usually order less common material if that is what you want.

Shrubs can be classified as specimens, accent plants, foundation plants, borders, screens, and hedges.

Specimen and Accent Plants

A specimen plant is one that has special qualities that warrant its use as an individual plant in such a way as to display those qualities. A specimen is usually a perfect example of the type it represents, and is outstanding in form, texture or color.

In general, use specimen plants by themselves where they can be enjoyed. You can use a plant as a specimen in a border, but it must be better than any other plant in the border, and it must be planted so that it can be viewed as an individual plant. A single specimen shrub can often take the place of a small tree. You may want to use a specimen shrub as the end feature of an axis (a major line of vision), or as a dominant element at the end of a straight line in a formal design.

If a specimen plant is not the same as the border plants, it must be at least similar to the group in size, shape, foliage, texture, and color. Do not use a totally different kind of plant. You can often use specimen plants at special points to frame a building, to accent a corner of special areas or flower beds, or to add interest to an open lawn area. Use these plants sparingly. Too many of them are distracting in a landscape design.

Accent plants are closely related to specimen plants. A specimen plant usually stands alone; an accent plant is part of the shrub mass but of a different height. It may also differ in form, color, and texture from the shrub mass.

Shrubs can be used for accent plants in both formal and informal gardens. Accent shrubs can be used to vary the height of the shrub border. They break up the silhouette and relieve the monotony of a group of plants of similar height.

Select plants for accent that are taller than they are wide. If you can't find deciduous shrubs that are suitable, you can use one of the pyramidal evergreens for accent in a deciduous shrub border. Using the same kind of accent plant at several locations in a long border, either singly or in groups of three, adds continuity and sequence to a garden design.

Arrange shrubs in masses or groups to give an appearance of strength to the border and to create line and good composition. Plants used as specimens might occupy 10 feet of lawn. The same plants would occupy only 6 to 8 feet in a shrub border because they would be planted more closely together to subordinate their specimen qualities.

Tall and thin plants with few leafy branches at the base are well suited for a shrub border. Tops can

Representative Shrub Forms

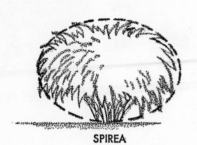

SPIREA

BARBERRY

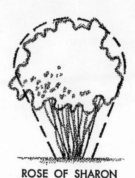

ROSE OF SHARON

MOCKORANGE

SAVIN JUNIPER

CREEPING JUNIPER

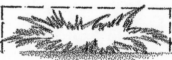

ANDORRA JUNIPER

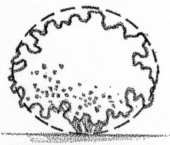

DWARF WINGED EUONYMUS

GLOBE ARBORVITAE

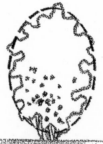

OREGONGRAPE

JAPANESE YEW

then grow freely to display flowers and foliage. Use smaller shrubs with lower branching habits in front of the tall ones to hide the bare branches and trunk at the base. Select two, three, or five different shrubs and use them together in large numbers. Keep the planting simple. Don't spot it with many different kinds of plants.

Foundation Plantings

Select shrubs for the foundation planting around your house that will make the house look natural and appropriate for its site. Choose shrubs that will not get large enough to need heavy pruning. Pruning destroys the natural shape of shrubs.

A few plants at the foundation are usually much more satisfactory than many plants. If you decide that your foundation planting calls for at least two

different kinds of plants, choose those that look well together. Examples are an upright Japanese yew in combination with three dwarf spreading yews, or a winged euonymus with dwarf Pfitzer or Andorra juniper around the base.

Branching habit is another important feature of foundation plants. Those with round or spreading shapes are preferable to those with a stiff, upright appearance. By selecting the correct type of shrub, it is easy to keep the planting proportions in scale with the house. This is not usually true with upright evergreen plants unless they are severely pruned. Select foundation plants that will blend man-made objects into the natural surroundings by providing a transition between the strong vertical lines of the house and the strong horizontal lines of the ground. For instance, the foliage should sweep to the ground so that the lower branches direct the eye to the grass.

TYPES OF SHRUB PLANTINGS

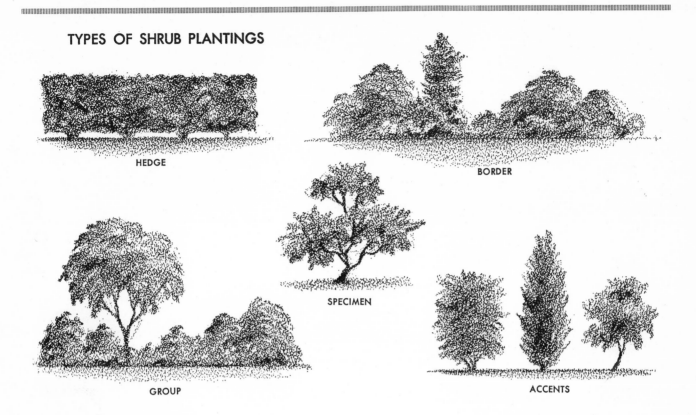

HEDGE

BORDER

SPECIMEN

GROUP

ACCENTS

USES OF SPECIMEN PLANTS

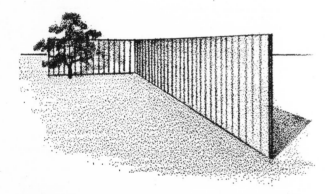

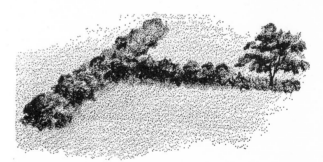

Specimen used as the terminus of the main axis of view. Fence shows off the plant's special qualities.

Specimen used as a part of a right-angle planting to emphasize the importance of an area.

Specimen adds interest in a shrub border when surrounded and framed by neutral plants.

Group Plantings

Three or four plants that are similar in form, color, and texture can be combined into a group planting. Group plantings should be interesting in outline and arrangement. They may be used against a fence to break up the monotony of its length, to divide areas, and to create interest near the patio or parking area.

One basic use for shrubs in the foundation planting is around doorways. The doorway is the center for all plantings in the design of the public area. It should provide a pleasing and attractive focal point. Doorway plantings should be interesting, but should not compete with the doorway for attention. They should be no higher than one-fourth to one-third the distance from the groundline to the eave.

A rule of thumb for corner plantings is that the maximum height of the mature plant should not be more than two-thirds the distance from the ground to the eave. Round-shaped plants tend to direct the eye to the ground and to break up vertical lines better than upright evergreens, giving a desirable transition between man-made objects and the natural surroundings. An upright evergreen at the corner emphasizes rather than softens the vertical line. If upright evergreens are used, there should be adequate room for additional plantings of low spreading evergreens to give a better transition.

Shrub Borders, Screens, and Hedges

In developing your landscape, remember that you are dealing with a cube of space. This space has sides, a ceiling, and a floor surface. You can create an outdoor living room and give form to this space by enclosing the sides with a shrub border. This border may act as a background for flowers, and create the walls of the outdoor living room. A shrub border may also serve as a screen if you need one for privacy or to block out an objectionable view.

Have a definite idea of the silhouette you want in your shrub border. Determine what size plants you need, and then select a few different varieties of shrubs. You may decide, for example, that four varieties will be enough for your particular border. Group several of each selected variety together (perhaps three in one group and five in another). Repeat each variety at several locations throughout the shrub border to get a unified effect (composition). Grouping or massing several shrubs of the same variety avoids the spotty, disjointed effect that results from using one forsythia, one mockorange, and one spirea. To avoid monotony, introduce accent plants of greater height or different habit or form of growth. Study the silhouette to get the sizes and shapes you want. Both foliage color and flower color should make a pleasing contrast with the color of the house and surrounding structures.

In choosing hedge and screen plants, you will want dense foliage that cannot be seen through and plants that are able to survive close together. Hedges can be either clipped (formal) or unclipped (informal). A formal clipped hedge demands a great deal of maintenance.

Shrubs for hedges must be able to tolerate a regular shearing. Shearing makes the plant thicker. Small twigs covered with leaves set close together eventually create a solid wall of foliage. Shrubs for hedges should also have a strong branching habit that will hold a load of ice and snow. (See Chapter 14 for suggested shrubs for hedges.)

To use shrubs as a screen, plant a solid mass of one kind to give the effect of a living wall. An ideal shrub for a screen would be tall and narrow but with heavy foliage to the ground. If you cannot find this kind of shrub, use tall plants that lack foliage at the base and put a lower growing type in front. This combination of plants may closely resemble a hedge, but since the plants aren't sheared, the screen doesn't have formal shape and is considered an informal screen. A screen planting can be a background for flowers, lawn, or a mixed shrub border.

The height of a screen or hedge will have to be a compromise between the height needed for screening and the limitation of scale given by the area. For example, in a small area where screening is necessary, a high screen might make the area seem even smaller than it actually is.

A border mass may be located along the property line or within the property as "arms" extending from the sides to divide or form areas. It might also serve as a background for flowers, to screen objectionable objects, to frame views, and to modify the effect of changes in ground elevation. If you use too many different types of plants in a border mass, you will have a plant collection rather than a pleasing composition. Select only a few varieties, and repeat them at various locations in the border. It is not necessary to repeat the variety in the same arrangement or number.

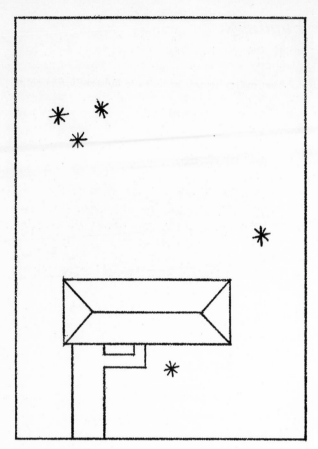 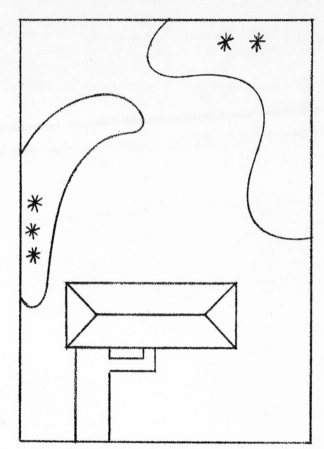

For a unified effect between plantings (foundation plantings, groups, border masses), repeat the same plant in several areas (left).   Repeat flowering shrubs at least once in the same general viewing area (right).

Screen plantings are usually made of neutral material arranged in harmonious groupings so that they do not draw attention. You don't have to block out an unpleasant view completely. A hedge or screen in harmony with the rest of the landscape will hold the viewer's attention to such an extent that he is not conscious of the unpleasant view behind the hedge or screen. You can also subordinate a building by placing some striking material in the foreground. Such special-interest plantings may even be placed at another angle to divert attention from what is being screened.

Planter Boxes

Planter boxes are often used in contemporary architecture. They may emphasize the horizontal lines of a house, define front-door areas, or, in many cases, simply parallel the front facade. There is much doubt about the value of a planter box as a planting area. Often the builder sets a planter box at such a point, scales it to such a height, and makes it of such proportion that it balances a particular area in front of the house. Adding plant material to the

height of the box, however, can completely throw the balance or continuity out of kilter.

Planter boxes are often tacked on wherever it suits the designer's or owner's fancy. Certainly some of the planter boxes that you see illustrated in popular magazines appear to be very desirable additions to a home. But to keep a planter box as neat and attractive as those shown in the magazine pictures would be almost a full-time job.

Plants in boxes or other containers above ground are subject to greater temperature and moisture variations than plants in the ground. As a result, they are much more sensitive to light, drouth, wind, and temperature. For example, soil in a masonry planter box will freeze and thaw much faster than the same soil in the ground. Planter-box materials must have the ability to survive these extremes of freezing and thawing and lack of moisture. Box plantings also demand special soil preparations and drainage.

Tubs, movable planter boxes, and other types of portable gardens also need special soil preparation, and the plants in them are subject to the same problems as those in fixed planter boxes.

Border Mass Plantings

To overcome monotony in a border mass, use shrubs that are of contrasting heights or that are outstanding in color, texture, or form.

Ground Covers

Ground covers have become one of the most useful types of material for landscape development. Ground covers are plant materials that improve the appearance of the ground and, in some cases, hold soil and prevent erosion. The proper ground-cover material will depend upon exposure to the sun and the degree of refinement or finish needed. In general, the nearer the observer is to the ground cover, the more refined and dense it should be; the farther away, the more loose the growth can be.

Ground covers are often used instead of grass. In the past, ground covers were used mostly on banks to hold soil and reduce mowing. But they can also be used in front of shrubbery, in shrub-bed areas, or in a large panel to increase the scale of a small area. They are often difficult to establish, and it takes some time for them to grow over an area.

Keep the soil moist with frequent watering while the cover is spreading, and cultivate carefully so that the roots are not damaged. You will need to hand weed until the bed is established. Once established, a ground cover should crowd out any weeds and be relatively weed-free.

Ground cover does not wear well, and should not be used in heavy traffic areas. Traffic areas need lawn or hard surfaces.

A formal hedge (above) requires maintenance to keep it well groomed. The plants must tolerate shearing and not break under the weight of snow. Material for a formal hedge should be spaced 18 to 24 inches apart. An informal hedge (below) is not pruned, and the plant material is allowed to grow in its natural form. Spacing varies with the plant selected, and can be as wide as 3 to 3½ feet between plants.

Screen plantings are used to obstruct movement, block vision, and reduce noises. A screen planting (above) is a low-cost means of obtaining an enclosure. Since many tall-growing shrubs may not have foliage at their bases, lower-growing shrubs can be planted in front of them (below). These "facer" shrubs mask the bare stems of the taller shrubs, and the increased foliage mass serves as a more effective sound barrier.

Vines

Vines are not used in American gardens as much as they should be. Perhaps they are not properly cared for, or owners are not familiar with the basic needs of vines. You can use them in your garden in many effective ways — for green foliage, screening, shade, overhead protection, or simply for their beauty. They are especially valuable in a small garden because they need little space to grow.

Vines are usually classified by their climbing habits. Some vines twist around for support, some have tendrils that reach out and attach to a support, others cling by little rootlets, and still others cling directly to stone or brick. Some sub-shrubs are not actually vines, but have long, flexible branches that can be tied in place to establish patterns.

Landscape designers divide vines into those that grow densely to form a solid covering, and those that grow loosely to provide a tracery effect that you can see through. You can thin out densely growing vines to get a tracery effect, but it is a lot of work. It is better to select the vine needed for the specific location. A light vine can be used as a tracery to break up the flat surface of a wall or fence. It can also be used to create an open tracery against the lattice or wire fence that serves as the vine's support.

Vines can be used for overhead protection over patios and other areas where shade trees might not be high enough to give the desired protection. This is an inexpensive way to get summer shade. A vine can help soften harsh construction lines, particularly on a two-story house. A vine across the porch can prevent the viewer's eyes from running up and down the full vertical height of the house. And vines can give a full, rich effect in narrow spaces.

The support for a vine should not be conspicuous unless it is a screen or baffle. A fancy trellis design against a house or fence is out of place and should not be used. A simple support of dowels and wire is far better than a highly designed, intricate support. A vine should blend into the total effect and not be shown off as an individual specimen.

If the vine is in direct sunlight, use insulated wire, slats, or wood dowels for support rather than bare wire. Wire heats up tremendously in the summer sun, and will burn the tips of young shoots.

You can often use two different types of vines for overhead or upright screening — one for dense foliage, and the other for its flowers. Usually the flowering vines are most satisfactory for the home garden.

Vines may be used on a porch for shade or as a screen. They may also be used over the patio and other areas where shade trees may not be high enough to give desired protection.

9: FITTING FLOWERS TO YOUR PLAN

Flowers must fit into the total landscape picture, but they should not be so spectacular that they stand out more than any other feature.

Since the house is the most important element in the total design of the public area, all planting and construction should complement the house, not compete with it for attention. Keep island flower beds, for example, out of the front yard.

As a general rule, flowers should be restricted to the rear of the property, to the outdoor living area, or to the service area. It is best if there are no flowers in the public area at all, although sometimes a planter box or an area within the foundation plantings can be planted to annuals satisfactorily. Only one type and color of flower should be planted, and the flowers should be planted in masses. Color in harmony with the house can give a pleasing contrast, but the color should not be so vivid and dominant that it holds the viewer's attention.

You'll hear frequent arguments that mother or grandmother had her flowers in the front yard. In grandmother's and even mother's day, people spent a great deal of their leisure time on the front porch; and since they wanted to see and enjoy their flowers, they put them in the front lawn. But outdoor living has moved to the rear of the house — flower beds should be there too, where you can enjoy them.

Flowers add considerable color and interest when seen from the patio or interior of the house. If you enjoy gardening, you can work a flower border into your landscape design that will provide contrast and variety to the overall composition. But if you want an attractive place with a minimum demand on your free time, you can create a pleasing landscape picture around your house through the use of trees, shrubbery, lawn, and ground covers only.

If you use a flower border in the outdoor living area, be sure that it does not dominate the entire garden. Flowers — like screening shrubs, flowering shrub borders, trees, and surfacing materials — should be only one element in the landscape picture. The only time a flower border should capture the complete attention of the observer is when it is used as a surprise feature tucked away behind an arm of shrubs that projects out toward the center of the lawn. Too lavish a display of color destroys the restful atmosphere of the outdoor living area.

The structure, form, and texture of the plants are important in a flower border. But if you intend to use flowers for indoor arrangements or garden club competition, the flower itself is of primary importance. A cut-flower garden in the service area will allow you to grow flowers in rows, as individuals. Then you will be able to give your flowers the necessary care to produce fine specimens.

Landscape design distinguishes between a flower bed and a flower border. A flower bed is designed to stand by itself. It is used in formal gardens as a display, and is not meant to supply cut flowers, since it is a definite design element surrounded by walks, lawns, or possibly a low hedge.

A flower border, on the other hand, consists of flowers planted in front of a shrub border. It has informal patterns, and its flowers are set off by the shrubbery. It is much easier to design a flower border than a flower bed. Since a flower border is seen from one side only, you simply plant low flowers in the front, medium-sized flowers in the middle, and tall flowers in the back. High shrubs provide the background.

To be most effective, flowers must be seen against a background that will show off their colors. It is a

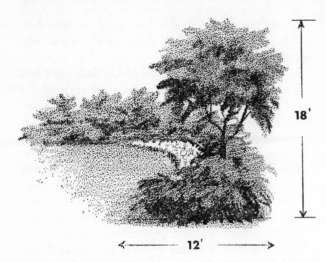

18'

12'

A planting border should be designed so that the incurve is located at the corner of the property. Locate flowers to the front of the incurve and shrubs behind the flowers for background. The shrubs in the outcurve should have a coarser texture than the shrubs behind the flowers. It is often desirable to use a small flowering tree in the outcurve. The tree should be approximately 1½ times as high as the bed is deep.

common mistake to plant flowers without this background. Most flowers need a dark background. This may be the green foliage of shrubs or the brown of a stained fence. Flowers planted against a light background lose much of their effectiveness.

A flower border located in a shrub border as a part of a long, sweeping curve is much more restful to the eyes than a flower border with sharp, angular lines. Curves preserve an informal effect. Limit flower borders to 5 feet in depth, since you will normally work in them only from the front.

Keep a flower border in reasonable proportion to the rest of the garden, especially to the shrub wall in the rear. For example, a 2-foot-deep border planting of flowers against a 10-foot-deep shrub planting would be only a shoestring of color rather than a garden feature. A 10-foot-deep flower border against a brick wall would also be out of proportion.

Annuals are plants that make all their vegetative growth, flower, and produce seed in one growing season, and then die. Most of them propagate by means of seeds. Biennials are plants that usually use at least part of two growing seasons to complete their life cycle, with a more or less dormant period in the middle. Perennials are plants that normally live more than two years.

Flower forms are a basic design element. The three major classifications are the spike form, the round form, either with individual flowers or flower clusters, and the intermediate shapes. Examples of the spike form include delphinium, lupine, and snap-

dragon. Peonies, oriental poppies, geraniums, and dahlias exemplify the round form. Bearded iris is considered intermediate.

In a flower border, the spike-form flowers are used as an accent comparable to the pyramidal form of evergreen in the general landscape. Used flagrantly, they become a disturbing force that may break up the entire composition. If you do not use the spike form at all, however, you run the risk of monotony and lack of interest.

Start your flower-border design with a scale plan on paper. Show each area to be planted to annuals, biennials, and perennials. Sketch in accent points, and then build a sequence of related sizes and shapes around them, making sure that the round flower form predominates.

The same basic color principles apply to flowers as to woody shrubs and all other ornamental plantings, and to such other color sources as structures, paving, house color, and trim. Color expresses individual tastes, and no one can tell you which colors you should use to dominate your own composition. Since you deal with color every day in wardrobe selection, home furnishings, and even the groceries and other package goods you buy, you can appreciate the important role color plays in human lives.

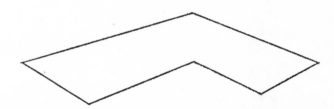

A planting border is a cultivated area in which the soil may either be exposed or covered with a mulch or an underplanting of ground cover. The border area should contrast sharply with the lawn and form a strong, dominant line and pattern in the design. Straight, angular lines (above) are usually uninteresting and monotonous because they are repeated in walks, drives, house, and property lines. Straight-line borders can be used, however, when the total design is composed of straight lines that form an overall design. (See Chapter 11 for illustrations of the use of straight-line borders.) A curved bed pattern (below) is more restful to the eye than a sharp, angular pattern, and preserves an informal effect.

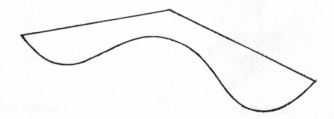

Color must please the eye. The color wheel is a good guide for obtaining pleasing color combinations. Red, yellow, and blue are the *primary* colors, and orange, green, and purple are the *secondary* colors. Red, orange, and yellow are *warm* colors. Blue, green, and violet are *cool* colors. A warm color is always opposite a cool color on the color wheel.

Since warm colors are closely related on the color wheel, they can be used together in vivid color combinations. As a general rule, use warm colors in a sequence. For example, a sequence could be a gradation from red to white. But the sequence must be smooth and gradual, such as from red to scarlet, to orange scarlet, to orange, to orange bronze, to orange yellow, to yellow, to pale yellow, to cream, and finally, to pure white. A jump from red to orange to yellow to white is too abrupt without the intermediate colors.

There is no rule of thumb for how much warm (or how much cool) color to use. But the smaller the area, the fewer warm colors you can use, and the shorter the sequence you can develop. If your proposed flower area is small, you may be able to develop a sequence from orange through light yellow or deep pink through white.

First, decide what color you want to use; then whether a light or a dark shade of this color will dominate.

Establish the largest amount of the dark color you will use (this will be determined by the scale of the area). The darker and purer or more intense the color, the more it will show up and dominate the scene. For this reason, you will not want to use too much of the darkest shade. Select your next lighter shade, and increase by one-third the number of plants used. Then go to the next lighter shade, and increase by one-third the number of these plants over the preceding group. Continue this ratio until you reach the lightest shade in your color graduation.

Use the darkest shades or the pure, intense flower colors at the point of principal interest, but avoid too much variety where it might add confusion.

Although cool colors (blue, green, purple) can be used in a sequence, they can be combined more effectively in a series of contrasts.

Those colors opposite one another on the wheel are *complementary* or *contrasting* colors. The purest or strongest of these complementary or contrasting colors, create a gay, lively effect — for example, the yellow of snapdragons with blue delphinium.

MAJOR FORMS FOR A FLOWER BORDER

SPIKE FORM   **ROUND FORM**   **INTERMEDIATE FORM**

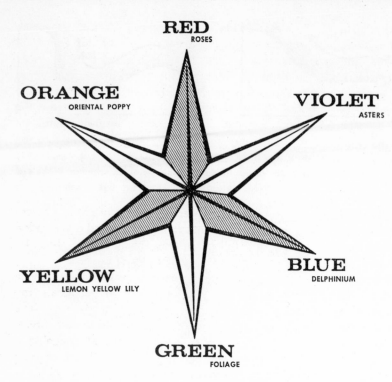

RED
ROSES

ORANGE
ORIENTAL POPPY

VIOLET
ASTERS

YELLOW
LEMON YELLOW LILY

BLUE
DELPHINIUM

GREEN
FOLIAGE

This color wheel lists flowers that are examples of the primary colors (red, yellow, blue) and the secondary colors (orange, green, violet). The warm colors (red, orange, and yellow) are closely related to one another. They are best used in sequence. The cool colors (violet, blue, and green) are used most effectively as contrasts to the warm colors.

You can obtain the most effective color contrasts by using the same shade of color opposites. Usually, you can also get pleasing contrasts by using a light shade of one color with a dark shade of its color opposite. For example, you might use light yellow columbine against dark violet lupine. But too many striking contrasts of light and dark shades can become disturbing contrasts in the composition, and give a mottled effect. Bright contrasting colors are useful for accent and emphasis, and contrasting muted or neutral colors result in a more restful picture.

Colors can create various illusions. Predominantly cool colors in a garden or at the back of a very short yard give an illusion of depth. Strong, warm colors at the rear of a garden or yard tend to make the garden or yard look shorter than it actually is.

The spacing of plants is important in flower border design. Some types spread rapidly and need frequent division, while others do not need to be divided for several years or more. The branches of trees and shrubs have permanent structure, but the stems of flowers die each fall. Since flowers do not have permanent structure, they should be used in groups rather than as individual specimens. Keep some space between groups and between plants within each group to avoid overcrowding and to give form to the border. Consider growth rates as well as the spreading habits of the different plants.

Flowers can be classified into three groups according to their spread and growth habits.

Group 1 plants spread rapidly and need to be divided and replanted every year, or at least every other year. This group includes asters, Michaelmas daisies, sunflowers, buttercups, goldenrod, helenium, wormwood, and rudbeckias.

Group 2 plants spread more slowly than those in Group 1, and need to be replanted every four or five years. This group includes artemisia, perennial spirea, bellflower, Shasta daisy, pink delphinium, comb flower, daylily, coral bells, flax, cinquefoil, painted daisies, violas, and violets.

Group 3 plants spread slowly and should not be disturbed for 8 to 10 years or more. Since the mature spread of these plants is quite wide, they shouldn't be planted close together. Examples in this group include heliotrope, clematis, bleeding heart, gas plant, globe thistle, baby's breath, lavender, lupine, bluebells, peony, and oriental poppy.

Decide the shape of each plant grouping or unit, and then space plants according to how often you will need to move them. Space Group 1 plants 6 to 8 inches apart and divide them every year. Space Group 2 plants 12 to 18 inches apart so that they will not be overcrowded before the end of four to five years. Place Group 3 plants at least 3 feet apart so that they won't have to be transplanted for years.

An informal planting bed is usually designed in a series of incurves and outcurves. Each outcurve reaches its greatest width at a certain point and

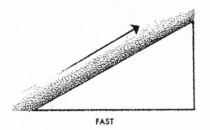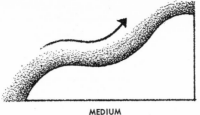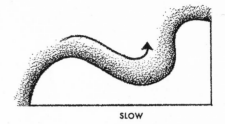

FAST   MEDIUM   SLOW

Snowdrift patterns formed by various wind velocities. The wind velocity parallels the rate at which the eye moves along a straight line, a slightly curved line, and a pronounced curve. These patterns are used in the design of a shrub border to concentrate the viewer's attention on the flower planting. A flower border is usually located in the incurve because any change in direction slows down the movement of the eye.

recedes from that point. These curves resemble snowdrifts as they build up against a fence. A snowdrift formed by a low-velocity wind has a very broad outcurve and a deep incurve, while a snowdrift built up by a moderate wind has less incurve. Drift buildup under a high wind is almost a straight line from the ground to the fence. The driftline is the result of wind velocity. The velocity of the wind parallels the rate of eye movement along these driftlines. The shape of the total shrub and flower-planting area should be developed by using these same principles.

In planning a shrub background for a flower border, you might allow the shrub groupings to come out to the edge of the bed at the point of the most extreme outcurve. Shrubs used at this point should have the coarsest foliage. Use deciduous shrubs with finer texture behind the flowers. A deep-bay inset of flowers framed on each side by a bold outcurve of coarse foliage grading into medium-textured foliage, and finally, into a finer foliage behind the incurve of flowers, makes an attractive planting picture.

Everything flows from the point of the outcurve to the point of the incurve — flower groups flow toward the center of the incurve, which is the focal point of the composition, and shrubs flow from the coarsest to the finest textures. Be sure to use bold curves. A number of wavy lines show direction feebly and can be irritating.

Relate planting height to border width. Usually, the shrub background or fence should be 1½ times as high as the bed is deep. For example, if the bed is 10 feet deep, the tallest planting should be about 15 feet high. But you don't have to conform strictly to this rule. Bold outcurves become planting high points, and these same outcurves, carefully located, can screen undesirable views or objects, or provide some of the privacy that you want for outdoor living.

Don't put an outcurve in the corner of your lot. That's the place for an incurve. Use facer plants in front of shrubs on the outcurve if you want to hide the "leggy" bare stems of the shrubs. You may want

to use some small flowering trees for height and accent at the center of an outcurve with ground cover underneath. The full-grown trees should also be about 1½ times as high as the deepest part of the bed.

Remember that herbaceous plants (those having little or no woody tissue), such as perennials and annuals, are *accessories* to the garden structure. The basic structure is made up of the trees and shrubs. Perhaps the most common mistake in designing a flower border is assigning the structural job of trees and shrubs to herbaceous plants.

Most herbaceous plants are attractive for only a short time. They need much more care than trees or shrubs, and are unattractive for long periods unless the area is constantly groomed. For this reason, short-term herbaceous plants should be backed up with good shrub plantings.

Flowers in the flower border should not be planted as individuals (right). Using flowers as plant groups and masses (below) will give a far more pleasing effect.

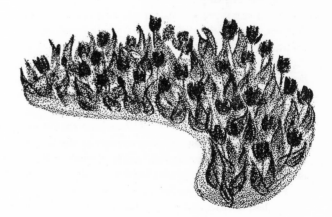

Colors can be used to create an illusion. Cool colors recede, while warm colors advance. If you have a short yard (above), use cool colors to the rear to make the yard appear deeper. If you have an extremely long, narrow yard (below), use strong, warm colors to the rear to make the yard appear shorter.

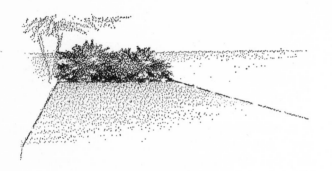

Plan the background to supplement the flower border rather than to compete with it. A background should be subtle and subordinate in the total picture. Walls and shrubs make effective backgrounds, but a fence design must be neutral without any detail or it will dominate. Another reason why you should not plant flowers against the house is that the house is architecturally "busy" with windows, doors, and trim. Flowers in the foreground must share interest with the house features.

Keep border plantings simple. Mass materials in drifts — don't spot them here and there. It is very difficult to keep a border in bloom all summer. If you are limited in space, you can expect only one good show a season. Plan for peak effectiveness either in the spring or fall, and depend upon flowering shrubs to carry the interest at other times.

All plants in a grouping should be sun-loving or shade-loving, and they should require the same conditions of soil, moisture, light, air, and temperature. The environmental needs of trees and shrubs discussed in Chapter 6 also apply to herbaceous plants. A wrong choice of plants will result in dead or dying plants, or a great deal of work to keep the plants going.

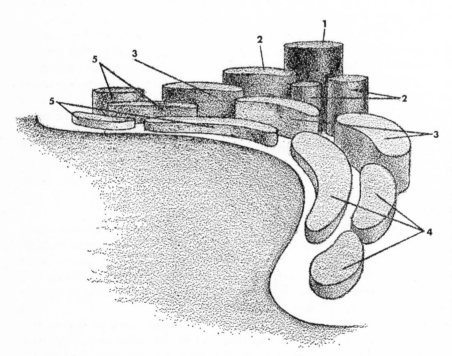

Since the darkest shade and pure intense color dominate a composition, it is wise to use the darker and more intense colors sparingly. You can balance the dominance of the dark color by selecting a lighter shade of harmonious color. To achieve this balance, increase the number of plants of the lighter shade by one-third. In this drawing, Group 1 represents the darkest mass, Group 2 the mass of the next lightest shade, etc. Notice the increase in the size of the masses as they become progressively lighter.

10: DESIGNING THE PUBLIC AREA

Every home needs a well-designed landscape to make it more livable, attractive, and valuable. Since the house is the most important element in the public-area landscape, all construction features (walks, drives, fences) and all plantings should complement the house, provide a proper setting for it, and not compete with it. Fundamental landscape principles for developing the public area are (1) to soften the architectural lines of the building, (2) to frame the building with trees, and (3) to maintain open lawn areas.

Your main purpose in developing the public area should be to blend the artificial structure of the house with the general surroundings so that the house looks natural on its site. You can do this by softening and blending the vertical house lines with the strong horizontal ground lines. A good transition between these two dominant lines creates a natural and attractive setting for the house.

The center of interest and balance point for all plantings is the doorway. The major planting areas to consider, then, are those at the corners where there are strong vertical lines and on each side of the doorway.

Before you can choose specific plants and arrange them in front of your house, you will need to analyze the architectural lines of your house. Study window locations, cornice detailing, doorway and porch arrangement, and any other architectural details or ornamentation. Ask yourself if all these various elements on the front facade are pleasing, tastefully detailed, and balanced into an attractive overall design. One element may seem awkward, poorly conceived, and ill-designed. If so, you can arrange plantings to soften, blend, or mask the awkward element so that it doesn't dominate the total picture.

In addition, study the balance of all the facade elements. Is the window arrangement on the left side of the door the same as that on the right side? Is the door exactly in the middle of the front facade? You may have true balance with a repetition of windows and other elements on each side of the door in the same proportion, or you may have an off-balance arrangement. If your door is off-center and the other elements of the front are not balanced, you can use a planting composition to restore visual balance.

Make a rough sketch to scale of the front of your house with windows, doors, and porches properly located. Or a black and white photograph is suitable if it shows only the front facade (not the sidewalls) of the house. Using a marking pencil, draw heavy black up-and-down lines at the corners of the house and at any jogs or projections on the front facade. To determine the balance, draw a small sawhorse in the center of the front foundation line and imagine the house as a teeter-totter to balance at this point. From this sketch, you can get an idea where you will need plantings to get better balance.

Exterior construction materials are also important to help set the scale of the plant textures to be used. For example, heavy siding calls for coarse plant materials. Any other construction in the public area would have to be identical with the siding or in scale and harmony with it.

You should also consider views to the outside from rooms that overlook the public area. Note on a pad of paper the views that you see; then decide whether they are acceptable. Outstanding views should be dramatized, while unsightly views need to be screened out. Note on your plan where plantings might be needed to frame a good view or screen a bad one, or where construction might be needed for

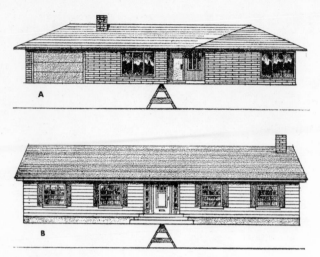

In (B) above, notice that the number, arrangement, and proportion of the elements to the left and right of the doorway are exactly the same, giving a formal design. In (A) the point of balance (fulcrum) is not the doorway, and different elements of different proportions and arrangements are located on either side of the doorway. This is an asymmetrical design. By making elevation drawings like these, you can study the massing, proportions, and balance of your house.

privacy. Also study the topography, drainage, and scale relationships of the foreground area between the house and street.

Proper grading for drainage will not only save you money in the long run, but may also prevent such disappointments as plant failure. If you have any doubt as to what is to be done and how, it is a good idea to consult with a professional landscape architect, a reputable nurseryman, or a contractor experienced in determining proper grades.

If your property has much slope, you may need a retaining wall. Decide well in advance where you want grade changes and how these changes will af-

fect your landscaping plans. With retaining walls, you can establish flat areas that help to solve erosion problems and give enough area for landscape development.

Ideally, the slope should be away from the house so that you get a series of terraces to look down upon. If you have to climb a flight of stairs to enjoy a flat garden area, you will probably make little use of it.

If your land slopes gradually or is almost flat, you may need only to grade a slope away from the house so that there will not be any standing water around the foundation.

Basic construction for the public area usually includes a drive, parking space, walks, screen, and baffles. The color and texture of the material used in the public area must harmonize with the house. For example, don't use a flagstone walk with a brick house. It is best to repeat home building materials in landscape construction. If this is not possible, use materials that will blend and harmonize pleasantly with your house — the focal point of the landscape.

Walls, fences, or baffles in the public area are not generally used as a barrier along the edge of the property. Usually you cannot justify building a fence along the side yard or across the front of the house. The best setting for any home consists of plantings across the front with an open lawn, uninterrupted except by trees and necessary walks and drives.

Large picture windows often open onto the public area and directly to the street. By building a baffle, small wall, or fence that fits the design of the house, you can cut off the view from the street directly into the house and create an intimate garden that can be seen from within the house. Plantings on the street side will soften the harshness of this added structure.

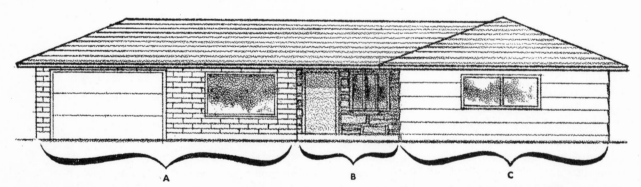

Do not combine completely different materials. The differences in texture, color, and scale often result in unpleasant contrasts.

Proportion and balance are lost when one material overpowers another. In the drawing above, (A) is brick, (B) is crab orchard stone, and (C) is board siding. (A) and (B) overpower (C) and dominate the entire facade. If areas (A) and (B) were either all brick or all stone, the result would be the same.

If (A) and (C) were siding, and (B) were either stone or brick, there would be proper proportion and balance. Brick and stone should never be used together. They are out of scale with each other, and give a poor contrast.

Doorway Plantings

Doorway plantings for a house with formal balance should carry out this balance. The plant used on one side of the doorway is repeated on the other.

If your house has asymmetrical balance, do not use the same plant on either side of the doorway. To determine the approximate height of the planting for each side of the doorway, make an elevation drawing of your house. From a point at the corner one-half to two-thirds the distance from the ground to the eave, draw a line to the center of the door's threshold. The distance from the ground to this line, as measured 3 to 5 feet from each side of the door or porch, will give you the height the plant should be to balance the asymmetrical design.

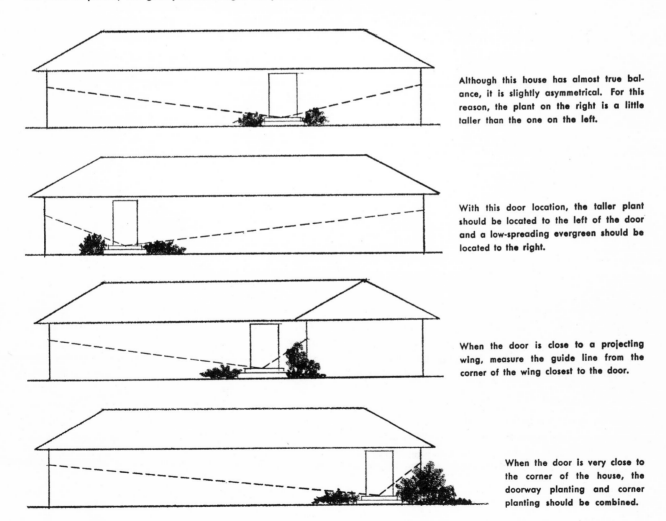

Although this house has almost true balance, it is slightly asymmetrical. For this reason, the plant on the right is a little taller than the one on the left.

With this door location, the taller plant should be located to the left of the door and a low-spreading evergreen should be located to the right.

When the door is close to a projecting wing, measure the guide line from the corner of the wing closest to the door.

When the door is very close to the corner of the house, the doorway planting and corner planting should be combined.

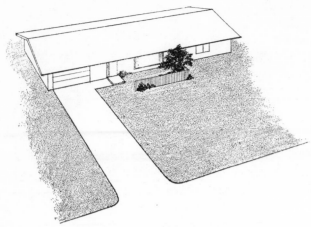

A small fence baffle may be used to create an interesting planting as viewed from a picture window facing the street, and may also serve to block the view into the house from the street. This fence baffle should be highly refined in detail, and should be constructed of the same material as the house or of a contrasting material that harmonizes in color, texture, and scale with the house.

Every landscape development needs walks and a drive. Since these are useful rather than beautiful, they should be as inconspicuous as possible. To keep your walks and drive from attracting attention (and to hold costs down at the same time), construct them in a minimum area and recess the surface of the drive.

In designing a short drive, paths, and walks, remember that curves are usually superfluous design features that do not direct either a pedestrian or an automobile the shortest way to your home. Although an unnecessary curve is not artistically successful, a long drive may curve toward the house to form a dominant line that helps direct the eye to the house.

The only time a short driveway or walk should curve is to go around a natural obstacle that cannot be removed, or when the planting around the house is so arranged that it seems natural for the walk or driveway to follow it.

Put walks where people naturally tend to go. You can also justify curves in walks and drives when the grade is too steep for people to walk in a straight line. In most contemporary homes, it is desirable for the driveway to handle both foot and car traffic. The walk to the front door from the drive then parallels the house. Keep the walk at least 6 feet from the house so that plantings will not run over on the side-

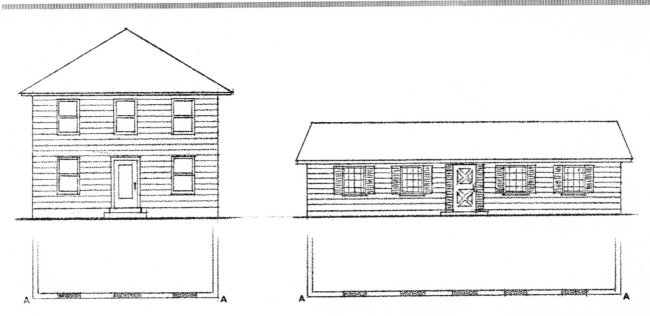

The primary objective in developing a foundation planting is to make the house look appropriate for the site on which it is placed by softening and blending the vertical house lines (A) with the strong, horizontal ground lines.

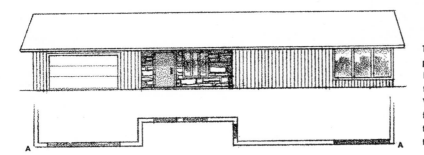

The center of interest and balance point for all plantings focuses on the center of the doorway. For this reason, the two major planting areas are the outside corners and each side of the doorway. Vertical lines formed by projections along the facade should be softened by plantings, although these plantings should not be as tall as those at the outside corners of the house.

walk. Otherwise, plants weighted down with rain will hang over the walk and prevent its use when most needed.

The width of the walk that leads to the front entrance must be in scale with the size of the house. Nothing looks worse than a narrow ribbon of concrete leading to a large house. The walk must be wide enough to allow two people to walk side by side. Since each person needs 2 feet the minimum width is 4 feet. A 5-foot walk is even better, since it is in proportion with most houses.

Do not pave secondary walks from the main entrance to the opposite side of the yard. Since secondary walks are used mostly by the family, stepping stones are usually satisfactory. Place them 24 to 28 inches on center for a natural step. If you want them spaced more exactly for your own pace, count your steps for a distance of 50 feet and divide 50 by the number of steps taken. Stones placed this distance apart will be ideal for your stride.

The town home drive usually needs to serve only the family car or cars. The minimum width for one

car is 9 feet, although 10 feet is better. Double these widths for two cars. If you also use the drive as a walk from the front road, add 3 feet to the drive width. Always keep the drive straight and direct when the house setback is relatively short.

Although many town homes have attached garages or carports, others have separate garages. You may want to provide a Y turnaround so that cars do not have to back into the street. A Y turnaround needs a turning radius of 18 feet as measured 28 feet from the front of the garage. The width of the Y at its narrowest point need not be more than 8 feet The radius of the short side of the Y should also be 18 feet.

A rural drive must be designed to accommodate traffic going to the house, and to allow continuous movement of business traffic between the road and the farm court. A rural drive needs to be at least 10 feet wide. This minimum width does not allow for the widest machinery that will occasionally move over the drive. It is important to leave the sides of the drive clear of all planting and fences or other objects for a minimum width of 15 feet.

Farm court and house traffic need to be separated. Daytime traffic to the house often gets in the way of business traffic. One solution to the problem is a circular drive. A circular drive should measure at least 70 feet across the widest part of the circle.

Traffic going to the house then moves along the curve closest to the house, while farm court traffic follows the outer curve. To find out whether you have the necessary width and clearance, drive the largest vehicle that you will use around the complete circle.

Or you might design a hammerhead or head-in area for parking at right angles to the drive. You will need at least 20 feet on the house side of the drive to park a car at right angles. Allow at least 10 feet for each car you wish to park. For instance, an area 20 feet by 20 feet would handle two cars.

The question "How can I make people use my front door?" is a difficult one for rural people to answer. A hammerhead parking area located at the front and to the side of the house will cause a car pulling into the parking area to face the door you want people to use. Then, if you have a straight walk from the parking area to the front door, your guests will use that door. If you have two doors at the front of your house, you may have to put up signs indicating which door you want guests to use.

To make this design work, have the parking area well-defined and do not allow enough space near the

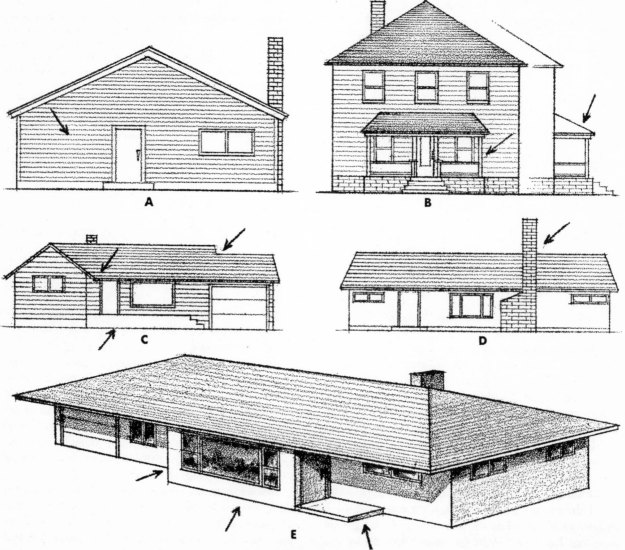

Study your elevation drawings for awkward and poorly designed elements or areas on the front facade that might be softened, screened, or balanced by plantings. (A) Poorly proportioned or large blank wall areas. (B) Large masses and dominant porches. (C) Disturbing angles, jogs, or changes in roof line (note dominance of massive porch across the front). (D) Disturbing contrasts of lines such as the strong vertical line of the fireplace chimney breaking up the dominant horizontal lines of the house. (E) Small jogs or recessed areas that have an "afterthought" or "tacked-on" appearance.

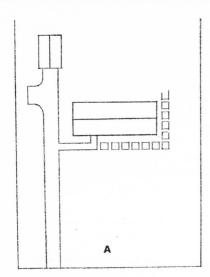
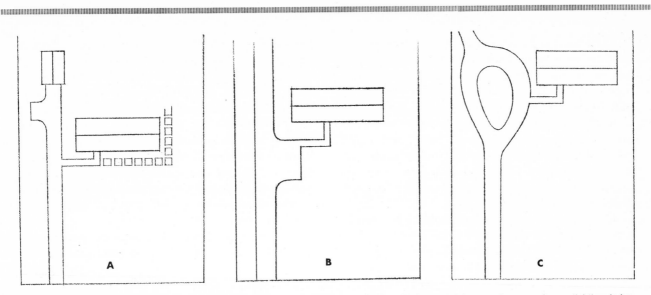
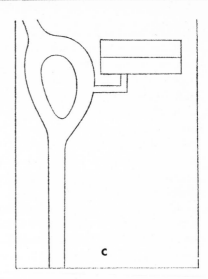

A broad, clear expanse of lawn is the best setting for your public-area design. Walks and drives cut into your lawn, dividing it into small sections. By using the driveway as both a walk and a drive, you eliminate one of these divisions and keep an uninterrupted foreground. Any secondary walks should be stepping stones to avoid additional hard lines of concrete. Notice (A) that the garage is located to the rear of the lot with a Y turnaround. This arrangement eliminates backing a long distance to the street and backing into traffic.

The hammerhead parking areas (B) require a depth of 20 feet beyond the edge of the drive. When located on the house side of the drive, as shown in B, the parking area should not overlap the front facade more than 2 feet.

The circle drive (C) requires more space than the hammerhead parking area. You can quickly determine if you have adequate space by driving over the area with the largest truck or car that will be driven regularly around the circle. The circle drive should be at the side of the house. Do not locate it across the front of the house.

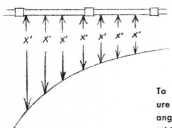

To locate a curved line, measure a number of points at right angles from a straight line established above the curve.

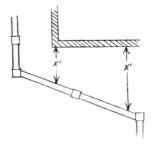

You can locate a straight line by measuring only 2 points at right angles from an established straight line.

rear or side entrance for vehicles other than the family car or cars.

Locate a circular or hammerhead drive at the side of the house, not directly in front of the house itself. Your house is the most important part of the public-area design, and the best setting for it is a broad expanse of unbroken lawn. Roads, parking areas, or circular drives cutting up the front lawn divide the lawn into sections or panels of grass similar to the division caused by a front walk from the doorway to the street.

Drainage is very important for a driveway or walk. Build drives and walks with a minimum drop of 1 inch every 10 feet. Lay them on a 4- to 6-inch gravel base that has been placed on well-compacted or undisturbed soil.

You can keep stones out of the grass by placing a metal or wooden strip or some other kind of divider between a gravel drive and the lawn. A border strip

also prevents weeds and grass from growing over the drive and helps to keep the edge of an asphalt drive from breaking away.

Ordinarily, plants at corners should be larger than those on either side of the entrance. Plants at the doorway should not be higher than one-fourth to one-third the distance from the groundline to the eave. If you stay within these proportions, you won't be faced later with a "peek-a-boo" situation in which your house is nearly hidden behind a mass of plantings.

Mature corner plantings should not be higher than two-thirds the distance from the groundline to the eave. The taller plants at the corners and the lower plants at the doorway form a concave line that directs the eye to the doorway.

A house with corner wraparound windows is an exception to this rule. Since the windows shouldn't be covered, the corner plantings will be lower than

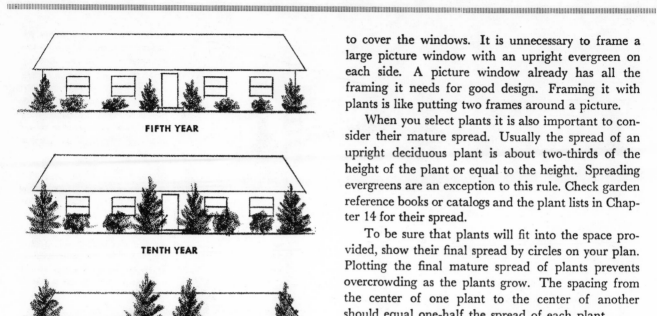

FIFTH YEAR

TENTH YEAR

FIFTEENTH YEAR

Know the mature height and spread of the plants you use. The "peek-a-boo" house (bottom drawing) shows the result of lack of information and planning.

the windows. A small flowering shrub or tree planted away from the corner will also give the desired blending effect without blocking the view.

Do not use conical or pyramidal evergreens for a foundation planting. A rare exception is a house with high-peaked gables, narrow windows or dormers, or a formal facade arrangement or natural surroundings that include pointed evergreens and sharp mountain tops. You cannot tie a house to the ground and soften its strong vertical lines with upright, pointed evergreens that emphasize these lines. If you have upright evergreens at the corners, you can soften this vertical effect by placing low-spreading plants around the evergreens. However, this kind of planting requires considerable space.

You can make a house look lower and wider by extending the foundation planting to add plant "wings" to the building. Wing plantings serve to "funnel" the view from the street toward the house and center it on the front door. This type of planting is particularly useful for two-story houses. It can also separate the public from the private living area.

It is not usually a good idea to plant under extremely low windows. Of course, if the foundation wall shows three feet of unattractive concrete or block, you can conceal it with plantings across the front. Do not place plants so that they will grow up

to cover the windows. It is unnecessary to frame a large picture window with an upright evergreen on each side. A picture window already has all the framing it needs for good design. Framing it with plants is like putting two frames around a picture.

When you select plants it is also important to consider their mature spread. Usually the spread of an upright deciduous plant is about two-thirds of the height of the plant or equal to the height. Spreading evergreens are an exception to this rule. Check garden reference books or catalogs and the plant lists in Chapter 14 for their spread.

To be sure that plants will fit into the space provided, show their final spread by circles on your plan. Plotting the final mature spread of plants prevents overcrowding as the plants grow. The spacing from the center of one plant to the center of another should equal one-half the spread of each plant.

You can drive down nearly any street and see homes lost in a forest of overplanting. The desire for a completed look immediately after planting is understandable, but you must have the patience to wait two or three years for a balanced and organized appearance that will last for many years. Most modern homes are attractive in themselves, and need only a few plants at the front foundation. This not only lowers landscaping costs but results in a more attractive composition.

You can combine deciduous and low evergreen plants for a highly interesting composition. Deciduous plants usually grow faster than evergreens, and offer interest throughout the year: flowers in spring, full foliage in summer, attractive fruit in late summer and early fall, fall coloring, and finally, after the leaves have fallen, twig patterns and shadows cast on wall areas. The addition of spreading evergreens with their permanent green foliage makes a pleasing combination. All evergreens or all deciduous plantings are also a possibility. The deciduous shrubs you select should be of the rounded, horizontally branched types.

If your house has a wide overhang, plant the materials at least one foot beyond the drip line so that they will get some natural rainfall. Plantings set under the eaves need regular artificial waterings to survive. If there is a walk in front of the planting, allow 6 to 12 inches in addition to one-half the total spread distance so that the plants will not overhang when laden with water or snow.

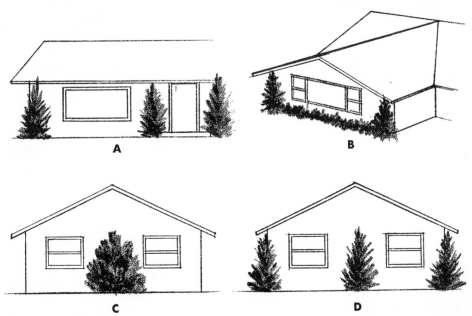

(A) DO NOT use conical and pyramidal evergreens at corners and doorways or to frame windows. These areas are already framed architecturally. Conical and pyramidal evergreens emphasize vertical lines and disrupt the scale relationship between the house and other plantings by growing too tall.

(B) DO NOT plant the projection of an L- or U-shaped house as a separate facade from the balance of the house. Elevation drawings are helpful in visualizing that the face of any projecting wing must be considered as being on the same plane as the other face areas of the house.

(C) DO NOT plant shrubs against every blank wall area, such as between windows at the side of the house. This type of planting tends to dwarf the house as well as to hide it.

(D) DO NOT plant upright evergreens or other plantings that divide an area into smaller parts. This makes the house appear tall and narrow.

The home should be framed with trees. Before you place trees, decide the point or points from which you want your home to look its best. Stand at this point or points and visualize where trees should be located to form a graceful frame for your home in later years. A small tree close to the sidewalk can frame your home well enough, but a small tree next to the house might not. The point of view is important in considering the types of trees to use.

Frame your house to concentrate interest on the house. A large house needs a large frame. For a small home, it is better to use large trees in the rear as background for the house and small to medium trees in front, unless a large tree is required to give adequate shade.

This doesn't mean that you should remove trees on your property that do not fit these proportions. But the fact that smaller trees fit best with low modern homes should guide your selection of new plantings. Keep in mind the scale relationship between the trees and the house. A two-story house demands large trees. Placing small trees against a large house emphasizes the size of the house, and results in a poor relationship between the tree and the house. A one-story house requires smaller trees. You can use a clump of small trees on one side of the house and a large tree on the other side for asymmetrical balance.

Repeat dominant lines in the house as often as possible in planting arrangements and structures.

Unless the foundation is high, it is not necessary to have a solid planting across the front of the house. A possible planting design is to have an area of ground cover (A) under a large window to tie the corner and entrance plantings together. (B) is a panel of grass or ground cover extending to the house. By breaking up the planting this way, the dwarfing effect of solid planting is avoided. Be careful not to have (B) out of scale with the house. It should be approximately one-third the length of the house.

Corner Plantings

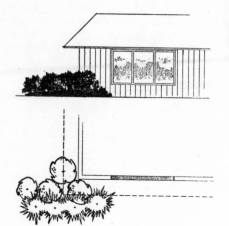

Use tall, medium, or low shrubs at the corners, with lower growing plants at their base to blend the vertical line of the corner into the horizontal line of the ground. Corner plantings should range in height from one-third to two-thirds the distance from the ground to the eaves, depending upon the size of the house.

For a small, low house where a tall corner planting would be too massive, the use of shrubs one-third the height from the groundline to the eaves would be desirable.

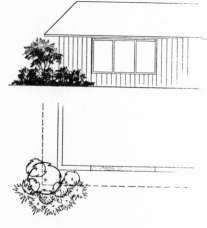

Taller shrubs used with lower growing types and low-spreading evergreens give a pleasing transition between the dominant vertical and horizontal lines. The distance that the planting extends along the front of the house will depend upon the distance of the window from the corner. The height of the window must also be considered. Begin or stop plantings alongside the house at a logical point — at window edges, jogs in the facade or roof, etc.

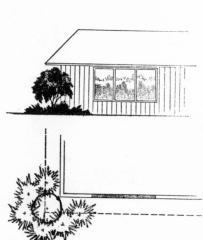

An example of tall deciduous shrubs combined with spreading evergreens at the base. Notice the effectiveness of rounded forms of deciduous shrubs in giving a smooth transition to the groundline.

Corner Plantings

Corner windows require different treatment so as not to obstruct the view. The planting in the top drawing is composed of a small tree with lower plantings located away from the house. Notice how the lower planting steps down toward the house corner, directing the eye to the front facade.

If the space from the side property line to the house is narrow (lower drawing), a small flowering tree can serve as a corner planting. Plant away from the house and to the front of the house. The corner plant can be a small or medium shrub.

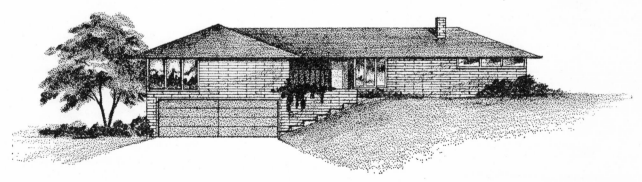

Select corner plantings for a split-level house according to the rule of thumb for height of shrubs at corners. In other words, keep the scale of the plants equal to the scale of the building. Plants will be taller on the higher corner, with the lower facer shrubs extending beyond the end of the house. The lower corner would be as shown in preceding drawings.

Tall two-story houses can be made to look lower and wider by extending the corner plantings beyond the house and angled toward the street. The planting at the corner is one-half to two-thirds the distance from the ground to the second story. The remainder of the material gradually increases in height as it extends from the corner, terminating in a small tree. This arrangement serves to "funnel" the eye toward the front door and reduces the effect of extreme height created by the house.

If a drive is located close to the house, the wing planting can be started on the other side. The viewer's eye will carry the line across the drive.

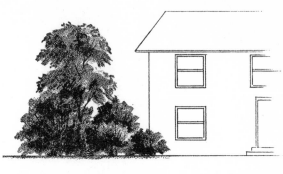

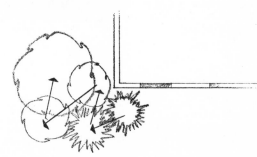

When space between the side property line and the house is limited, a modified wing planting can be achieved. Plant the lowest plant on the front facade near the corner, and build up the height of the plants in the direction of the arrows.

Horizontal lines call for trees with horizontal branching habits. Don't choose a tree just because you happen to like it. Many trees will not fit a small home at all, and later become towering giants that overshadow the house and throw the entire picture out of proportion. Carefully study tree lists in reference books and in Chapter 14, and note which trees are suitable for lawn or street trees and which are suitable only as lawn or shade trees.

Another element of good public-area design is an open lawn. This may be the most unpopular principle. Front lawns cluttered with circular and diamond-shaped flower beds, gazing balls, bird baths, petunia patches, unnecessary lattices, pergolas, and specimen shrubs or perennial flowers are a hangover from the Victorian era. If you feel you really want to

use these items, locate them in the living or service areas, not in the public area.

The best setting that you can give your home is a broad expanse of open lawn from street to house, with foundation plantings and framing trees broken only by needed drives and walks. The more compact the drives and walks and the less cut up the lawn, the more pleasing the total picture will be.

Vines may be useful in the public area if your house is too tall for its width. A vine can make a conspicuous horizontal line across part or all of the front of a building to keep the observer's eye from running in an unbroken line to the top of an awkward house. When planting space is limited by the closeness of the sidewalk, vines can also be used to relieve the harshness of the house.

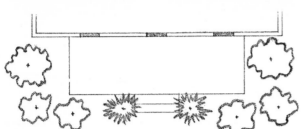

Porch Plantings

Porch plantings vary according to the height of the foundation, the type of porch railings (open or solid), and the general balance of the facades. If the railing is open, use lower plants; if the railing is solid, use larger growing plants. Wing planting can be continued beyond corners if house is tall.

When the porch entrance is off to the side, locate largest shrub at corner of house (inside the front walk) and lower shrubs off street side of steps. Remainder of planting is similar to plantings shown in preceding drawings.

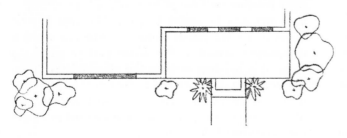

When the porch is to one side of the front facade, low shrubs are used at the entrance, medium shrubs at the porch corners, and larger shrubs at the house corners. Vines are used to soften the vertical line in middle of facade and to create a dominant horizontal line along the porch eave. This horizontal line keeps the viewer's eye from moving up the full height of the house.

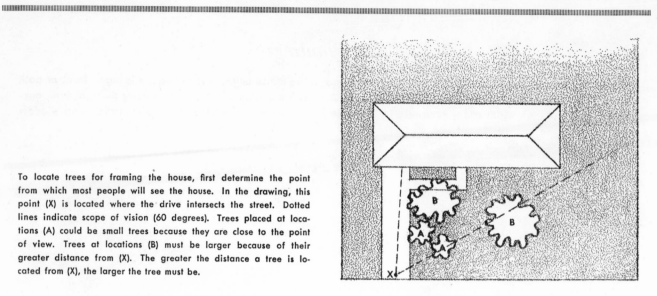

To locate trees for framing the house, first determine the point from which most people will see the house. In the drawing, this point (X) is located where the drive intersects the street. Dotted lines indicate scope of vision (60 degrees). Trees placed at locations (A) could be small trees because they are close to the point of view. Trees at locations (B) must be larger because of their greater distance from (X). The greater the distance a tree is located from (X), the larger the tree must be.

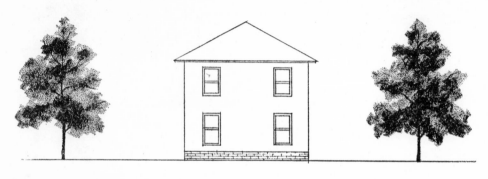

Roof lines forming strong, pointed shapes, such as gables, should be repeated in plant form whenever possible. For example, the small-leafed linden tree in the top drawing repeats the form and line of the roof. In the drawing below, the gable shapes are repeated through the use of pyramidal evergreens.

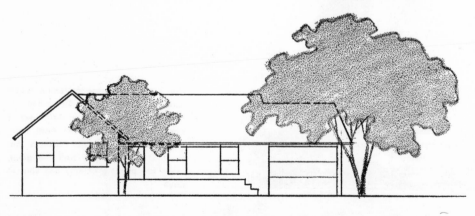

Trees for framing may also be used to screen, soften, or break disturbing angles, jogs, or changes in construction (roof lines, small projections, etc.).

Side Plantings

It is not necessary to have a solid planting across the end of the house unless the foundation is high. Plant at both corners. The planting may be extended from either corner with low plants of the same variety that run from one-third to two-thirds the width of the house. It is desirable to start or stop plantings at a logical point — at window edges, jogs in the facade or roof, etc.

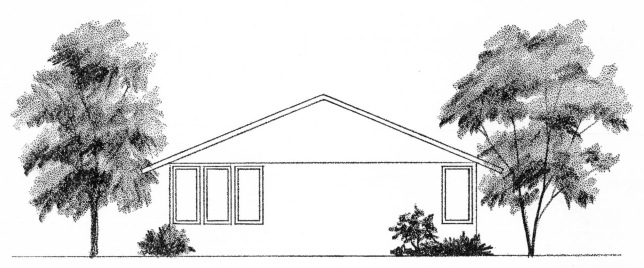

A long blank wall can be monotonous. Divide the wall into a small area and a large area, perhaps one-third and two-thirds, as shown above.

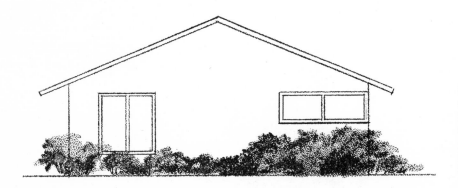

If one kind of small shrub spanning the area would be monotonous, use two kinds of shrubs. One should be slightly taller than the other. Do not divide the plantings in half. Plant two-thirds of the area to a low shrub and one-third to slightly higher plants.

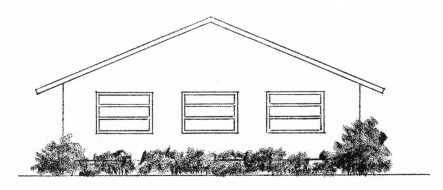

Use a planting across the entire length of a house with a high foundation. At the back corner, select a shrub that is somewhat shorter than the front foundation planting. If the distance between the two corners isn't too great, use a low planting of only one kind of shrub.

Never use a window box in the public area if the house is attractive without it. Window boxes can be used, however, to disguise badly proportioned architectural features. For example, window boxes can prevent the viewer's eyes from wandering all the way up the vertical lines of a tall building front. They may also improve window proportions by extending beyond the sides of windows that are too tall or too small. Horizontal lines are much more pleasing than vertical lines because the viewer's eyes and head move naturally in a horizontal plane.

Flowers also do not belong in the public area.

Many people insist on planting them there because they love flowers. One way to have flowers in the public area and still not have them dominate the home is to put them behind "wing" plantings so that they can be seen from the house but not from the street. Or you can plant flowering bulbs between shrubs in the public area if you place them carefully so as not to create a vivid splash of color. Don't plant bulbs in rows like little soldiers. Throw them on the ground and plant them where they land. Remember that splashes of color in the public area detract from the house.

The window boxes on the side of this house keep the viewer's eye from moving up the full height of the house.

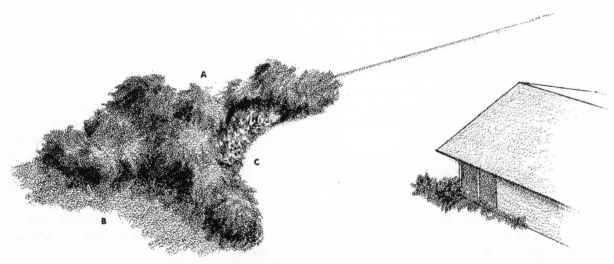

Since flowers attract so much attention in the public area, their location must be carefully planned. This drawing shows one possible location of a flower border. The planting has been extended along the side property line (A), and then curved toward the center of the lot (B) to form a bay (C) for flowers. The flowers can be seen from the house, but are screened from the street so that they do not compete with the house for attention.

11: DESIGNING THE LIVING AREA

What you do with the private living area depends upon your interest in gardening, outdoor living, and other activities. Your family inventory and your own good taste will determine the design of the private living area.

Private-area design is so flexible that there is no formula to use, but don't try to put all of the design elements (plants, surfacing materials, walls or fences) into one landscape. Choose only those that meet your family's needs and interests. Think of the private area as an extension of the house to the outdoors. In effect, you are creating another room for the house with walls, floor, and ceiling. For this reason, it is important to consider enclosures for privacy and protection, particularly on small lots in town with houses close together. Enclosure and screening are not as necessary in the country, where the property is surrounded by natural beauty.

A fence is one of the most popular and efficient ways to enclose the private area. Building a fence along the property line results in maximum space and reduces maintenance of land outside the fence. In a large yard, fencing inside the property line can give a better screening effect than a property line fence. Clotheslines, storage space, and other items in the service area also need to be screened by barriers located inside the property line.

A fence gives privacy, protects the garden, provides a background for flowers and shrubs, screens out unsightly views, and shelters the patio or terrace from the wind. It may be used as a barrier to keep people from crossing the yard or to keep children and pets within a yard, or as a strictly ornamental feature. The kind of fence you should build will depend upon its purpose. For example, an open-wire fence is less expensive than a solid wood fence, and will keep out animals. You can plant dense shrubs against it as a screen.

Use only a simple, plain fence as background for garden plants. Fancywork on a fence is expensive and detracts from the garden design. You need not limit yourself to one type of fencing. For example, you can use an expensive panel fence around the patio and a less expensive board fence in the rest of the garden. Do not change fence style at a corner — it will draw attention to that particular spot. The fence at the rear of the property should be the same height as that along the sides.

You can use short sections or panels of fencing for interest. By dividing the garden, they make it appear larger and stimulate curiosity. A panel set at a right angle on a diagonal or curve may emphasize a specimen tree or vine, or serve as a place to put a garden feature or sculpture. You can also add interest by introducing contrasting materials for a single panel or a few panels of a long fence. For example, you can use one plastic, asbestos, or brick panel in a wood fence, or one or more panels of a contrasting design achieved by different use of the same material.

Plant materials can also create an enclosure. Use a group of shrubs or small trees to form a border. An informal shrub border makes a good screen for most properties. A plant screen has the advantage of relatively simple upkeep. It will need pruning only every two or three years. But it should not become a collector's museum. Limit the number of shrub varieties and repeat these varieties in series to get the plants you need. Avoid the dot-and-dash system of having only one of each variety. Masonry, concrete, or rock walls outlining property lines can also give enclosure.

Any garden development involves arranging open spaces and plantings. More of one means less of the other. Your personal wants and needs will determine how much of each you will use.

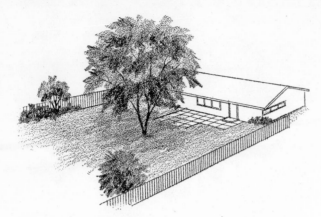

Although fences along the property line will provide privacy, they often cannot be built high enough to screen views effectively from surrounding higher elevations. If space is available, tall shrub plantings or trees might be more effective. Since a fence does not require as much ground space as plants, it is often used on small properties.

Fencing within the property line can give better screening effect and climate control than a property-line fence. Fences close to the living areas need to be more refined (such as panel or solid fences) than those used along property lines.

An outdoor living room needs some type of surfacing. Different surfaces give different effects. The most popular and most functional is a lawn. Lawns have certain advantages that no other surface can match. They are cool and pleasant to sit or lie on in hot weather. They make a good play surface for small children. They provide an attractive foreground to set off plants and flowers in the garden. Their one disadvantage is that they need almost constant care. Keeping the lawn in good condition is a never-ending job from the moment you start to build it.

Not all surfacing has to be lawn. You can use ground covers for additional green surfacing in areas where there is no traffic, or you can provide usable open space with other kinds of paving materials. Many loose surfacings are both inexpensive and

attractive. You can get many sizes of gravel ranging from very small pebbles for a sitting area to large rocks for an entrance driveway. Tanbark, brick chips, and other materials are also available for surfacing "light-use" areas.

Surround lawn and ground covers in the garden with a flat edging of paving or a strip of lumber. This makes trimming easier and separates the lawn from ground covers to prevent their intermixing. A wide strip separating gravel and lawn keeps gravel out of the grass and prevents mower damage.

DO NOT use fancy, highly embellished gates. They clash with the remainder of the fencing. Gates should be of the same material as the fence and of the same basic design. If contrasting material is used, it must harmonize with the fence in color, texture, and pattern.

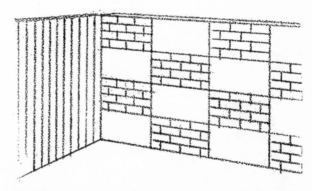

DO NOT change fence designs at a corner. A change in design emphasizes that particular spot and draws attention to itself.

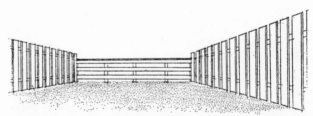

DO NOT use fencing at the rear of the property that is lower than the fencing along the side property lines.

Fence Forms

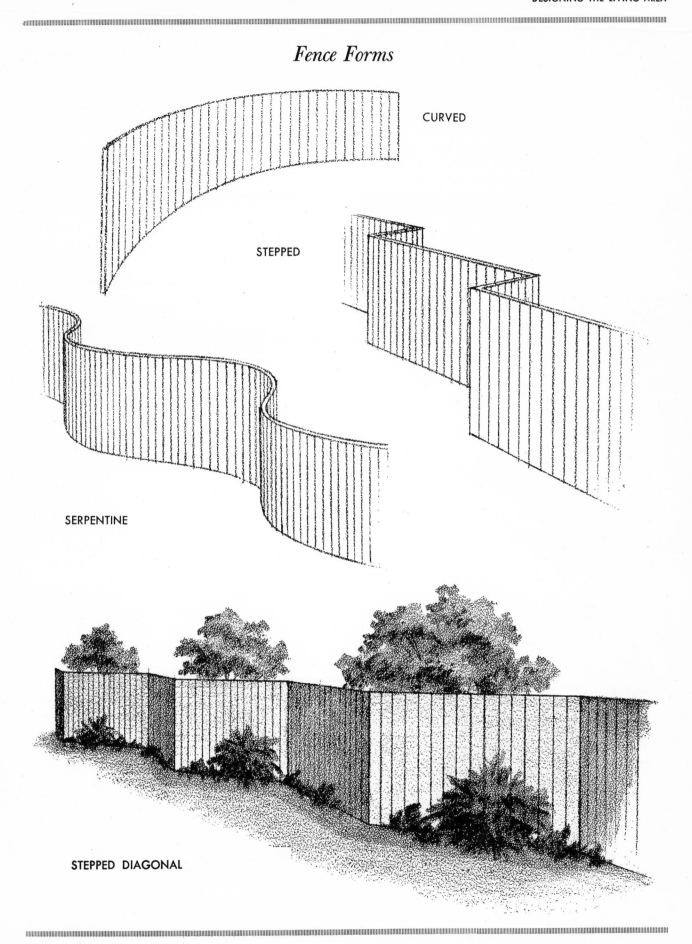

CURVED

STEPPED

SERPENTINE

STEPPED DIAGONAL

Several surfacing materials such as hard paving, loose surfacing, ground covers, or lawn can be used together to make a design. The pattern may be a simple combination of paving and lawn, or paving with loose surfacing. Three surfacing materials can be made into more complicated arrangements by carefully working out interesting area shapes and using materials with pleasing texture and color contrasts.

You can develop an unlimited choice of patterns for various surfacing materials. A pattern can be formed with straight, curved, or diagonal lines, and one shape may help form another. The edgings that hold the ground cover or paving will emphasize the pattern.

Terrace or patio areas are usually designed with a hard surface. Since the private area extends the indoors to the outdoors, you will need a door at grade level for easy access. This area should also be located close to the kitchen so that it is handy for cookouts and outdoor eating.

Fence panels or plantings help divide the garden into sections, create space, define areas, and stimulate curiosity.

Baffle effect created by low shrubs and a tree.

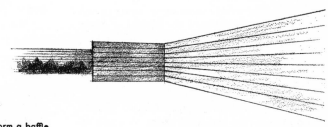

Panels used at right angles to form a baffle.

Baffle effect created by trees and ground cover at right angles to shrub border.

Header or divider boards are used between two types of surfacing materials to keep one from intruding upon the other. The divider boards should be redwood, cypress, cedar, or a wood that has been treated with wood preservatives. (A) Headers dividing loose gravel and lawn or other surfacing materials. (B) Headers dividing ground cover and lawn. (C) Headers dividing brick and lawn.

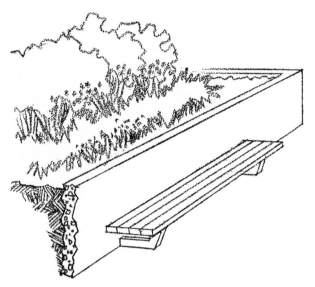

Several low retaining walls make a better design than one high wall. If a high wall cannot be avoided, the addition of a seat bench against the wall gives a strong horizontal line that helps to reduce the effect of height.

Locate the terrace or patio on your plan early in the designing process, and plan the rest of the garden to take advantage of the patio location. A patio in a small home-grounds design gives a good vantage point from which to enjoy the yard.

Raised planting beds are another design element you can use. They can be created by building low walls of masonry or wood. You can put a cap on top of the wall so that it will serve as a seat as well as a retainer for the raised bed. The walls or retainers used to create these raised beds emphasize specific lines, and are important design features where strong patterns are to be developed. They can be used to divide the garden into areas, or as a special feature in conjunction with the patio. They are also useful in breaking the monotony of level ground. Plant flowers, shrubs, or specimen plants in these raised beds.

A raised edge provides interest in a flat yard. Even as little as 4 inches of change can emphasize a partic-ular planting mass, a tree planter, or specialized planting areas close to the terrace, patio, or sitting area.

Slopes can be handled in several ways. Grading in the private area is the same as that for the front lawn. A steep slope may need to be filled in behind a retaining wall to get a usable flat area. These flat areas should slope away from the house and drop at least 2 inches every 10 feet. A slope is less expensive than a retaining wall, but the latter requires less space, is permanent and attractive, and weathers well over the years.

You can work out some interesting effects with retaining walls. They may be curved, angled, or straight. A series of low walls is far more pleasing than a large single wall on a steep slope. If your wall is too tall for a seat wall, consider building a low bench against the wall to make the wall look lower and emphasize its length.

Steps may serve both as a retaining wall and as a means for getting from one level to another. Or you may need a ramp to roll a wheelbarrow and other equipment up and down a grade change. A ramp is easier and cheaper to build than steps, but steps offer many interesting design arrangements.

Garden steps do not have to be in a straight flight. Various turns or angles may be used as long as they do not look abrupt or pinched. Garden steps should have a wide tread and a low riser. The general recommendation is a 15-inch tread with a 5-inch riser.

The height of a flight of garden steps should not be greater than the width. If the flight is extremely long, break up the steps into smaller groups and separate with landings. You can change direction at a landing.

You may want to set aside a special area for the children. Put all play equipment — sandbox, swings, teeter-totter, etc. — in this area. You can partially hide the play area with shrubs, although it should be easy to see from the kitchen window so that Mother can supervise while doing her regular work. Sand or tanbark is suitable under play equipment, since you

Raised planter beds create interest and dramatize a tree or other plantings. Top of retainer may serve as an excellent potted-plant display shelf.

Steps can serve both as a retaining wall and as a means of access from one area to another. Outdoor steps should be of greater scale than indoor steps. Avoid making them so narrow that they look pinched. Garden steps should have a wide tread and low risers. The height of a flight of steps should not be greater than the width.

Make any change in the direction of the steps at landings only.

If the flight is extremely long, break the steps into smaller groups and separate these groups with landings.

can't grow grass successfully in the play area. Don't build anything in this area with sharp corners or angles, and avoid ornamental details that children can damage.

Since a child quickly outgrows the need for a restricted play area, the ages of your children will determine how permanent this development should be. It should be located and arranged so that it can be easily incorporated into the landscape after the children have outgrown it.

You can put in standard volleyball and basketball courts, if you wish. Although these usually do not improve the appearance of the property, they can be justified if sports are an important part of your family's activities.

Place any pools or water effects in your garden so that they can be seen easily from the terrace or patio. Water in a garden always gives a pleasant, cooling effect, and you can add interest to a pool by using one of a variety of shapes. Add motion with a circulating pump, or leave the water quiet as a clear reflecting pool.

If you have an off-property view to develop, make your garden a foreground opening up and framing it. Use broad, flowing lines of plants, walls, and paving to lead the eyes from the house toward the view. Use planting arms to dramatize or emphasize any part of the view.

A garden should appear wider than it is deep to dramatize a view. If your property is lengthy in the direction of the view, you can create an illusion of width by putting in or emphasizing lines running across the garden. For instance, you can make a change in level by building steps across the width of the garden or by running a low wall across the middle toward the view. Everything else in the garden should be on a large scale. Anything delicate or small will be dwarfed by the size of the view off the property.

A flat, open space, such as a lawn and paving or gravel, should be the foreground to the view. There should be nothing to mark the end of the property — the garden should flow right into the view. If you can see housetops or other disturbing elements at the bottom of the view, you can block them off with a low hedge or fence or other low planting. Plant only a few varieties and repeat them often. Avoid specimen plants that draw attention from the view.

You can use special points of interest to dress up a garden just as knickknacks are used in a room. These attention-catchers could well be some of the objects banished from the public area, such as a gazing ball or a bird bath. Unusual construction or a bright spot of color becomes an immediate point of interest important enough to make the use of other garden ornaments unnecessary. A special design, mosaic in

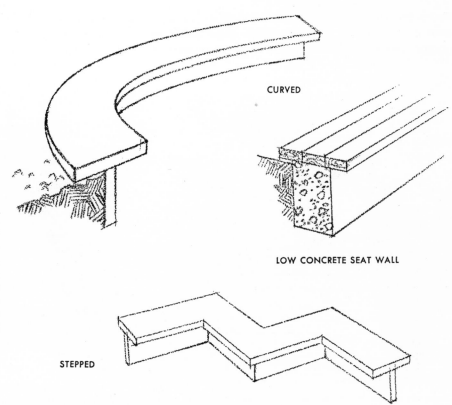

CURVED

LOW CONCRETE SEAT WALL

STEPPED

Low seat walls can have many forms. They can be constructed entirely of wood or brick, of brick support with wood top, of concrete with wood top, or of concrete block with wood top. A seat wall may be freestanding to give additional seats and line, pattern, or division of space; or it may retain or hold soil, creating a raised bed for a change in grade.

It is often desirable to incorporate off-property views into the landscape. To be effective, these views should be framed with plant materials. The general garden layout should have dominant flowing lines from the house or terrace leading the eye to the view.

If the character of the view is predominantly vertical, use trees as the framing elements to repeat this vertical quality.

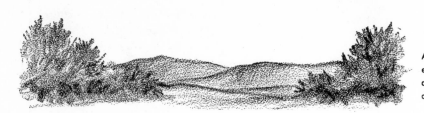

A view that is predominantly horizontal can be emphasized by tapering the ends of planting arms to the ground to repeat this horizontal character.

the pavement, unusual stepping stones, statues, a small fountain, bird bath, a piece of driftwood or carving, a special panel or design on a fence — all are attention-getters.

But just as too many knickknacks can clutter a room, so can too many clutter a yard. If a special garden ornamentation is used, create a setting for it and place it as a focal point. The setting usually requires a background such as plants or fence to set off the feature. Be sure it is well located and in scale with the rest of the design.

Although the public-area design must complement your home and be in keeping with other homes along the street, your outdoor living area should be private and not seen as one of a series at the rear of other homes. It can have traditional style with symmetrical balance, or, for a more natural setting, be informal with an asymmetrical balance. Or it can be an architectural-type garden with definite patterns, lines, forms, and shapes contrasting with one another in a geometric design.

An irregular, asymmetrical layout tends to have more interest. Symmetrical balance is rigid and formal; asymmetrical balance is more subtle. Informal design has the advantage of not needing to be as spic-and-span as a formal design.

Narrow spaces between walks, structures, lawn, and fences may be planted to flowers or vines.

Usually a formal garden should be longer than it is wide. Its rectangular shape should have a ratio of 7 to 3 or 7 to 4. One major axis should lead from the terrace or picture window to the rear of the property. Any special feature midway down the line must be low and unobtrusive. A formal garden is symmetrical, with regular and balanced shapes and patterns for each element of lawn, paving, and shrubbery. The basic shape is rectanglar, even when curves are added for ornamentation.

Shapes should be informal in an informal garden. The number of shapes is limited only by your imagination. They don't have to be pleasing in themselves, but they should fit together in a pleasing combination. A broad, simple curve is usually preferable to a series of small curves. Pattern shapes should be well proportioned and not too long, narrow, or irregular. There should be enough difference between lengths and widths to create interest.

Plan a design that you believe would be most comfortable for you and your family. As you work out your plan, think first only of shapes and locations. Allow yourself plenty of time — ideas sometimes come slowly.

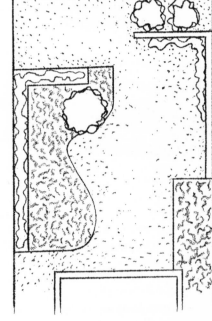

An informal design has asymmetrical balance and more natural lines, and is not confined by rectangular forms or straight lines.

A formal design has symmetrical balance on each side of a major axis (A). In other words, whatever appears on one side of this axis is duplicated exactly on the other. Every formal design also has a secondary axis (B). This secondary axis is used primarily for developing minor focal points (Y). Major focal points are always at (X). Formal gardens require a rectangle of 7 to 3 or 7 to 4 proportions. All shapes in the design are geometric figures or segments of them.

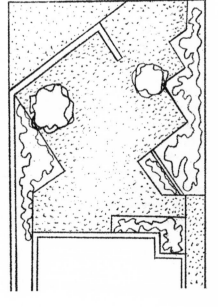

The architectural or stylized informal design has definite lines, patterns, and shapes. These can be either straight or curved, but tend to be geometrical. The design shown here is characterized by asymmetrical balance.

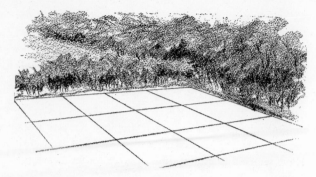

Low plants, seat walls, or low retaining walls give line and pattern to the design and create space by serving as divisions. They do not have to extend the full width of the yard. A short distance is sufficient, since the imagination will carry the effect of a division.

To start your garden design, tape a clean sheet of tracing paper over the base plan of your house and yard. Pencil in the various areas — terrace, utility space, vegetable garden, shrub borders, paved and soft-surface areas. Then locate trees and fencing for shade, windbreaks, and privacy. Keep in mind the relationship of open spaces and plantings. Decide which will be dominant. Consider needed grade changes and how you will get them — whether by retaining walls, steps, or improved slope.

When you have worked out a simple, well-proportioned pattern, lay another sheet of paper over your base plan to refine the paved areas. The size and shape of a paved area will depend upon the use of that area. A desirable minimum size for a patio is about 15 feet by 20 feet. Don't be afraid to experiment in working out relationships. Draw over, erase, or change anything that looks wrong. Tracing paper

is inexpensive, and it is certainly worth a few sheets to insure a good investment.

Now designate the planting areas. They can vary in depth from about 1 foot to 15 feet. Plant a narrow space with flowers, a vine, or low shrubs. Shrubs will grow about the same width as their height, so you should allow 8 feet of depth for an 8-foot screen.

Flower beds should be from 2 to 5 feet deep. Beds that are too narrow look sparse and out of scale, and those that are too wide are difficult to work in. An ideal flower bed should be about 2 to 5 feet deep backed by 6-foot shrubs to make the flowers stand out. Or you can back up flowers with a fence and avoid the problem of competition between shrub and flower roots when they are planted too close together.

You should also consider what part of the garden will be used in good weather and what part you will simply look at from within the house. Try to make each view as pleasant as possible. Move from room to room at the back of the house to determine if what you see outside is attractive and should be featured, or whether it is unattractive and should be screened.

After making this inside survey, look over the property from the outdoor sitting area. Notice where you will have to protect your privacy or screen out an unsightly view. Locate all fencing on your garden plan. Then sketch in all trees and shrubs needed for privacy. Put in any flower beds. Study and locate seat walls and retaining walls to be sure that their lines and forms blend in with the area. Now recheck your studies on paving and surfacing and decide whether you need more of these materials. Perhaps you will want more ground cover or soft-surface material added to the lawn and hard-surfaced areas.

Shrubs used with a fence (or wall) should be shorter or taller than the fence, and the exposed portion of fence should be wider than it is tall.

You can achieve variety in the silhouette of a border mass by using plant groups of different heights. Accent plants, such as upright evergreens, focus attention on a specific area and give a sharp contrast to the dominant round forms.

Now it is time to polish and refine your plan. You can emphasize the important lines in your garden in many ways. In addition to retaining walls or seat walls, fencing, and shrubs, perhaps special brick or concrete edging would work. A short line of low plants, either clipped or allowed to grow naturally, can emphasize shapes and divisions. Plants or a low seat wall do not necessarily have to extend the full length of the line. The viewer's imagination will carry the line beyond a small section.

Study the shapes and line directions in your plan. The eye tends to follow long lines to their terminus. They are useful to draw attention to some special object or section of the garden, but they can be disturbing if they do not lead to a particular point. One line should meet another at a right angle or as close to a right angle as possible. Avoid a junction of two lines that is sharp or pinched. This applies to the meeting points of curves as well as those of straight lines.

You may want to rework your design on the basis of some of these tips. Don't worry about an occasional feeling that your design might not be a good one. Remember that your garden will undoubtedly be far better than if you had not planned it at all. There is no one best way, but any arrangement should be based on your own imagination, needs, and desires. It is not a matter of what is right or wrong, but what is attractive, satisfying, and functional to you and your family.

Thus far you have tried to make the plan look pleasing on a flat sheet of paper. Since a garden has three dimensions, however, height and space must be considered in the planning. The basic rule is that different things should be of different heights, while similar things should be of similar height. For example, matching planter boxes and groups of similar

It is a rule of thumb that everything in the landscape should be wider than it is tall.

A flowering shrub border is more effective if masses of the same shrubs are located in several places in the garden. The shrubs do not necessarily have to be in the same arrangement or number — possibly 3 in one location and 5 or 6 in another.

plants in different parts of the garden should be the same height.

But real interest in the garden is a result of height contrasts. Different groups of shrubs should definitely be of different heights — medium shrubs with tall ones, low ones with ground cover, and so forth. Shrubs near a fence should be taller or shorter than the height of the fence.

Proportion must be considered along with height. Everything in a garden should be definitely wider than it is tall. That is why shrubs are recommended in groups of two or three or more of a kind. If you have two plantings, both of which are higher than the fence, the exposed portion of the fence should be wider than it is high.

The third dimension to consider is the ceiling to the outdoor living room. The sky makes a good ceiling, but there is also a need for a sense of enclosure above as well as along the sides. Because they help give this sense of enclosure, trees are an important asset to any landscape design. If you are fortunate enough to have trees already on your property, you may not have much of a problem. But most people have to start with young trees. Put in several young trees, and in a few years they will begin to spread out and arch over the garden to give a feeling of overhead enclosure.

Small trees in a shrub border give a pleasing contrast in height and plant form. But too many upright plants tend to break up a planting composition.

The location of background trees is important. These trees should provide shade for the sitting area, patio, or terrace, serve as a backdrop for the house as seen from the street, and act as a canopy over the living area. Put them where they might also screen an object or frame a view. Plant trees that are both deep-rooted and rapid-growing. It is difficult to find trees with both of these qualities, but they are available.

Look at your rough plan. Are the tall shrubs and trees in balance, or is there more tall material on one side than on the other? Do your plantings interrupt the tops of fences and walls to help soften these structures and blend them into the design? Try to visualize how the plants will look when they are mature so that you allow enough room for them to grow.

To apply the final polish to the rough sketch, you might ask yourself several additional questions. For example, would raised beds or low retaining walls around part of the planting be worth the effort? Will you want to put any ornamental objects in the garden? Recheck designated flower-bed areas, tree locations, lines, forms, and patterns to be sure that they are free-flowing and not cramped or twisted. Is the garden easy to move through? Garden openings must be larger than those in the house, with minimum openings about 10 feet wide. After you have checked over your detailed plan and asked yourself these or other questions, you should have a plan that will show the proposed layout and arrangements of your garden.

Thus far in your planning you have not selected any building materials nor decided on specific plants. Now, with your completed plan, you are at last ready to choose construction materials and the best plants to use in your design. Don't be afraid to make changes as you select plants and materials. It is almost impossible to plan ahead for everything.

In designing the private area, remember that both plant materials and fences or walls can be used to create enclosures. Since plants require more space than structures, your choice will be determined by the amount of available space. For example, a shrub planting may require 8 feet, while a fence would require about 1 foot.

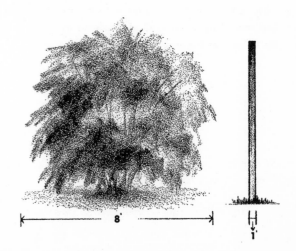

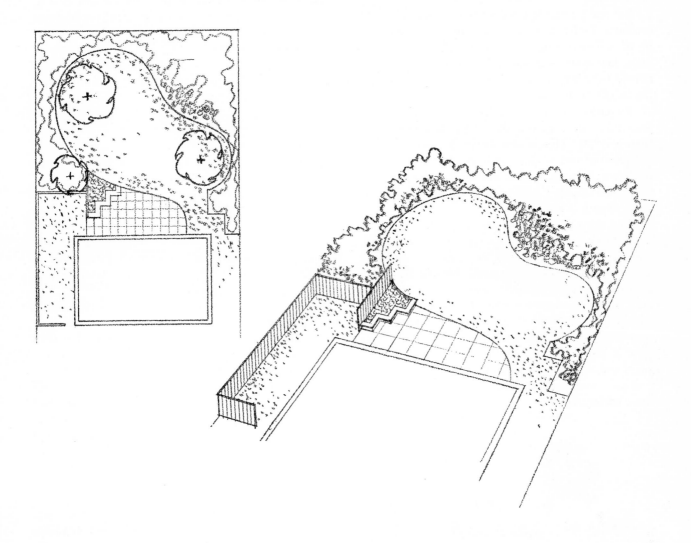

Many patterns can be created by combining various surfacing materials, shrubs, trees, and vertical structures into the overall design. In this drawing, dominant patterns have been evolved from the use of curved and straight lines. Notice the wood fence used to screen the service area and create an enclosure along one side at the same time. The raised planting bed created by a seat wall adds interest by giving a change in grade on a level lot. The patio has a hard surface, and the balance of the area is in lawn and planting.

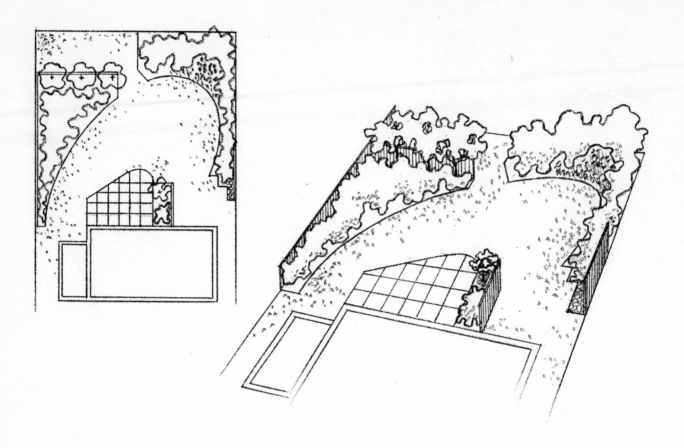

One principle of art — repetition — is illustrated here. Notice repetition of curved bed line in the line and form of the patio. The small planting bed to the right of the patio is devoted to a specimen plant (stag horn sumac) and ground cover (Japanese spurge). At the rear of this planting is a fence panel which provides a backdrop for the planting and screens the neighbors' view at the same time.

An additional section of fence is located on the property line to extend privacy on the right side of the yard. The same fencing is used to screen the service area and give protection on the left. The strong patterns formed by the beds, lawn, and patio add interest, and the repetition of line and material gives unity and harmony to the design.

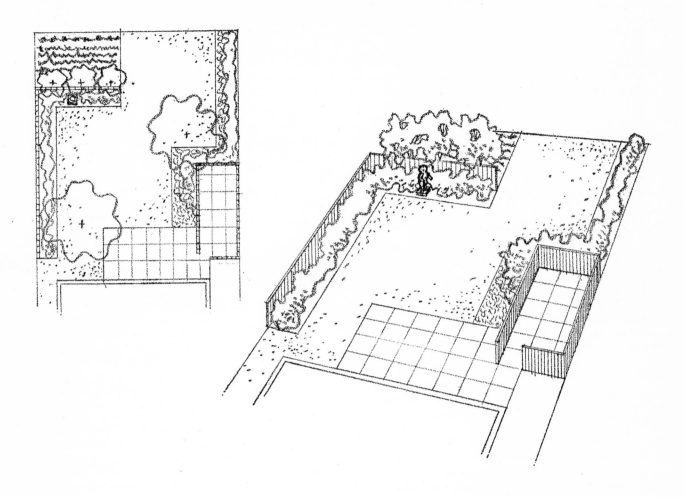

This asymmetrical design has been worked out entirely with straight lines. It shows good space organization for the various use areas — service area, leisure area, sports area, and vegetable garden area. The service area is located close to the utility room, and there is easy access to the outdoor living area from the kitchen. An interesting scene has been created for viewing from within the house as well as from the patio.

The fence screening the vegetable garden may be continued along the property line, depending upon the need for screening or privacy. The fence screening the service area may be more refined than that along the property line and vegetable garden because of its nearness to the patio. Notice use of gravel and ground cover surfacing in addition to lawn and patio surfacing. Remember — straight lines should lead to something. For example, the fence panel by the vegetable garden should have sculpture or a specimen plant as a terminus for the straight line.

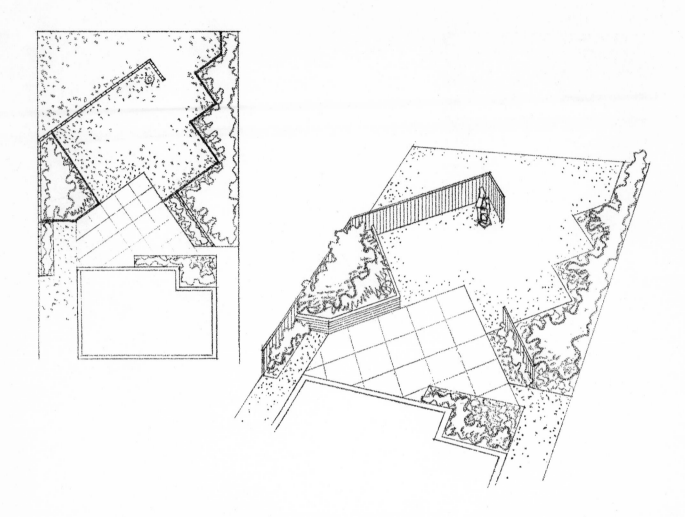

This design was created through the use of straight lines in a diagonal pattern. Notice that the irregular shapes of lawn, paving, and planting beds all fit together. It is the pattern formed by the relationship of these shapes, rather than the individual shapes themselves, that is of primary importance. The line that separates shapes can be straight or curved, a series of steps or jogs, or simply an irregular shape. But it must define an interesting shape on both sides — not just one side. Be sure that the dividing line is pleasing, not complicated with unnecessary bumps or jogs. Consider the proportions of the two areas it defines. There should be enough difference between the length and width of each area to create interest.

Notice the diagonal fence screening the service area. The panel of fence set at right angles creates a focal point for a specimen plant, sculpture, or other garden ornamentation. The dark lines in the drawing could be raised beds or well-defined dividers between lawn and planting beds to emphasize shapes and patterns. The diagonal fence panel to the right of the patio provides protection from the wind and helps tie the design together.

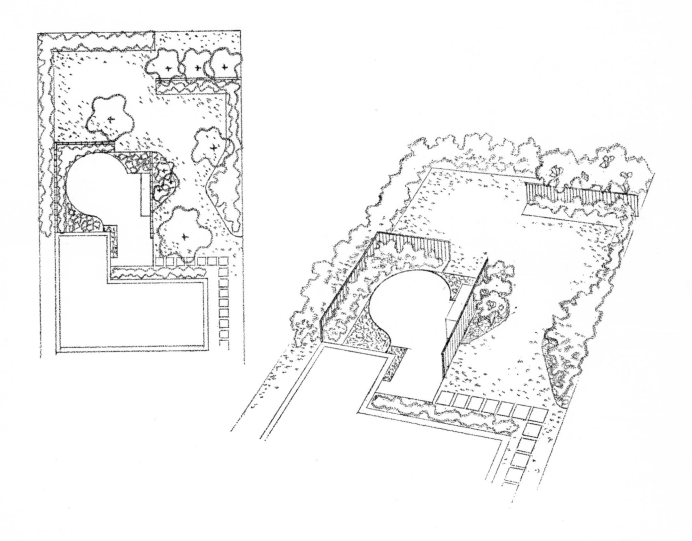

This informal design combining curves and straight lines shows one way to treat a long, narrow lot. The only highly refined and intensely developed area is the patio. The patio is set off from the remainder of the private area by a fence that also gives privacy. The wide opening at the upper righthand corner allows a view of the balance of the yard, preserving a sense of spaciousness even with three sides enclosed. Notice the contrast of shapes in the patio. The hard surfacing is curved in sharp contrast to the strong rectangular shape of the area. Loose surfacing material is used adjacent to the circular patio area.

Trees behind the service yard fence soften the harshness and relieve the monotony of a length of fence. The added height of the trees also screens the property from a large two-story house on a high foundation. A single row of screen plantings finishes off the area along the property line between the patio and service yard. A screen planting of greater interest and variation has been developed along the right side of the property.

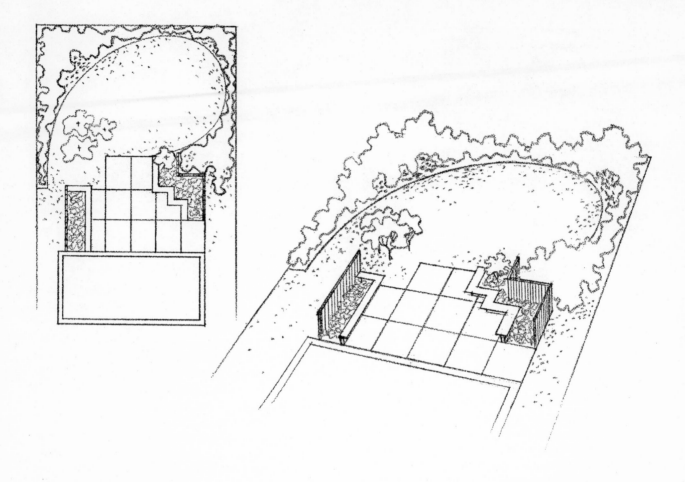

This is an informal design using curves and straight lines. The strong curved line dividing the lawn and plantings blends into the patio with a transition to straight lines achieved by a stepped seat wall, fence panels, and planting area in the righthand corner of the patio. The effect is repeated in the lower lefthand corner along the fence that screens the service area. Access to the patio is from the living room, and access to the service area is from the kitchen.

This design lends itself well to incorporating flowers at the upper left and right incurves of the planting bed. Notice small clump of flowering trees to balance seat walls and bed at upper righthand corner of patio. Fencing for screening or privacy is not required, since the plantings give sufficient protection to the areas at the rear.

12: BUYING AND PLANTING PLANTS

You may be confused by the many places to buy plants and about what to look for to be assured of vigorous and healthy stock.

The first suggestion is to buy locally grown material, if possible. Local plants are adapted to your climate and are most likely to be in good condition. Shipping plants long distances may dry them out too much and lower their vigor and chances for survival.

A possible source of plants, particularly trees, is from a native grove. You may have to mark the plants you want when they are in bloom or in foliage, and then move them out later when they are dormant.

One disadvantage of transplanting trees from a woods is that the roots are often long and straggly. Since their root systems are not as compact as those of nursery stock, trees from a woods are harder to reestablish than trees from a nursery.

Another disadvantage of transplanting native trees is that they grow so close together in the woods that it may be difficult to find well-shaped specimens. Try to choose trees that are growing in a large open area because these trees are more likely to have well-formed crowns. They will also be easier to dig out with more root system.

Small trees do not need to be root-pruned, but large trees from woods should be root-pruned for two years before moving them. A root-pruned tree has a much better chance to survive transplanting. Root pruning will encourage the development of fine hair roots on the remaining roots. To root-prune, draw a circle on the ground a few feet from the trunk and divide it into 6 pie-shaped sections. In the spring or fall, trench and backfill around the outside of every other section, cutting all roots. The following year, trench and backfill the other three sections.

Nursery-Stock Standards

The American Nurserymen's Association and the American Standards Association have set up standards to describe the quality and grades of nursery stock. Some of these standards are discussed below.

The height of deciduous shrubs (those that lose their leaves in winter) is usually given in inches up to 24 inches. For plants taller than 24 inches, the height is stated in feet. When measurements are stated in series (for example, 12 to 15 inches, or 2½ to 3 feet), the height of the material will not be less than the smaller figure nor greater than the larger figure.

In buying a deciduous shrub, actual height is not as important as the number of stems. It is important to select a plant with a dense, well-shaped crown and a root system that is as undamaged as possible. Consider the plant's general condition and appearance, too.

Evergreen shrubs keep their foliage all year, and their measurements depend upon the type selected. Evergreens include spreading types such as Andorra or Pfitzer junipers, and upright types such as pines and spruce. Measurements for the spreading types give the spread, not the height. Spread measurement is usually an average rather than the largest diameter of the plant. Height measurement for the upright type is given in inches up to 24 inches, and in feet for plants taller than 24 inches. The term "specimen" indicates exceptionally heavy, well-shaped plants that are larger than the average.

Tree standards are given either as height or caliber measurements. Height is expressed in feet as a minimum to maximum height for the species or variety listed. Caliber refers to the diameter of the trunk. This measurement is usually taken 6 inches

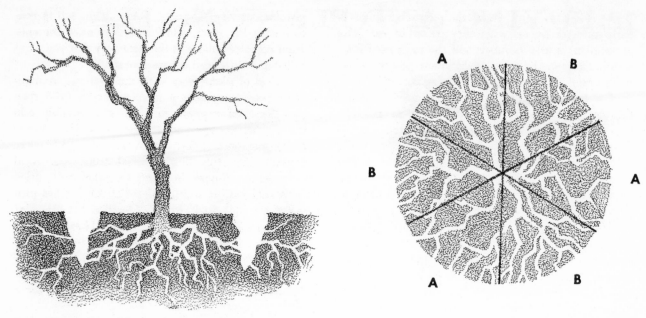

To root-prune a large tree, draw a circle around the trunk. The distance from the trunk should be about 5 inches for each 1 inch of trunk diameter. Divide this circle into 6 pie-like sections. The first year, dig a trench deep enough to cut all roots in the areas marked (A). Mix excavated soil with well-rotted manure or commercial fertilizer before replacing it in the trench. The second year, follow the same procedure for sections marked (B). The tree can be moved in the third year.

above the ground for those trees whose caliber does not exceed 4 inches, and 12 inches above the ground for tree caliber larger than 4 inches. Height is not as important as caliber in tree selection.

Tree quality is determined by a bushy crown and a well-developed root system. Because of extreme differences in growth rates and habits of trees, it is difficult to set standards for crown height and breadth in relationship to total height or caliber.

Handling Materials

An understanding of the way a nursery retail yard or garden center handles plant materials will help you to choose vigorous material that will quickly adapt to its new location. Plant material will be handled in the salesyard either as bare-root, balled and burlapped, or container stock.

You will have better luck with transplanting if you can select locally grown plants in the field. Since these plants are freshly dug, they will be subject to the least amount of moisture loss and shock between digging and replanting.

Balled and burlapped plants, often referred to as "B & B," are plants dug with a ball of soil around the root system. This ball is then wrapped with burlap.

Evergreen plants must be balled to be moved, and deciduous plants must be balled when moved in leaf. The ball of earth containing undisturbed roots

must be wrapped to keep it from breaking apart during the moving. Always carry a balled and burlapped plant under the ball, and handle it carefully.

Keep the ball as small as possible so that it will not crack open under its own weight. You will have to take enough soil for the plant to reestablish itself in its new location. Standard ball diameter is about one-third or one-fourth of the plant height. Exceptions are extremely small or extremely large plants, when the relative size of the ball may be larger for a small plant and somewhat smaller for a large plant.

To take out a balled plant, dig a trench around the plant a little farther out than you want the ball. Widen the trench as you dig deeper, and shape the ball as you go down. Slip a piece of burlap under the ball as you cut underneath, and roll the ball onto it. When the ball rolls free, carefully wrap the burlap around it. Hold the burlap in place with nails and tie securely with twine or rope.

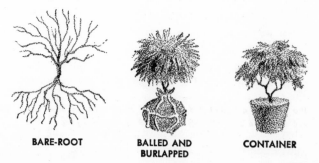

BARE-ROOT   BALLED AND   CONTAINER
                 BURLAPPED

It is best to move deciduous plants bare-root in early spring or late fall when they are out of leaf. The entire plant is then dormant and the roots need little water. Dormant, bare-rooted deciduous plants are less likely to suffer from the shock of being moved.

For bare-root transplanting, you need only dig up the plants, saving as many roots as possible. Don't let the roots dry out after digging — cover them immediately with burlap, soil, or sawdust while moving the plant to its new location. Even a few minutes in the air will dry roots out enough to kill the plant. You can store plants for several weeks or more by heeling them in and keeping the roots damp.

Many evergreens and deciduous materials come from a nursery in containers. The soil starts to dry out as soon as the container is cut open, and it is difficult to keep the roots moist. Set these plants out immediately in the ground, or store them with moist soil or sawdust covering the roots. Keep all the soil in contact with the roots, and plant the entire contents. Plant container plants in the same way that you plant balled and burlapped or bare-root stock.

Prices of plants vary with their source. A mail-order house may offer a more attractive price than your local nurseryman, but you must usually add the cost of postage and express or freight charges to the mail-order price. The final cost may be close to that of freshly dug material from your local nurseryman. Shipped-in plants are often badly dried out when you get them, unless the shipper has protected the roots and crowns. Question the origin of cut-rate material, how long the material has been dug, and how well it has been handled, cared for, and protected since it was taken from the ground.

Some people will pay 4 to 5 dollars for a steak dinner, but will object to paying that amount for a

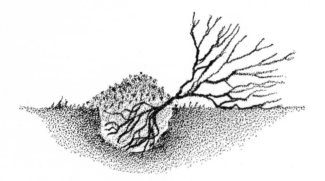

If you can't place a new plant in the ground immediately, protect its roots from drying out. This plant has been heeled into a trench with soil covering its roots.

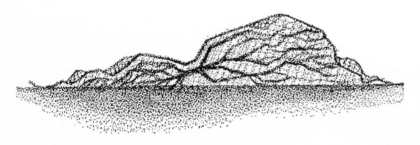

If the plant is going to be planted soon, it is usually sufficient to cover the entire plant with burlap or canvas. Dampen after covering.

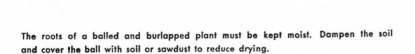

The roots of a balled and burlapped plant must be kept moist. Dampen the soil and cover the ball with soil or sawdust to reduce drying.

handsome evergreen or deciduous shrub or tree. The desire to get your money's worth is understandable, and cut-rate prices may appeal to your sense of economy. But the nursery industry as a whole tries to maintain a price level that will result in a fair price for the buyer and a reasonable return to the grower. The important point is to buy only from a reputable local dealer or a mail-order firm that will back up its material with a guarantee.

Neighbors, relatives, and friends who offer their surplus stock are a good source of plants. But don't put everything in your yard that is offered to you. Discipline yourself to follow through with your landscape plan, and if what is offered doesn't fit into your plan, express your thanks and decline the offer. After all your work in planning your design, you can appreciate the importance of using the right material in a chosen spot.

Before you plant anything, you have to prepare the soil properly — perhaps even condition it. Conditioning means more than just fertilizing. It means altering the physical makeup of the soil. For example, you must correct the physical balance of soil that has too much clay in it, or sand that contains too little organic matter. Topsoil is usually better for plant growth than subsoil because it has larger amounts of decayed organic matter in it. For best growth, topsoil should be at least 8 to 12 inches deep. If your soil is poor and you can't afford to add 6 inches of topsoil, you should have at least enough good soil on hand to fill planting holes properly.

Unless sandy soil has enough organic matter, it will lose needed water and plant nutrients through leaching. If the soil has too much clay, it may not drain well. Improve sandy soils by mixing in topsoil and organic matter, and improve clay soils by adding such coarser materials as sand, calcined clay, and humus. Peat moss, sewage sludge, and compost are common forms of organic material.

A soil test will tell you the fertility level of your soil. You can get a soil test by sending a soil sample to the farm adviser in your county cooperative extension office.

To take a proper soil sample for a test, dig in random areas over the entire property. Dig out a shovelful of soil, and then slice a thin section from the hole and put it on a sheet of paper. When you have slices from all the different places in your yard, mix them thoroughly in a jar and send them in for your soil test. If you are interested in the soil from one area, take soil only from that area.

Your soil test will tell you how much of each kind of fertilizer to add. Fertilizers may be organic (such as bonemeal, fishmeal, and sewage sludges), synthetic, or inorganic. Inorganic fertilizers are readily available to plants, while organic fertilizers break down slowly and become available over a longer time.

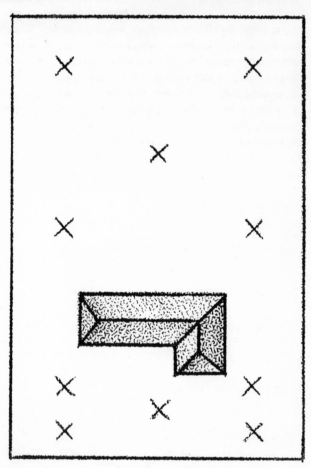

Take samples for a soil test of your yard in a random pattern similar to that indicated by the X's in the drawing.

To dig a soil sample, remove one shovelful of soil. Then slice a thin section from the hole and place in a bucket or on a sheet of paper.

All plants need nitrogen, phosphorus, and potash for satisfactory growth. These elements are listed in that order by numbers on fertilizer bags. For example, a 10-6-4 combination indicates 10 percent nitrogen, 6 percent phosphorus, and 4 percent potash. A fertilizer containing all three of these nutrient elements is referred to as a "complete" fertilizer. Use a high-nitrogen fertilizer on foliage plants. Nitrogen is important for growth of new leaves and stems.

However, too much nitrogen supplied to flowering plants will cause them to produce leaves and stems rather than flowers. For this reason, use a high-nitrogen fertilizer primarily on trees, shrubs, and lawn. Use a high-phosphorus fertilizer, perhaps a 5-10-5 (5 percent nitrogen, 10 percent phosphorus, and 5 percent potash) on plants to encourage flowering.

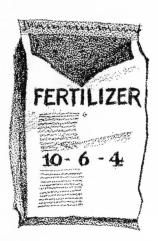

A bag of complete fertilizer. The numbers indicate the percentages by weight of nitrogen, phosphorus, and potash in that order.

Soil pH indicates the relative acidity or alkalinity of the soil. The neutral point is 7.0 in a scale that runs from 0 through 14. Soil that tests below a pH of 7.0 is acid, and soil above 7.0 is alkaline. These pH values are based on logarithms, and a pH of 5.0 is 10 times more acid than a pH of 6.0. Most plants will thrive in a pH of 5.5 to 7.0. Some plants are indifferent to soil pH, while others are definitely sensitive and prefer either a strongly acid or alkaline soil.

Soil pH can be changed by adding certain materials. For instance, if a soil test shows that your soil is too acid to grow most plants successfully, you can raise the pH by adding lime to the soil.

Some plants grow best in acid soils. If your soil is not acid enough for the plants you want, you can add small amounts of aluminum sulfate or dusting sulfur. Too much aluminum sulfate can be fatal to some types of plants. Acid-loving plants often need partial shade, a rich organic soil, plenty of water, and good drainage.

Although plants need water, few plants do well if water collects around them in the soil without draining away. Water can shut off the air supply in the soil and "drown" the plants. If you have this problem, you can put in "pockets" of topsoil for growing plants in tight soil. Before planting and backfilling with new soil, be sure that the subsoil allows for good drainage.

When you get ready to plant, have some good topsoil on hand that is high in organic matter and rich in nitrogen, phosphorus, and potash. Good topsoil pays big dividends in the speed with which the plant adapts itself to its new location and to its early growth.

For best results, dig the holes before the plants are delivered, and get the plants in the ground as soon as they arrive. If the root system dries out, you can do nothing to repair the damage and the plant will die. If you can't get the holes dug first, cover the roots with moist material while waiting to plant. Heel the plants into a trench to keep the roots covered with moist soil until you can plant them.

Dig the hole for bare-root stock wide enough so that you can spread out the root system naturally without cramping or twisting it. Hold the plant in the air — the pattern that the roots take should be the planted pattern. Dig the hole about 4 inches deeper and 4 inches wider than the spread of the root system. It is foolish to put a 25-dollar plant in a two-bit hole.

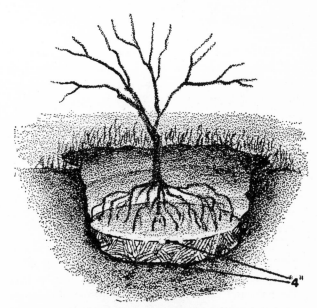

When transplanting, prepare a hole that is 4 inches wider and 4 inches deeper than required by the plant. Place 4 inches of prepared soil in the bottom of the hole. Add more soil if necessary to bring plant to about the same depth as that at which it was planted previously.

To enrich the soil that has been taken from the hole, mix it with some well-rotted manure or other organic matter. Put a 4-inch layer of this mixture in the bottom of the hole, and use it for backfill.

Never let fertilizers come in contact with newly planted roots. Cover the fertilizer mixture with 2 inches of plain soil. Evergreens should not be buried any deeper than the depth at which they originally grew, although they may be planted slightly higher. Deciduous materials should be planted at their original depth or slightly lower. Use the prepared soil mixture in the bottom of the hole to get the correct height.

Plant so that you can see the best side of the tree or shrub from the terrace or patio. Fill in soil around the roots so that there are no air pockets. Tamp the fill with a shovel handle or your foot. When the roots are about half-covered, soak well with water, finish filling the hole, tamp, and then soak again to settle the soil around the roots for good soil and root contact. Finally, make a ridge of dirt around the edge of the fill to hold water over the roots.

Follow this same procedure with canned or balled plants. Make the hole twice as wide and twice as deep as the ball, if you can. Put the prepared soil mixture in the bottom of the hole, and then fill with plain soil until the top of the ball is slightly higher than the surrounding ground. Plant balled and burlapped plants with the burlap still around the plants. Loosen it around the top, if you wish. Burlap rots away quickly and causes no problem.

Remember that there is a balanced relationship between the roots and the top of a plant. The roots below the surface spread laterally as well as descend into the soil. When roots are cut, the reduced root system will slow top growth. When you move a large tree, it may stay about the same size for several years while restoring its root system. If too few roots are left, the plant may not get enough water and may die.

When root loss has been severe, prune back the top for compensation. An overbalance of leaves over roots will draw more water than the roots can supply, and the plant will wilt and die. Branches taken off at transplanting time will grow back as fast as the root system develops to handle them. In pruning after transplanting, try to keep the natural shape of the plant, but take off about one-fourth to one-third of the top to balance root loss.

You can prune back a branch to a bud, or all the way back to the main stem. In either case, always make a prune cut on a slant and as close to the bud as possible. Prune back to buds on the outside of the branch. If stubs of branches are left above the bud, they will eventually rot and offer easy access to insects or disease.

It may be best to prune the tree before planting so that you can reach the top easily. When you prune during the dormant season, you need not worry about painting the wound to halt bleeding. But such profuse "bleeders" as birch and beech cannot be pruned in spring.

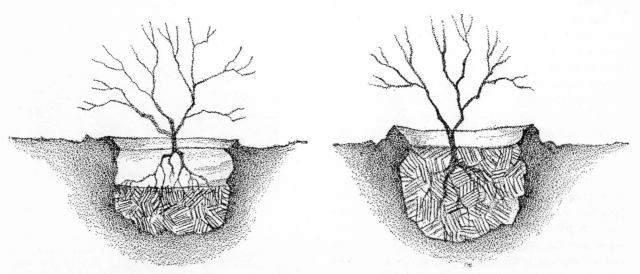

After plant is located at proper depth in the hole (left), backfill with topsoil to ½ the depth of the hole. Tamp thoroughly to remove air pockets. Allow water to filter through the filled area. Complete the backfilling of the hole to ground level (right), tamp, and water again. Then use remaining soil to form a dish or basin around the plant. This basin will facilitate watering.

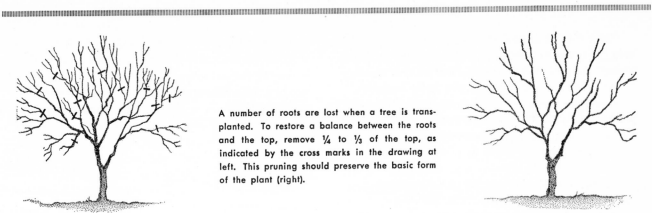

A number of roots are lost when a tree is transplanted. To restore a balance between the roots and the top, remove ¼ to ⅓ of the top, as indicated by the cross marks in the drawing at left. This pruning should preserve the basic form of the plant (right).

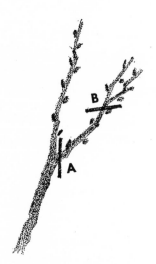

Branches should be pruned flush to parent branches (A) or to a bud (B). Be sure that the bud is facing in the direction in which you want the new growth. Make the cut at an angle, and as close to the bud as possible.

Water newly planted trees and shrubs well. Soak the soil around them thoroughly twice a week for the first month or two after planting. One way is to let the hose run gently into the basin around the plant. But be sure that the running water doesn't erode the soil around the roots or the ridge.

During the rest of the growing season, water new plants once a week. In the second growing season, water every second or third week. Watering deep is the secret to success. Make sure the water gets into the soil where the roots are. Watering by sprinkler only wets the surface. Fill the basin around new plants several times at each watering. It is hard to overdo watering if drainage is good, but it is easy not to water enough.

It is normal for most plants to wilt slightly soon after transplanting. Shade severely wilted plants by covering them with heavy paper, cloth, or burlap. Keep this shade material wet and the ground soaked. A critical period for wilting may last for two or three weeks or even longer in hot weather. If the plant does not recover in a week or two, prune severely to lessen the amount of water lost by the plant.

Some plants will drop their leaves when transplanted in foliage and will develop a new set later.

If you suspect that your plant is dead after it has dropped all its leaves, scrape the bark with your fingernail. A green underlying surface indicates that the plant is still living and should not be pulled up. Don't damage the plant or kill it with too much scraping.

If you plant evergreens in the fall, provide some sort of protective shade from winter winds and sun to cut down moisture loss from the foliage. This is particularly important if the plants are planted on the south or west sides of the house. Winter winds can have a great drying effect on evergreens.

Wrap deciduous trees with sisal kraft paper whether you plant them in spring or fall. Spiral the paper from the ground level to the first branches. Secure the paper with twine wound around the full length of the trunk. The paper helps to protect the trunk from sunscald, which injures so many newly planted trees. An unprotected trunk may split when the sun warms up the bark on the south and west sides during the winter months. This alternating freezing and thawing action may crack the trunk lengthwise. Leave the tree wrapped for at least two growing seasons.

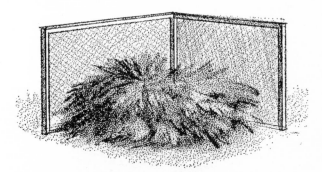

If your new plants become severely wilted because of loss of moisture from sun and wind, they may need artificial protection. You can protect plants with burlap screens attached to a wood frame, or by wrapping the plant with burlap to reduce moisture loss. Do not wrap the plant so tight that air movement is restricted beneath the burlap.

Stake newly planted trees to keep them from being whipped and loosened by high winds. Wind whipping can injure the root system. Fasten the tree to a 2- by 2-inch or 2- by 4-inch stake with wire. Loop the wire around the tree in three places — where the first branches start, midway down the trunk, and about 6 inches above the groundline. Use plastic tubing or rubber hose to keep these loops from cutting into the bark. Unprotected wire loops can girdle and kill the tree. Keep the wires tight.

One way to stake a tree is to "plant" the stake against the trunk when you plant the tree. Bind the stake to the trunk with wide strips of rubber inner tubing, cloth, or burlap. Where trees are subjected to extreme wind conditions, it is a good idea to stake in two directions. The stakes should be directly opposite each other. Tie the tree in the three locations described above. Keep the tree tied to the stakes for at least two years.

You can transplant successfully in the Midwest in both spring and fall. Spring planting may be better because the plant has a full growing season to reestablish its root system before going through the rigors of winter. The important thing is to move deciduous materials when they are dormant. Evergreens have dormant periods, too, and it is best to move them in early spring or early fall.

You can move balled and burlapped plants or plants in cans at any time, but you must also shade and water them to be sure that they survive.

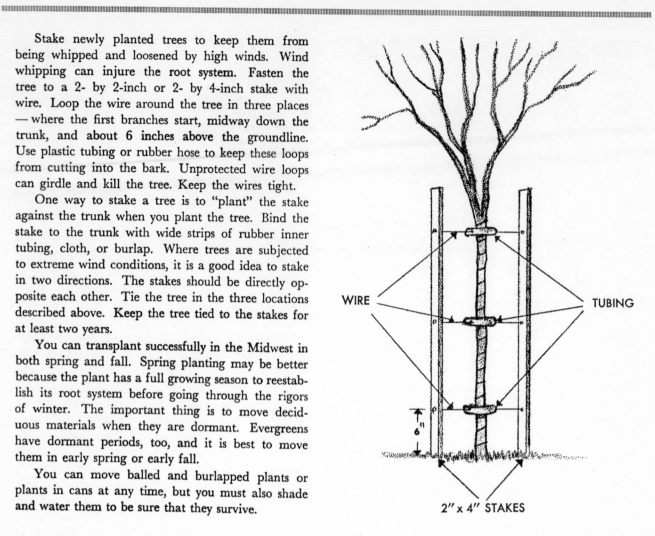

WIRE   TUBING

6"

2" x 4" STAKES

13: TAKING CARE OF YOUR PLANTS

Every landscape needs some maintenance to stay attractive. You will be working with living, growing material that is constantly changing and demanding water, fertilizer, spraying, pruning, and cultivation.

In selecting plants for your landscape, first consider their environmental requirements — light, temperature tolerances, wind and climate effects, and water needs. Each yard has its own environment. You can reduce care and maintenance considerably by choosing plants whose normal needs are closest to the environmental conditions in your garden.

To care for outdoor plants properly, you should understand how plants grow and know some general facts about soil. Soil is the growing medium for plants. A knowledge of soil structure, pH reactions, amendments (materials added to the soil to improve the soil), and fertilizers will help you give your plants better care.

Finally, an understanding of plant function is basic in plant care. Plants need light, water, air, and mineral elements to carry out their life processes.

Soil Conditioning

Putting lime on your soil can correct acidity, change soil structure, hasten bacterial action and the decomposition of organic materials, and speed the liberation of plant foods. You can apply lime either as ground limestone or in the hydrated form. Hydrated lime acts more quickly than ground limestone, but does not last as long. Put the lime on the surface and then work it into the soil. Successive applications may be harmful, so ask your county extension office for recommendations as to the amount you need.

To increase soil acidity, apply either dusting sulfur or aluminum sulfate. You can put on any reasonable amount of aluminum sulfate if you add phosphorus at the same time. Otherwise, aluminum sulfate may be toxic to plants. Dusting sulfur is slower to act than aluminum sulfate but longer lasting. Common powdered sulfur is not recommended, since it takes three to six months to produce results.

Sand, calcined clay, sawdust, and ashes may be used as amendments to improve such fine-textured soil as clay. Decayed sawdust and peat have a beneficial effect on soil structure, but the bacteria responsible for this decay require large amounts of nitrogen. For this reason, add extra nitrogen as you put sawdust or peat on the soil, or they will tie up available nitrogen and slow plant growth. Ashes from nonlignite coal can be used after screening out the clinkers. Although wood ashes improve soil structure, they have little fertilizing value.

Humus is also important for good soils. Compost, peat, manure, sawdust, and shavings are all sources of humus.

Fertilizing

Commercial fertilizers are the most economical way to add plant nutrients to the soil. Nitrogen, phosphorus, and potassium are the three nutrients most important to plant growth. (See the discussion of fertilizers in Chapter 12.)

Nitrogen is essential for plant growth, but too much nitrogen stimulates an overgrowth of foliage at the expense of flowers and fruits and keeps new growth from maturing before freezing weather sets in. Since nitrogen tends to disappear from the soil, it must be replaced with commercial fertilizer.

One source of nitrogen alone is ammonium sulfate, which can be applied at the rate of 1 to 2 pounds per 100 square feet of garden area. Another source is urea, a synthetic form of nitrogen that should be applied at the rate of 1 pound per 100 square feet.

Phosphorus is also essential for plant growth. It aids redevelopment and encourages flower and fruit production. Phosphorus becomes "fixed" in the soil when it is applied — it does not leach out or move in the soil. For this reason, it is important to apply phosphorus where you want it to be available to the plants.

The chief source of phosphorus is superphosphate, which is applied at the rate of 2 or 3 pounds per 100 square feet. Bonemeal contains up to 25 percent phosphorus, but releases it so slowly that its value is questionable.

Potassium is important to the general vigor of plants. It increases disease resistance and has a general balancing effect on other plant nutrients. One source of potassium is potassium chloride. The recommended application rate is 1 pound per 100 square feet.

Some trace elements are needed for plant growth, although only minute amounts are required. Complete fertilizers often contain several of these trace elements, such as iron, boron, manganese, and sulfur.

A complete fertilizer in the ratio of 10-10-10, 10-6-4, or 10-8-6 will usually produce desirable results on Midwest lawns, shrubs, and trees. Since phosphorus encourages flowers and fruit production, a 5-10-5 fertilizer works well on flowers and other plants where flower and fruit production are important.

You can fertilize shrubs and trees anytime from early spring to midsummer, and from September 15 to the last of November. Application between July 15 and September 15 may stimulate a late succulent growth. This growth would not have a chance to harden off properly before the killing frosts of fall caused dieback of the twigs.

Since the feeding roots of large trees extend as far as or even beyond the spread of the branches, apply fertilizer around this "dripline" area. Drive holes 24 to 30 inches apart and 18 to 24 inches deep in concentric circles around the trunk under the spread of the branches. Do not punch holes closer than 3 to 5 feet from the trunk. Put a complete fertilizer in each hole; then fill the holes with water to dissolve the fertilizer. Use a funnel to put the fertilizer in the holes, particularly on lawn areas where spilled fertilizer might harm the grass.

To fertilize a mature tree, you must get the fertilizer in the area of the hair roots so that they can take advantage of it. These roots are usually located at the dripline of the crown. Drill holes 18 to 24 inches deep and 2 to 2½ feet apart in this area. Be sure that you have one circle of holes beyond the dripline and several circles within the dripline. Fill these holes with fertilizer and water.

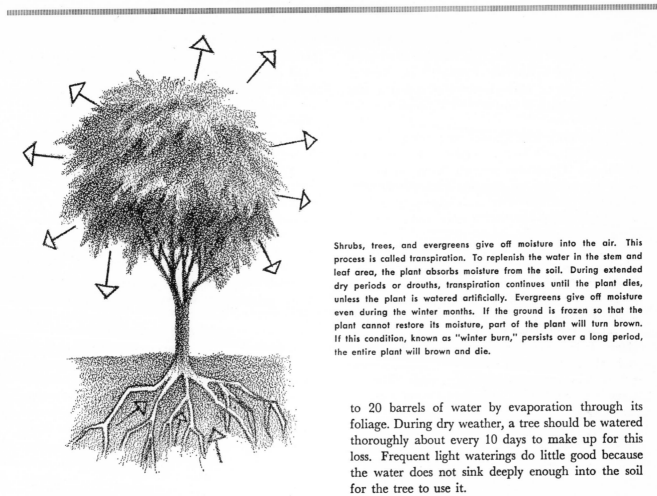

Shrubs, trees, and evergreens give off moisture into the air. This process is called transpiration. To replenish the water in the stem and leaf area, the plant absorbs moisture from the soil. During extended dry periods or drouths, transpiration continues until the plant dies, unless the plant is watered artificially. Evergreens give off moisture even during the winter months. If the ground is frozen so that the plant cannot restore its moisture, part of the plant will turn brown. If this condition, known as "winter burn," persists over a long period, the entire plant will brown and die.

to 20 barrels of water by evaporation through its foliage. During dry weather, a tree should be watered thoroughly about every 10 days to make up for this loss. Frequent light waterings do little good because the water does not sink deeply enough into the soil for the tree to use it.

There are no exact rules for watering plants. Use the condition of the soil and plant as a general guide. Consider the environmental needs of the plants you have used in your landscape. Those that resist drouth may not need much water between rains. Other plants that grow in shade and like moist conditions should have frequent waterings to survive in very hot summer weather. A watering lance is useful for getting water into the root zone.

Shrubs and flowers also benefit from fertilization, although there is little information available on what they need for best growth. Use a balanced fertilizer, and vary the amount with the size of the shrub and the frequency with which you apply it. A 10-6-4 fertilizer is a good one to use for shrubs. Apply it from near the base of the plant to the outer spread of the branches. Most of the feeding roots are in this area. Use from 1 to 3 cups of fertilizer, and work it into the upper soil surface.

Certain fertilizers can burn the foliage of growing plants. Apply any fertilizer only when the foliage is dry. Water thoroughly immediately after fertilizing. Put on enough water to carry the fertilizer down into the soil.

For flowers, work a handful of fertilizer into the soil around the base of both perennials and annuals. Use a fertilizer that is high in phosphorus content, such as 5-10-5.

Watering

Shrubs and trees may lack expected vigor because they aren't getting enough water. On a warm summer day, a mature tree may lose as much as 10

Water lawn, trees, or shrubs slowly. Soak the soil to a depth of 8 to 10 inches to encourage deep root penetration. If the planting is new, apply the water slowly in the basin or dish formed when transplanting. Water an area for 15 minutes, and then dig to find depth of moisture penetration. This method will help you determine the length of time required for a deep watering.

Apply water slowly so that it will soak into the soil. To get an idea of how slowly water penetrates, water an area for 15 minutes or so, then dig down to see how far the water has gone. Rate of penetration will depend upon soil type. If runoff occurs, you have probably watered too much or too rapidly.

Soak the soil deeply to encourage root development. Never water by spraying only the surface of the soil. This encourages shallow root development that may result in plant damage if you don't water for a day or two and there is a sudden hot spell.

Don't water in late afternoon, since this encourages disease on many plants. And don't water too much. Water passing through the soil may dissolve nutrients and carry them away, causing nutrient deficiencies. Excess water standing in the root zone can "drown" a plant by shutting off its soil air supply.

One deep watering every 5 to 7 days is enough for most plants under most weather conditions. Don't forget the plants close to a wall or under the eaves. These plants don't get much natural rainfall, and will need to be watered.

Pruning

Pruning is a very important part of caring for and maintaining plants that is often either overdone or completely ignored. Pruning is the art of cutting out unwanted growth to make a plant respond as desired. Most plants need some pruning to serve as intended in the landscape. But if you have selected plants with the correct form and mature size, you won't have to prune severely at any time.

Pruning helps to produce more or better blooms, develops and keeps desired shape, rejuvenates plants by removing older stems and encouraging vigorous young growth, repairs injuries, removes diseased or injured parts, and removes winterkilled and dead wood. It differs from shearing or barbering.

You can find evidence in almost any neighborhood of the "frustrated barber" approach to pruning shrubs. The tops are sheared round or cut straight across to give a "butch haircut" appearance. Pruning involves selection and judgment. Shearing merely involves clipping.

If you cut back a branch only part way, many new shoots will grow out below the cut at awkward angles. These shoots then grow upward to create the unattractive "butch haircut" design. To prevent this, cut off a branch only where it joins a larger branch, and cut it off flush so that no stub is left.

Cut off a main stem at the ground level. Do not leave any stub. A stub not only produces new branches below the cut that disfigure the plant but is also subject to decay and a point of entry for disease and insect damage. If a branch extends beyond the rest of the crown, do not cut it back only to the length of the other branches. Cut it back to where it joins a larger branch or back to the ground level. A pruned bush may look a little thin when you finish, but it will fill out nicely.

Don't prune too much at one time. Too severe pruning encourages the growth of suckers — long branches with larger than normal foliage. A rule of thumb for pruning flowering shrubs is to remove one-fourth to one-third of all older wood at ground level. This stimulates growth of new wood from that area. Old wood is larger and has darker-colored bark than new wood.

Pruning also emphasizes a plant's natural shape by making each branch stand out separately. This is especially desirable for specimen plants.

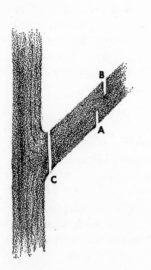

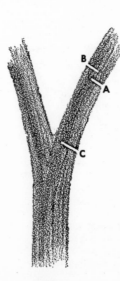

Remove a large limb from a tree in three steps. The first cut (A) should be made from the underside of the limb 1 foot from the trunk (left). The second cut (B) is made from the top about 2 inches from the undercut. Continue this cut until the limbs falls. By using this method, you avoid peeling away the trunk bark (middle). The third cut (C) is made flush with the trunk to remove the stub. Notice the procedure for a split crotch (right). Cut (C) has to be made from underneath to avoid damaging the remaining limb.

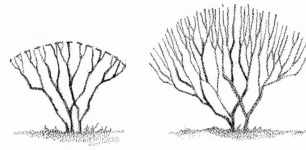

Plants should be allowed to grow into their natural shape. Don't shear plants (left) into balls, squares, or other rigid and unnatural shapes. These artificial shapes fit only into formal designs. Shearing is not pruning. Excessive sucker growth (right) develops as a result of shearing.

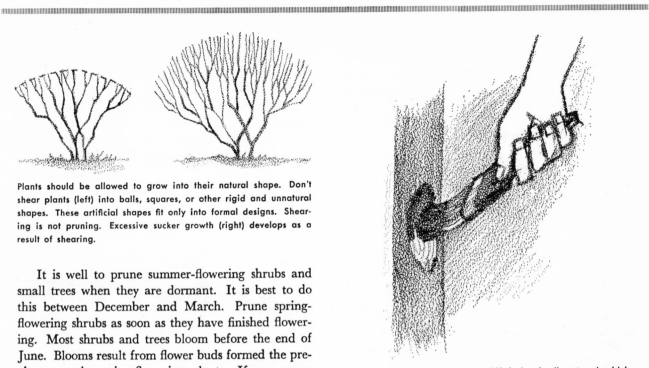

Pruning cuts that are larger than 1½ inches in diameter should be dressed with a commercial tree paint or shellac to prevent excessive bleeding. If large cuts are unattended, they may cause disease and insect problems.

It is well to prune summer-flowering shrubs and small trees when they are dormant. It is best to do this between December and March. Prune spring-flowering shrubs as soon as they have finished flowering. Most shrubs and trees bloom before the end of June. Blooms result from flower buds formed the previous year in spring-flowering plants. If you prune these plants before they bloom, you will cut off most of the flower buds. Forsythia, spirea, deutzia, and mockorange are examples of spring-flowering plants.

Shrubs that bloom after June usually do so on growth made the same year. As a result, they have plenty of time to grow their flowering stems. Prune this group of shrubs in the winter when they are dormant. Examples of this group include buddlea, crepe myrtle, althea, white hydrangea, and vitex. They produce their flowers on the new wood that grows each spring.

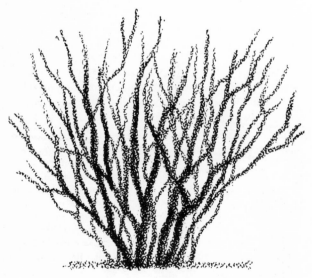

Prune the oldest wood from an established shrub at ground level. This wood is easily recognized because it is the largest and has the darkest color. Remove ¼ to ⅓ of this wood annually to preserve the shrub's natural form and to stimulate flowering.

Shade trees need relatively little pruning. Remove dead or diseased wood and cut out crowding or interfering branches. Pruning small, dead branches will often keep large branches or the trunk from rotting. To remove a dead branch, cut into live wood where it joins a larger branch. To remove large branches, cut from below part way through the branch, and then finish the cut from the top a short distance from the undercut. The lower cut will keep the weight of the branch from ripping off a section of bark just before the saw cuts through. After the branch has fallen, cut the stump that remains to a flat surface flush with the parent branch or trunk, and cover it with a wound dressing. You can make small cuts without danger of the tree bleeding, but large cuts should be protected with pruning paint or dressing wax.

Mulching

Mulching is recommended for plants to prevent erosion, control weeds, conserve moisture, and protect the plants. Nature mulches plants with fallen leaves and other organic materials. Mulching, as practiced by gardeners, is simply an adaptation of this natural process. Since most mulch is organic material, it helps to improve soil structure by adding humus as the mulch decays.

The greatest advantage of mulching over clean cultivation is the moisture-saving ability of mulch. Mulch greatly reduces evaporation losses by protecting the soil from the sun and wind. It absorbs rainfall, keeps the soil from packing, and controls erosion.

Another advantage of mulching is weed control. Mulching is especially important in controlling weeds around shallow-rooted plants that cannot be cultivated, such as azalea, rhododendron, and camellia. Using a chemical weed killer with mulch increases the benefits even more.

Mulch also helps to control soil temperature. A lower soil temperature in summer favors plant growth. And in winter there is less frost penetration under mulch. This is important for evergreens, since they need moisture in winter as well as in summer. A winter mulch for evergreens helps to keep a supply of moisture available for a longer period and minimizes the effects of alternate freezing and thawing.

Although the advantages of mulching far outweigh its disadvantages, there are a few drawbacks. Mulching materials are sometimes costly or difficult to obtain. Some mulches, such as straw and dried leaves, are a fire hazard at certain times. Rodent problems may increase around mulched plants. And you may get a nitrogen deficiency when you use corncobs or sawdust as a mulch, since the bacteria that decompose these materials use nitrogen. Add nitrogen fertilizer when you apply this type of mulch to prevent nitrogen deficiency.

Sawdust is easy to obtain in many parts of Illinois. Apply it 3 to 4 inches deep. It is low in nutrients, decomposes slowly, and tends to pack. If you mulch with sawdust, wood chips, or shavings, add ammonium nitrate or sodium nitrate at the rate of 1 pound per 100 square feet.

A corncob, sawdust, or straw mulch prevents the soil from freezing as quickly as exposed soil and reduces the depth of frost penetration. As a result, mulching helps keep the plant supplied with moisture during the winter. To prevent winter burn from excessive moisture loss during the winter, water evergreens thoroughly before the ground freezes in mid-November. Water again during mid-winter thaws.

Peat moss is another attractive and readily available mulching material, but it is usually too expensive for large areas. Apply it to a depth of 1 to 2 inches. Before spreading, dampen the bale thoroughly for easier handling. Ground corncobs are also easy to get in several Midwestern states, and are excellent for mulching and for improving soil structure. They should be applied to a depth of 4 to 6 inches.

Controlling Weeds

In addition to mulch, several chemicals are available to help in the fight against weeds. Weeding may be a definite problem for the first year or two after planting and fertilization. It is important to keep weeds controlled before they can go to seed.

Weed seed will continue to germinate in the soil until controlled by good cultural practices. You can kill most weed seedlings by hoeing about 1 inch deep and letting the soil dry out. Dry surface soil acts much like a mulch, helping to reduce the number of weed seeds that sprout.

Controlling Diseases and Insects

Plant diseases are hard to diagnose. If part of the plant dies, or if the leaves turn brown and fall off too early, the cause may be either a disease or an environmental condition. For example, too much water in the soil will cause these symptoms.

A good preventive program provides the best disease control. Clear all weeds and debris out of your garden each spring and fall. In the spring, cut out all dead wood and turn under or remove winter mulch. In the fall, remove and burn all dead flower stalks, leaves, and annual plant stalks so that diseases and insects will not be carried through the winter.

Insect problems will vary from season to season. Apply preventive sprays to plants that are attacked each year by such insects as aphids, bagworms, or red spiders. Be continually on the alert for signs of insect damage to foliage, bark, or flowers. Apply control measures promptly to check the damage and keep the insects from spreading.

Protecting Plants

Be sure to provide adequate winter protection for your plants. The amount of protection needed depends upon the natural hardiness of the plant and the severity of the climate.

Extreme cold will cause twigs, stems, and branches to freeze. Too much moisture loss or severe cold often causes winterkilling, particularly in ever-

Place a lath frame over plants close to buildings to prevent damage from snow sliding off the roofs.

greens. Most winter moisture loss results from strong drying winds on sunny days. The plant may die if the roots can't supply enough moisture.

For this reason, one of the most important ways to prepare all woody plants, especially evergreens, for winter is to make sure that the soil has a large reserve supply of moisture. If autumn rainfall has been light, thoroughly soak the ground around the plants before the first hard freeze. Then put on a heavy 4- to 6-inch mulch of ground corncobs or another good mulch to keep the ground from freezing too deep. The plant will then continue to supply moisture from the ground to replace the moisture lost by winter evaporation. Since the plants under the eaves do not receive adequate moisture, it is especially important to water these plants thoroughly before the ground freezes.

You can shield less hardy evergreens from winter sun and wind damage with burlap, straw, or boxes. Attach burlap to a frame around the plant as a screen, or wrap the burlap on the plant itself. Leave the wrapping loose enough to allow some air movement through the burlap. An evergreen located under the roofline may need a lath shield to prevent damage from snow sliding off the roof.

You will have a chance to replenish moisture loss from the plants and soil during the customary winter thaws in the Midwest. Whenever the ground is not completely frozen, you can water the plants well to get moisture back into the soil. Check the mulch during the winter to be sure that it is still in place and not washing away.

Do not remove such winter-protective devices as screens, wrappings, and snow supports too early in the spring. The Midwest is subject to many late heavy snowstorms and temperature extremes, and early mulch removal might be a serious mistake. Leave mulch on until well into the spring to be sure that your plants get maximum protection.

You will set the stage for winter plant protection by the kinds and numbers of plants that you choose for your garden. If you like to work outdoors with plants, you may want to use a few semi-hardy plants to get the variety you want. But you will have to take extra precautions to keep these plants flourishing.

If you do not have the time or the inclination to test semi-exotic plants in your yard, choose hardy plants that need only minimum care.

Wrap upright evergreens with burlap or straw mats to protect them from the drying effects of winter sun and wind. Do not wrap the plants so tight that air movement inside is restricted.

14: SELECTED LIST OF PLANT MATERIALS

The plant list in this chapter is divided into two sections: groupings of shrubs and trees according to their use in the home landscape, and descriptive outlines of shrubs, vines, trees, and ground covers. This list is, of course, a selected one, and many materials suitable for ornamental plantings are not included.

Shrubs are grouped as accents and specimens or on the basis of their use in certain planting areas (doorway, corner, border, etc.), and trees are grouped as lawn trees and street trees. The fact that a shrub appears in a particular group does not mean that the shrub is restricted in its use to that group. For example, a shrub listed under "Corner Planting" may be used with equal effectiveness in a shrub border or group planting. This is not the case with lawn trees and street trees. Although any of the street trees can be used as lawn trees, the reverse is not true. Only the trees listed as street trees are satisfactory for that use. These are not all of the trees that can be used for street plantings, but the varieties listed are dependable and readily available.

The detailed descriptive outlines of shrubs, vines, trees, and ground covers have been organized so that you can find whatever information you require quickly and easily. Height and spread, texture, flower and fruit effects, fall color, exposure requirements, and suggested landscape uses of each plant are set in heavy type for easy reference.

For your convenience, each plant is listed alphabetically by its common name. The botanical name is given after the common name. Be sure to include the botanical name when ordering your plants. There may be several common names for a plant, but the botanical name identifies the plant without question.

Before choosing a tree, shrub, or vine for your home landscape, make sure that it will grow in your area. The word *hardiness* is used to express a plant's tolerance to temperatures and climates. Each zone represents an area of winter hardiness for certain ornamental plants. The zone number that appears after each plant name in the descriptive outlines refers to the hardiness of that particular plant. These hardiness zones are based on average minimum winter temperatures.

Although these minimum temperatures are of primary importance for plant survival, there are other conditions that determine whether a plant will survive in a particular zone. These include frost occurrence, seasonal rainfall distribution, humidity, soil characteristics, and duration and intensity of sunlight.

A plant species that lives in one part of a zone can be expected to live in other parts of the same zone or in a warmer zone provided that growth conditions (rainfall, soil, summer heat, etc.) are comparable or capable of being made comparable through irrigation, soil correction, wind protection, partial shade, or humidity control. Despite your best efforts, however, a plant considered adapted to your zone may not survive the winter. This may be the result of cultural conditions affecting the plant's hardiness, or a more severe winter than usual.

The zone number for each plant is followed by a brief description of the plant's habits of growth and any qualities or problems worthy of special notice. The average mature height and spread is given for each tree and shrub, the height only for vines, and the height and spacing for ground covers. The spacing measurements are from the center of one plant to the center of the next plant.

The climbing method of each vine is given to help you determine the kind of support that will be required, and the rooting habit of each tree is listed so that you can select the tree that best fits your situation. Deep-rooted trees do not compete with lawn and nearby plantings for nutrients and water and seldom interfere with underground water or sewer lines, but trees with shallow or spreading roots should not be located close to underground utilities.

Some plants will grow only in shade and others demand sun. The preferred exposure of each shrub and ground cover is included so that you can easily select a plant that will thrive in any of the exposures on your property.

Soil preferences or special soil requirements are noted. For those plants that will tolerate a general soil condition, no comments are made about soil.

The texture of each plant is given to help you develop a design that has a pleasing textural quality. This information should also be helpful in achieving texture contrasts with other landscape elements. You might want to review the discussions of texture in Chapters 6, 7, 8, and 9 before making your final decision.

Flower and fruit effects are described unless they are not outstanding or do not contribute significantly to the design. In that case, they are either omitted or indicated as "not showy." Consider color carefully to be sure of a harmonious color scheme. Remember that the flowers are usually of interest for only a short time. Don't base your selection entirely on the flower effects of a plant.

Fall color is a quality that contributes to the late-season effects of the landscape. When a plant has outstanding foliage color in the fall, the color is indicated; otherwise it is omitted.

The landscape uses to which each plant is particularly adapted are given at the end of each descriptive outline.

Here's how the list works. Let's say, for example, that you want a shrub with a certain texture, flower color, or height. A quick check through the list will tell you which shrubs will generally meet these requirements. Then, by comparing the shrubs you have checked, you can quickly find the one that will do the job best. Or perhaps you need a tree for shade close to a flower-shrub border. In this case, you will want a tree with descending roots so that they will not compete with the flowers and shrubs for food and water. Or possibly you need a plant that will tolerate shade, moisture, sandy soil, etc. Again, a check of the appropriate subhead under each plant will give you a list of plants from which to select the one that best suits your needs.

All of the plants listed here can be obtained in the nursery trade. Your nurseryman may not have some of these plants in stock, but he can order them for you. Be firm in your demands. Don't clutter up your landscape with plants of mediocre ornamental qualities simply because your nurseryman has these plants or because your neighbors offer them to you as gifts.

The author wishes to acknowledge use of the following books as references in compiling the list of plants in this chapter:

Useful Trees and Shrubs by Florence Bell Robinson. The Garrard Press, Champaign, Illinois, 1960.

Shrubs and Vines for American Gardens by Donald Wyman. Macmillan Company, New York, 1949.

Trees for American Gardens by Donald Wyman. Macmillan Company, New York, 1951.

You may wish to refer to these books for information about other plants for the home landscape.

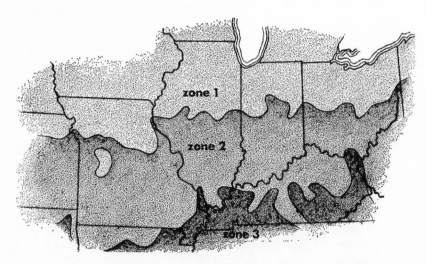

HARDINESS ZONES of the Midwest. This map and the maps appearing with the descriptive outlines are reproductions of a portion of the United States map prepared by the U. S. Department of Agriculture and the American Horticultural Society. For convenience, the USDA zone numbers have been changed to Zones 1, 2, and 3. Zone 1 is the same as USDA Zone 5; Zone 2 is the same as USDA Zone 6; and Zone 3 is the same as USDA Zone 7.

Shrubs Grouped According to Use

CORNER PLANTINGS

Abelia, Glossy
Almond, Flowering
Barberry, Wintergreen
Bayberry
Buckthorn, Common
Cherry, Manchu
Cinquefoil, Farreri Bush (Gold Drop)
Cinquefoil, Klondike Bush
Cotoneaster, Spreading
Deutzia, Lemoine
Dogwood, Yellowtwig
Euonymus, Dwarf Winged
Euonymus, Spreading
Euonymus, Winged
Firethorn
Honeysuckle, Winter
Hydrangea, Hills-of-Snow
Jetbead
Juniper, Blue Rug
Juniper, Compact Pfitzer
Juniper, Henry Sargent
Juniper, Pfitzer
Juniper, Prostrate
Juniper, Waukegan
Lilac, Persian
Nandina
Ninebark, Dwarf
Pine, Dwarf Mugho
Plum, Flowering
Privet, Regels Border
Quince, Japanese Flowering
Viburnum, American Cranberrybush
Viburnum, Arrowwood
Viburnum, Burkwood
Viburnum, Compact American Cranberrybush
Viburnum, Compact European Cranberrybush

(Corner Plantings, continued)
Viburnum, Doublefile
Viburnum, Fragrant Snowball (Carlcephalum)
Viburnum, Koreanspice
Viburnum, Leatherleaf
Viburnum, Mapleleaf
Weigela
Yew, Dwarf Spreading Japanese
Yew, Spreading Japanese
Yew, Taunton Anglojap
Yew, Upright Japanese
Yew, Wards Anglojap

BORDER PLANTINGS

Almond, Flowering
Azalea, Exbury Hybrids
Azalea, Karens
Barberry, Japanese
Beautybush
Buckeye, Bottlebrush
Buckthorn, Common
Cherry, Manchu
Cotoneaster, Peking
Cotoneaster, Spreading
Deutzia, Lemoine
Dogwood, Gray
Dogwood, Redtwig
Dogwood, Yellowtwig
Euonymus, Spindle Tree
Euonymus, Spreading
Euonymus, Wahoo
Euonymus, Winged
Forsythia, Beatrix Farrand or Karl Sax
Forsythia, Showy Border
Hazel, American
Holly, American
Holly, Burford Chinese
Holly, Foster's

(Border Plantings, continued)
Holly, Winterberry
Honeysuckles
Hydrangea, Hills-of-Snow
Jetbead
Kerria
Lilacs
Lilac, Persian
Mockorange
Pearlbush
Peashrub, Siberian
Plum, Flowering
Privet, Amur
Privet, Ibolium
Privet, Lodense
Privet, Regels Border
Quince, Flowering
Rhododendron, Catawba
Rhododendron, P. J. M. Hybrid
Rhododendron, Wilson
Rose, Father Hugo
Rose of Sharon
Serviceberry
Spirea, Bridalwreath
Spirea, Van Houtte
Weigela
Witchhazel, Chinese
Witchhazel, Common
Viburnum, Arrowwood
Viburnum, Burkwood
Viburnum, Compact American Cranberrybush
Viburnum, Compact European Cranberrybush
Viburnum, European Cranberrybush
Viburnum, Fragrant Snowball (Carlcephalum)
Viburnum, Koreanspice
Yew, Spreading Japanese

Shrubs Grouped According to Use

FACER PLANTS
Abelia, Glossy
Barberry, Japanese
Barberry, Mentor
Bayberry
Bluebeard
Cinquefoil, Bush
Cinquefoil, Farreri Bush (Gold Drop)
Cinquefoil, Klondike Bush
Coralberry, Chenault
Coralberry, Indiancurrant
Cotoneaster, Cranberry
Cotoneaster, Rock
Currant, Alpine
Deutzia, Compact Lemoine
Deutzia, Slender
Euonymus, Dwarf Winged
Forsythia, Bronx
Holly, Convexleaf
Holly, Heller
Hollygrape, Oregon
Honeysuckle, Clavey Dwarf
Juniper, Blue Rug
Juniper, Compact Pfitzer
Juniper, Henry Sargent
Juniper, Prostrate
Juniper, Waukegan
Kerria
Ninebark, Dwarf
Quince, Dwarf Japanese Flowering
Rhododendron, Wilson
Roses, Floribunda
St. Johnswort, Sungold
Spirea, Anthony Waterer
Sumac, Fragrant
Viburnum, Dwarf European Cranberrybush
Yew, Dwarf Spreading Japanese
Yew, Taunton Anglojap
Yew, Wards Anglojap

HEDGE (C = Clipped, U = Unclipped)
Arborvitae, Mission U
Barberry, Japanese C-U
Barberry, Mentor C-U
Barberry, Truehedge Columnberry C
Barberry, Wintergreen C-U
Buckthorn, Common U
Cotoneaster, Peking C
Currant, Alpine C-U
Deutzia, Slender U
Euonymus, Dwarf Winged U
Euonymus, Saracoxie C
Euonymus, Wintercreeper C
Germander U
Honeysuckles U
Jetbead U
Ninebark, Common U
Ninebark, Dwarf C-U
Pachistima U
Privet, Amur C-U
Privet, Ibolium C-U
Privet, Lodense C-U
Quince, Flowering C
Quince, Japanese Flowering C
Roses, Floribunda C-U
Rose of Sharon U
Spirea, Anthony Waterer U
Yew, Dense C-U
Yew, Hicks or Hatfield C-U

PLANTERS OR TUBS
Azalea
Bayberry
Cotoneaster, Bearberry
Cotoneaster, Peking
Dogwood, Kelsey Redtwig
Euonymus, Saracoxie
Euonymus, Wintercreeper
Germander
Holly, Convexleaf

(Planters or Tubs, continued)
Holly, Heller
Pachistima
Pine, Dwarf Mugho
Viburnum, Dwarf Cranberrybush
Yew, Dense
Yew, Dwarf Spreading Japanese
Yew, Hicks or Hatfield

SPECIMEN PLANTS
Azalea, Karens
Buckeye, Bottlebrush
Cherry, Manchu
Cotoneaster, Cranberry
Cotoneaster, Rock
Cotoneaster, Spreading
Euonymus, Spindle Tree
Euonymus, Winged
Firethorn
Hazel, Contorted European
Holly, American
Holly, Burford Chinese
Holly, Foster's
Lilacs
Magnolia, Saucer
Magnolia, Star
Plum, Thundercloud
Rhododendron, P. J. M. Hybrid
Rose, Father Hugo
Rose of Sharon
Sandcherry, Purpleleaf
Serviceberry
Sumac, Staghorn
Viburnum, Doublefile
Viburnum, Fragrant Snowball (Carlcephalum)
Viburnum, Leatherleaf
Witchhazel, Chinese
Witchhazel, Common
Yucca

Shrubs Grouped According to Use

DOORWAY PLANTINGS

Azalea
Barberry, Mentor
Barberry, Truehedge Columnberry
Bayberry
Cinquefoil, Farreri Bush (Gold Drop)
Cinquefoil, Klondike Bush
Cotoneaster, Cranberry
Cotoneaster, Rock
Currant, Alpine
Deutzia, Compact Lemoine
Deutzia, Slender
Dogwood, Kelsey Redtwig
Euonymus, Dwarf Winged
Euonymus Saracoxie
Euonymus, Wintercreeper
Holly, Convexleaf
Holly, Heller
Hollygrape, Oregon
Honeysuckle, Clavey Dwarf
Juniper, Blue Rug
Juniper, Compact Pfitzer
Juniper, Henry Sargent
Juniper, Prostrate
Juniper, Waukegan
Pine, Dwarf Mugho
Quince, Japanese Flowering
Spirea, Anthony Waterer
Viburnum, Compact European Cranberrybush
Viburnum, Dwarf European Cranberrybush
Yew, Dense
Yew, Dwarf Spreading Japanese
Yew, Taunton Anglojap
Yew, Wards Anglojap

ACCENT PLANTS

Holly, Burford Chinese
Redcedar, Canaert Eastern
Yew, Hicks or Hatfield
Yew, Upright Japanese

GROUP PLANTINGS

Almond, Flowering
Azalea, Exbury Hybrids
Azalea, Karens
Cherry, Manchu
Cinquefoil, Farreri Bush (Gold Drop)
Cinquefoil, Klondike Bush
Cotoneaster, Cranberry
Currant, Alpine
Deutzia, Lemoine
Euonymus, Spindle Tree
Euonymus, Wahoo
Euonymus, Winged
Forsythia
Forsythia, Beatrix Farrand or Karl Sax
Forsythia, Bronx
Holly, American
Holly, Foster's
Holly, Winterberry
Honeysuckle, Winter
Honeysuckle, Zabel Tartarian
Hydrangea, Hills-of-Snow
Juniper, Blue Rug
Juniper, Henry Sargent
Juniper, Prostrate
Kerria
Lilacs
Mockorange
Nandina
Pearlbush
Plum, Flowering
Plum, Thundercloud
Privet, Lodense
Privet, Regels Border
Quince, Flowering
Redcedar, Canaert Eastern
Roses, Floribunda
Rose of Sharon
Sandcherry, Purpleleaf
Serviceberry
Spirea, Bridalwreath

(Group Plantings, continued)

Viburnum, American Cranberrybush
Viburnum, Burkwood
Viburnum, Compact American Cranberrybush
Viburnum, Compact European Cranberrybush
Viburnum, Doublefile
Viburnum, European Cranberrybush
Viburnum, Fragrant Snowball (Carlcephalum)
Viburnum, Koreanspice
Viburnum, Wayfaringtree
Weigela
Witchhazel, Chinese
Witchhazel, Common
Yew, Taunton Anglojap
Yew, Wards Anglojap

SCREEN PLANTS

Arborvitae, Mission
Euonymus, Eastern Wahoo
Forsythia, Showy Border
Holly, Foster's
Holly, Winterberry
Honeysuckles
Lilacs
Lilac, Persian
Mockorange
Peashrub, Siberian
Privet, Amur
Privet, Ibolium
Redcedar, Canaert Eastern
Viburnum, American Cranberrybush
Viburnum, Arrowwood
Viburnum, Doublefile
Viburnum, European Cranberrybush

Trees Grouped According to Use

SMALL LAWN TREES
(35 feet or under)

Ash, Moraine
Birch, Gray
Cherry, Kwanzan Oriental
Crabapple, Flowering
Dogwood, Corneliancherry
Dogwood, Flowering
Fringetree, White
Goldraintree, Panicled
Hawthorn, Washington
Hornbeam, American
Magnolia, Saucer
Magnolia, Star
Magnolia, Sweetbay
Maple, Amur
Mountainash, European
Mulberry, White
Redbud
Sassafras, Common*
Serviceberry
Silverbell, Carolina
Smoketree

MEDIUM LAWN TREES
(60 feet or under)

Ash, Green
Birch, Canoe
Birch, White
Corktree, Amur
Crabapple, Flowering
Hornbeam, Hop
Horsechestnut, Common
Horsechestnut, Ruby*
Linden, Crimean
Linden, Greenspire Small-Leafed

* Height varies through a range exceeding the maximum height of the group in which it is listed.

(Medium Lawn Trees, continued)

Linden, Littleleaf
Maple, Fassen Black
Maple, Norway
Maple, October Red and
   Autumn Glory
Maple, Red
Maple, Schwedler
Oak, Pin*
Pagodatree, Japanese*
Pear, Bradford
Sweetgum
Yellow-wood, American
Zelkova, Japanese*

LARGE LAWN TREES
(over 60 feet)

Ash, Blue
Ash, Marshall Seedless
Beech, American
Beech, European
Coffeetree, Kentucky
Cypress, Common Bald
Ginkgo
Hackberry, Common
Hackberry, Southern (Sugar)
Honeylocust, Thornless
Linden, American
Maple, Sugar
Oak, English
Oak, Northern Red
Oak, White
Planetree, London
Tuliptree
Tupelo (Black Gum)

* Height varies through a range exceeding the maximum height of the group in which it is listed.

STREET TREES

Ash, Green
Ash, Marshall Seedless
Ash, Moraine
Cherry, Kwanzan Oriental
Corktree, Amur
Dogwood, Flowering
Ginkgo
Goldraintree, Panicled
Hackberry, Common
Hackberry, Southern (Sugar)
Hawthorn, Washington
Honeylocust, Thornless
Hornbeam, American
Linden, Crimean
Linden, Greenspire Small-Leafed
Linden, Littleleaf
Maple, Amur
Maple, Norway
Maple, October Red and
   Autumn Glory
Maple, Red
Maple, Schwedler
Maple, Sugar
Mountainash, European
Oak, Northern Red
Oak, Pin
Pagodatree, Japanese
Pear, Bradford
Planetree, London
Redbud
Silverbell, Carolina
Sweetgum
Tuliptree
Zelkova, Japanese

Descriptive Outlines of Shrubs

ABELIA, GLOSSY (Abelia grandiflora).   **Zones 2–3**
Medium rate of growth. Dense plant, excellent foliage and small flowers appearing during most of the summer.

Height: 5 feet.   **Spread:** 4–5 feet.

Exposure: requires sun.

Texture: medium.

Flower effects: pink throughout summer.

Fruit effects: not showy.

Fall color: bronze to purple.

Use: corner, facer, hedge, informal hedge.

ALMOND, FLOWERING (Prunus glandulosa).   **Zones 1–3**
Slow to medium growth. Upright. Single- or double-flowering varieties available. Subject to verticillium wilt.

Height: 4 feet.   **Spread:** 4 feet.

Exposure: requires sun.

Soil: prefers rich, moist soil.

Texture: medium.

Flower effects: pink or white in May (according to variety).

Fruit effects: red, not showy.

Fall color: yellow.

Use: border mass, facer, group.

ARBORVITAE, MISSION (Thuja occidentalis var. Techny).   **Zones 1–3**
Fast growing, dark green foliage, columnar growth that tolerates shearing. Valued for color and low mature height.

Height: 8–10 feet.   **Spread:** 5–6 feet.

Exposure: sun or shade.

Soil: prefers moist soil but tolerates good humus soils.

Texture: fine.

Use: hedges, screens.

AZALEA (Azalea mollis).   **Zones 1–3**
Slow-growing, low, well-shaped, symmetrical plant. Attractive foliage, showy flowers. Many varieties available in numerous flower colors.

Height: 3–6 feet.   **Spread:** 3–5 feet.

Exposure: prefers sun, will stand shade.

Soil: best on slightly acid, light soils with much humus.

Texture: medium.

Flower effects: yellow in early spring (before leaves).

Fruit effects: not showy.

Fall color: red bronze.

Use: good in group or mass; also can be used singly for doorway or tub.

AZALEA, EXBURY HYBRIDS (Rhododendron hybrid crosses).   **Zones 1–3**
Moderate rate of growth, well-shaped, rounded to spreading form dependent on hybrid selection. Large flowers and striking colors in early June. Non-evergreen. Buy named clones.

Height: 4–5 feet.   **Spread:** 4–5 feet.

Exposure: partial sun for best flower effect.

Soil: rich, well-drained, acid.

Texture: medium.

Flower effects: large, showy, ranging from near-whites to pink, orange, rose, and red.

Use: group, border mass.

AZALEA, KARENS (Rhododendron kurume var. Karens).   **Zones 1–3**
Medium rate of growth, dense, twiggy. Showy flowers. Excellent plant.

Height: 3–4 feet.   **Spread:** 3–5 feet.

Exposure: sun or partial shade.

Soil: rich, well-drained, acid.

Texture: medium.

Flower effects: lavender.

Use: specimen, group, border mass.

BARBERRY, JAPANESE (Berberis thunbergi).   **Zones 2–3**
Slow-growing, dense, round plant, good in all seasons. Red-foliage variety also available.

Height: 5–7 feet.   **Spread:** 4–7 feet.

Exposure: either sun or shade.

Texture: fine.

Flower effects: yellow in May, but not showy.

Fruit effects: red in summer.

Fall color: scarlet.

Use: border mass, facer, hedge, planter, tub, on slopes, and for undergrowth.

BARBERRY, MENTOR (Berberis mentorensis).   **Zones 2–3**
Slow-growing, upright semi-evergreen plant. Withstands dry summers and low winter temperature. Good substitute for wintergreen barberry.

Height: 5–6 feet.   **Spread:** 4–5 feet.

Exposure: either sun or shade.

Texture: fine.

Flower effects: yellow in May, but not showy.

Fruit effects: red in fall.

Fall color: red.

Use: doorway, facer, hedge.

BARBERRY, TRUEHEDGE COLUMNBERRY (Berberis thunbergi erecta).   **Zones 2–3**
Medium-slow growing. Excellent, upright, requires little pruning when used as a hedge.

Height: 4 feet.   **Spread:** 2–3 feet.

Exposure: sun or shade.

Texture: fine.

Flower effects: yellow in May, but not showy.

Fruit effects: red in late summer.

Fall color: red.

Use: doorway, hedge.

BARBERRY, WINTERGREEN (Berberis julianae).   **Zones 2–3**
Slow- but strong-growing, dense, upright evergreen plant with prominent spines.

Height: 6 feet.   **Spread:** 4–5 feet.

Exposure: requires sun.

Texture: medium to fine.

Flower effects: yellow in May, but not showy.

Fruit effects: blue to black in fall.

Use: corner, group, hedge, specimen.

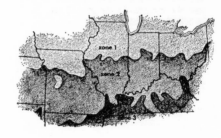

Descriptive Outlines of Shrubs

BAYBERRY, NORTHERN (Myrica pensylvanica). Zones 1–3
Slow to medium growing. Compact, rounded, with excellent semi-evergreen foliage and fruit. Sexes separated. Combines well with junipers.
Height: 5 feet. Spread: 3–5 feet.
Exposure: requires sun.
Soil: tolerates both moist and dry sterile soils.
Texture: medium.
Flower effects: not showy.
Fruit effects: blue to white in late summer and fall.
Use: corner, doorway, facer, planter box.

BEAUTYBUSH (Kolkwitzia amabilis). Zones 1–3
Slow growing, broad, vase-shaped.
Height: 6–10 feet. Spread: 6–9 feet.
Exposure: prefers sun.
Soil: requires well-drained soil.
Texture: medium.
Flower effects: pink in May and June.
Fruit effects: not showy.
Fall color: reddish.
Use: border mass.

BLUEBEARD (Caryopteris clandonensis). Zones 1–3
Fast growing, round, and spreading. Valued for late flowers. In Zones 1 and 2, top of plant will die back to ground and plant will require heavy pruning in early spring.
Height: 3–4 feet. Spread: 4 feet.
Exposure: requires sun.
Texture: medium fine.
Flower effects: blue in late summer and fall.
Fruit effects: not showy.
Use: border mass, facer, group.

BUCKEYE, BOTTLEBRUSH (Aesculus parviflora). Zones 1–3
Medium to fast rate of growth, broad, rounded, many-branched shrub. Can be trained into a tree form. Showy flowers.
Height: 8–12 feet. Spread: 8–16 feet.
Exposure: sun.
Texture: coarse.
Flower effects: white pyramidal clusters in July.
Use: specimen, border mass.

BUCKTHORN, COMMON (Rhamnus cathartica). Zones 1–3
Medium rate of growth, round and dense, handsome foliage. Tolerates pruning.
Height: 12 feet. Spread: 10–12 feet.
Exposure: either sun or shade.
Texture: medium to coarse.
Flower effects: not showy.
Fruit effects: black berries in fall.
Fall color: holds deep green foliage into late fall.
Use: border mass, corner, hedge.

CHERRY, MANCHU (Prunus tomentosa). Zones 1–3
Fast growing, broad, spreading, rounded. Showy when in flower.
Height: 8–10 feet. Spread: 10–15 feet.
Exposure: either sun or shade.
Soil: prefers rich, moist soil.
Texture: medium.
Flower effects: white to pink in April.
Fruit effects: red in June and July.
Fall color: reddish.
Use: border mass, corner, group, specimen.

CINQUEFOIL, BUSH (Potentilla fruticosa). Zones 1–3
Slow growing, bushy, dense. Can be pruned heavily. Chief value lies in its long period of flowering. Tolerates pruning.
Height: 3 feet. Spread: 3 feet.
Exposure: requires sun.
Texture: fine to medium.
Flower effects: yellow from early summer to fall.
Fruit effects: not showy.
Use: facer, hedge; combines well with perennials.

CINQUEFOIL, FARRERI BUSH (GOLD DROP) (Potentilla fruiticosa var. Farreri). Zones 1–3
Medium rate of growth, dwarf, compact. Leaves very small.
Height: 2 feet. Spread: 3 feet.
Exposure: sun.
Texture: fine.
Flower effects: deep yellow in summer to fall.
Use: doorway, corner, facer, group.

CINQUEFOIL, KLONDIKE BUSH (Potentilla fruiticosa var. Klondike). Zones 1–3
Medium rate of growth, dwarf, compact. Showy flowers from summer to fall.
Height: 2–3 feet. Spread: 3 feet.
Exposure: sun.
Texture: medium to fine.
Flower effects: deep golden yellow summer to fall.
Use: facer, group, doorway, corner.

CORALBERRY, CHENAULT (Symphoricarpos chenaulti). Zones 2–3
Fast growing; low, loose growth. Larger fruit than Indiancurrant Coralberry.
Height: 3–4 feet. Spread: 4 feet.
Exposure: either sun or shade.
Soil: prefers well-drained soil.
Texture: fine.
Flower effects: pink in July.
Fruit effects: red to white in fall.
Use: facer, group, underplanting in woodland plantings.

CORALBERRY, INDIANCURRANT (Symphoricarpos orbiculatus). Zones 1–3
Fast growing, round, dense. Good in shade but tolerates sun. Clustered fruit persists.
Height: 3–4 feet. Spread: 3–4 feet.
Exposure: prefers shade.
Texture: medium to fine.
Flower effects: not showy.
Fruit effects: pink to coral in fall.
Use: banks, facer.

COTONEASTER, BEARBERRY (Cotoneaster dammeri). Zones 2–3
Slow-growing, prostrate, evergreen plant.
Height: 12 inches. Spread: 6–12 inches.
Exposure: either sun or shade.
Texture: fine.
Flower effects: pink in June.
Fruit effects: red in late summer.
Use: planter box, slope, tub.

COTONEASTER, CRANBERRY (Cotoneaster apiculata). Zones 1–3
Medium to fast rate of growth. Low, mounding plant with large fruit.
Height: 2 feet. Spread: 5–8 feet.
Exposure: sun or partial shade.

Descriptive Outlines of Shrubs

Soil: well-drained.

Texture: fine.

Flower effects: small, pink in June.

Fruit effects: red berries in fall.

Fall color: reddish.

Use: doorway, facer, group, specimen, at top of retaining wall. Handsome with rocks.

COTONEASTER, PEKING (Cotoneaster acutifolia). Zones 1–3

Slow growing, erect, and spreading. Requires little care. Tolerates pruning. Withstands wind.

Height: 8–10 feet. Spread: 8–10 feet.

Exposure: requires sun.

Soil: does well even on poor soils.

Texture: fine.

Flower effects: white to pink in June.

Fruit effects: black berries in fall.

Use: border mass, hedge, tub.

COTONEASTER, ROCK (Cotoneaster horizontalis). Zones 2–3

Slow-growing, low, dense, horizontally spreading plant, with excellent foliage and persistent fruit. Difficult to transplant.

Height: 2–3 feet. Spread: 4–6 feet.

Exposure: requires sun.

Soil: requires well-drained soil.

Texture: fine.

Flower effects: pink in May and June, but not showy.

Fruit effects: red in fall.

Fall color: red-orange.

Use: doorway, facer, specimen, and at top of retaining wall. Handsome with rocks.

COTONEASTER, SPREADING (Cotoneaster divaricata). Zones 2–3

Medium rate of growth. Arching and spreading. Withstands wind. Difficult to transplant. Excellent fruiting habit.

Height: 6 feet. Spread: 5–6 feet.

Exposure: requires sun.

Texture: fine.

Flower effects: pink in May and June.

Fruit effects: red in late summer; persists into fall.

Fall color: red.

Use: border mass, corner, specimen.

CURRANT, ALPINE (Ribes alpinum). Zones 1–3

Medium rate of growth. Compact and dense, attractive foliage. Does well in shade. Tolerates pruning.

Height: 4–6 feet. Spread: 4–5 feet.

Exposure: either sun or shade.

Texture: medium.

Flower effects: not showy.

Fruit effects: red berries during summer.

Fall color: yellow.

Use: doorway, facer, group, hedge (clipped or unclipped).

DEUTZIA, COMPACT LEMOINE (Deutzia lemoinei compacta). Zones 1–3

Medium growth rate, dense, compact; abundant flowers.

Height: 4 feet. Spread: 3–4 feet.

Exposure: either sun or partial shade.

Texture: medium fine.

Flower effects: white in June.

Fruit effects: not showy.

Use: doorway, facer, group.

DEUTZIA, LEMOINE (Deutzia lemoinei). Zones 1–3

Vigorous, fast growing, dense, upright; handsome and reliable. Showy flowers.

Height: 6–7 feet. Spread: 4–6 feet.

Exposure: either sun or partial shade.

Texture: medium fine.

Flower effects: white in June.

Fruit effects: not showy.

Use: border mass, corner, group.

DEUTZIA, SLENDER (Deutzia gracilis). Zones 1–3

Slow growing, low, compact, abundantly flowering, reliable. Easy to transplant.

Height: 3–4 feet. Spread: 3 feet.

Exposure: either sun or partial shade.

Texture: fine.

Flower effects: white in May.

Fruit effects: not showy.

Use: doorway, facer, unclipped hedge.

DOGWOOD, GRAY (Cornus racemosa). Zones 1–3

Erect and spreading, medium in rate of growth. Tolerates pruning.

Height: 8–15 feet. Spread: 8–12 feet.

Exposure: requires partial shade.

Soil: prefers moist soil.

Texture: medium.

Flower effects: white in June.

Fruit effects: white in fall.

Fall color: dull red.

Use: border mass, underplantings.

DOGWOOD, KELSEY REDOSIER (Cornus stolonifera Kelsey). Zones 1–3

Slow growing, valued for its dwarf, round, compact form. In warmer zones (2 and 3), leaf blight is often a serious problem.

Height: 18–24 inches. Spread: 12–18 inches.

Exposure: either sun or shade.

Texture: coarse.

Use: doorways, planter boxes, under low windows.

DOGWOOD, REDOSIER (Cornus stolonifera). Zones 1–3

Slow-growing, broad, spreading shrub valued for its winter color. Bloodtwig Dogwood (C. sanguinea) is similar to this variety.

Height: 8 feet. Spread: 8–10 feet.

Exposure: either sun or shade.

Texture: coarse.

Flower effects: white in April and May.

Fruit effects: white to blue in late summer.

Fall color: red to bronze.

Use: border mass, woodland gardens.

DOGWOOD, YELLOWTWIG REDOSIER (Cornus stolonifera flaviramea). Zones 1–3

Medium to slow growth rate. Spreading shrub valued for yellow twigs during winter.

Height: 8 feet. Spread: 6–8 feet.

Exposure: either sun or shade.

Texture: coarse.

Flower effects: white in May and June.

Fruit effects: white to blue in late summer.

Use: border mass, corner, group.

Descriptive Outlines of Shrubs

EUONYMUS, BIGLEAF WINTERCREEPER (Euonymus fortunei vegetus). Zones 2–3
Slow-growing evergreen subshrub. Thick, leathery, glossy leaves. Grows upright with support, but otherwise forms a mounded mass. Subject to scale infestations.
Height: 2–4 feet.
Exposure: either sun or shade. Often needs shade in winter.
Texture: medium.
Flower effects: not showy.
Fruit effects: orange in fall.
Use: doorway, hedge, planter box, tub.

EUONYMUS, DWARF WINGED (Euonymus alatus compactus). Zones 1–3
Slow growing, dense, compact, outstanding fall color. Transplants easily.
Height: 6 feet. Spread: 4 feet.
Exposure: either sun or shade.
Texture: medium in summer; coarse in winter.
Flower effects: not showy.
Fruit effects: pink in fall.
Fall color: rose-red.
Use: corner, doorway, facer, unclipped hedge.

EUONYMUS, EASTERN WAHOO (Euonymus atropurpureus). Zones 1–3
Slow growing, treelike, spreading, with outstanding foliage and fruit color.
Height: 15–20 feet. Spread: 8–15 feet.
Exposure: either sun or partial shade.
Texture: medium.
Flower effects: not showy.
Fruit effects: red in fall.
Fall color: purple to red.
Use: border mass, group, screen.

EUONYMUS, SARACOXIE (Euonymus fortunei Saracoxie). Zones 1–3
Slow-growing, handsome, upright broadleafed evergreen. Tolerates pruning.
Height: 6 feet. Spread: 3–4 feet.
Exposure: requires sun.
Texture: medium.
Flower effects: not showy.
Fruit effects: not showy.
Use: doorway, hedge, planter box, tub.

EUONYMUS, SPINDLE TREE (Euonymus europaeus). Zones 1–3.
Medium rate of growth. Medium-dense, oval shrub, sometimes tree-like, valued for profuse and colorful fruiting. Excellent foliage. Aldenham variety produces heavier fruiting.
Height: 15–30 feet. Spread: 10–25 feet.
Exposure: sun or partial shade.
Texture: fine.
Flower effects: not showy.
Fruit effects: brilliant rose-pink capsules, persistent.
Fall color: reddish.
Use: specimen, group, border mass.

EUONYMUS, SPREADING (Euonymus klautschovicus). Zones 2(?), 3
Slow-growing, bushy, round semi-evergreen. Flowers attract flies.
Height: 5–6 feet. Spread: 6 feet.
Exposure: requires partial shade.
Texture: medium.
Flower effects: not showy.
Fruit effects: pink to red in fall.
Use: border mass, corner, group.

EUONYMUS, WINGED (Euonymus alatus). Zones 1–3
Slow growing, dense, broad, horizontally branched; outstanding fall color. Reliable and transplants easily.
Height: 8–10 feet. Spread: 6–8 feet.
Exposure: either sun or partial shade.
Texture: medium in summer, coarse in winter.
Flower effects: not showy.
Fruit effects: pink in fall.
Fall color: rose-red.
Use: border mass, corner, group, specimen.

FIRETHORN, SCARLET (Pyracantha coccinea). Zones 2(?), 3
Medium rate of growth. Broad, spreading, deciduous in north, evergreen in south. Fruit adds vivid color to winter scene. Prominent thorns. Tolerates pruning. Subject to fireblight.
Height: 6 feet. Spread: 6–10 feet.
Exposure: requires sun but needs protection against sun and wind in winter months.
Soil: prefers well-drained soil.
Texture: medium.
Flower effects: white in June.
Fruit effects: orange to red in fall and winter.
Use: corner, espalier, specimen, tub.

FORSYTHIA (Forsythia varieties). Zones 1–3
Fast growing; erect, arching, and trailing varieties available. Reliable shrub, easily transplanted. Showy flowers and good foliage.
Height: 8–10 feet. Spread: 10–15 feet.
Exposure: requires sun.
Soil: prefers well-drained soil.
Texture: medium.
Flower effects: yellow in early spring.
Fruit effects: not showy.
Use: border mass, group, screen. Avoid overcrowding from planting too close.

FORSYTHIA, ARNOLD DWARF (Forsythia var. Arnold Dwarf). Zones 1–3
Medium to slow rate of growth, plants wide-spreading with branches rooting when touching soil. Dense, mounding form. Flowers, if any, not outstanding.
Height: 4–5 feet. Spread: 8–10 feet.
Exposure: sun.
Soil: prefers well-drained soils.
Texture: medium.
Flower effects: not showy.
Use: slopes.

FORSYTHIA, BEATRIX FARRAND OR KARL SAX (Forsythia intermedia var. Beatrix Farrand or var. Karl Sax). Zones 1–3
Fast rate of growth, upright, ascending habit with hardier flower buds than most varieties. Large showy flowers.
Height: 6–10 feet. Spread: 6–10 feet.
Exposure: sun.
Texture: medium.
Flower effects: deep golden yellow with orange center.
Use: group, border mass.

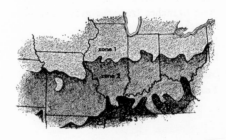

Descriptive Outlines of Shrubs

FORSYTHIA, BRONX (Forsythia viridissima Bronxensis).   **Zones 1–3**
Medium rate of growth, very dwarf habit of growth with small but abundant flowers.
Height: 2 feet. **Spread:** 2–4 feet.
Exposure: sun.
Texture: medium.
Flower effects: small, yellow.
Fall color: green to yellow.
Use: group, facer.

FRINGETREE, WHITE (Chionanthus virginicus).   **Zones 1–3**
Slow growing, round, spreading, tree-like. Particularly tolerant to city conditions. Leaves appear late in spring. Subject to scale insects. Sexes usually separate.
Height: 10–20 feet. **Spread:** 8–20 feet.
Exposure: requires sun.
Soil: likes moist soil.
Texture: coarse.
Flower effects: white and fragrant in May and June.
Fruit effects: blue in early summer.
Fall color: yellow.
Use: corner, group, specimen.

GERMANDER, CHAMAEDRYS (Teucrium chamaedrys).   **Zones 2–3**
Medium to slow growing. Low, dense evergreen subshrub. May need winter protection in Zone 2 and northern half of Zone 3.
Height: 10 inches. **Spread:** 8–12 inches.
Exposure: either sun or shade.
Soil: prefers well-drained soil.
Texture: medium to fine.
Flower effects: rose to purple in summer.
Fruit effects: not showy.
Use: low border hedge, planter box.

HAZEL, AMERICAN (Corylus americana).   **Zones 1–3**
Fast rate of growth, rounded mass with erect branches from the ground. Tends to sucker.
Height: 3–8 feet. **Spread:** 5–10 feet.
Exposure: sun.
Soil: tolerant.
Texture: coarse.

Flower effects: yellow catkins in early spring.
Use: woodland, border mass in large areas.

HAZEL, CONTORTED EUROPEAN (Corylus avellana contorta).   **Zones 1–3**
Medium to slow rate of growth, irregular growth habit with twigs curled and twisted.
Height: 6 feet. **Spread:** 4–5 feet.
Exposure: sun or shade.
Texture: medium-coarse.
Use: specimen.

HOLLY, AMERICAN (Ilex opaca).   **Zones 2–3**
Slow rate of growth, densely branched pyramidal form with branches to ground. Foliage evergreen. Difficult to transplant. Dense, spiny tips, popular Christmas decoration. Sexes separate, require male and female for fruiting.
Height: 18–40 feet. **Spread:** 12–20 feet.
Exposure: shade or partial shade.
Root habit: tap, with laterals spreading wider than top.
Soil: light, well-drained.
Texture: medium-coarse.
Fruit effect: red berries.
Flower effect: not showy.
Use: group, border mass, specimen.

HOLLY, BURFORD CHINESE (Ilex cornuta burfordii).   **Zones 1–3**
Slow-growing, dense globose shrub with short spreading branches, glossy, evergreen leaves with deep rich color. Tolerates shearing; requires winter shade.
Height: 6–25 feet. **Spread:** 6–8 feet.
Exposure: sun or shade.
Soil: moist, slightly acid.
Texture: medium.
Flower effects: not showy.
Fruit effects: clusters of red berries.
Use: specimen, border mass, accent.

HOLLY, CONVEXLEAF JAPANESE (Ilex crenata convexa). **Zones 1(?),2,3**
Slow-growing, broader than it is high; good substitute for boxwood. Broadleafed evergreen. Tolerates pruning — can be held to any size preferred.

Height: 4–20 feet. **Spread:** 4–15 feet.
Exposure: tolerant but prefers partial shade.
Soil: prefers moist, slightly acid soil.
Texture: medium.
Flower effects: not showy.
Fruit effects: not showy.
Use: doorway, planter box, facer, specimen, hedge.

HOLLY, FOSTER'S (Ilex myrtifolia × opaca hybrid: Foster's II).   **Zone 3**
Slow, open type of growth. Upright or conical in shape. Small dark evergreen leaves and bright red fruit.
Height: 25 feet. **Spread:** 10–15 feet.
Exposure: shade or partial shade.
Rooting habit: shallow.
Soil: acid.
Texture: medium.
Flower: white.
Use: group, border mass, screen, specimen.

HOLLY, HELLER JAPANESE (Ilex crenata convexa Heller). Zones 1(?),2,3
Slow-growing, dwarf compact evergreen. Tolerates pruning.
Height: 3 feet. **Spread:** 3–6 feet.
Exposure: either sun or partial shade.
Soil: prefers moist, slightly acid soil.
Texture: medium.
Flower effects: not showy.
Fruit effects: not showy.
Use: doorway, facer, hedge, planter box, specimen.

HOLLY, WINTERBERRY (Ilex verticillata).   **Zones 1–3**
Slow growing, spreading; excellent foliage; fruit persists to midwinter. Interesting the year around. Easily transplanted.
Height: 6–8 feet. **Spread:** 3–5 feet.
Exposure: requires partial shade.
Soil: requires rich soil; tolerates damp or wet locations.
Texture: medium.
Flower effects: not showy.
Fruit effects: red in fall and winter.
Fall color: yellow.
Use: border mass, group, or screen.

Descriptive Outlines of Shrubs

HOLLYGRAPE, OREGON
(Mahonia aquifolium).   **Zones 2–3**
Medium rate of growth. Round, upright evergreen. Interesting holly-shaped, lustrous foliage and grapelike clusters of fruit.
Height: 3–5 feet. **Spread:** 2–3 feet.
Exposure: requires partial shade and often winter protection.
Texture: coarse.
Flower effects: yellow in spring.
Fruit effects: blue to purple in fall.
Fall color: bronze to purple.
Use: doorway, facer, group.

HONEYSUCKLE (Lonicera
varieties).   **Zones 1–3**
Medium-fast growing. Varieties broad, spreading, rounded. Vigorous shrubs with an abundance of small flowers and small bright-colored fruit.
Height: 5–12 feet. **Spread:** 5–12 feet.
Exposure: either sun or partial shade.
Soil: some varieties tolerate dry soils, others tolerate wet soils.
Texture: medium.
Flower effects: white to pink, early to middle spring.
Fruit effects: red, summer and fall.
Fall color: blue-green.
Use: border mass, group, informal hedge, screen.

HONEYSUCKLE, CLAVEY DWARF
(Lonicera var. Clavey).   **Zones 1–3**
Medium to slow growing, compact, dense.
Height: 6 feet. **Spread:** 4–6 feet.
Exposure: either sun or shade.
Texture: medium.
Flower effects: white in spring.
Fruit effects: red in summer.
Use: border mass, group.

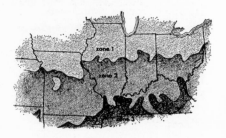

HONEYSUCKLE, WINTER
(Lonicera fragrantissima).   **Zones 2–3**
Medium rate of growth. Round spreading, with handsome foliage. Flowers are fragrant and appear in very early spring. Tolerates pruning.
Height: 6 feet. **Spread:** 6 feet.
Exposure: either sun or partial shade.
Texture: medium.
Flower effects: white before leaves appear.
Fruit effects: red in early summer.
Use: border mass, corner, group, hedge.

HONEYSUCKLE, ZABEL TARTARIAN
(Lonicera tartarica zabelli). **Zones 1–3**
Fast growing, upright to spreading structure, vigorous grower, free of disease and insect pests. Good appearance in all seasons.
Height: 7–10 feet. **Spread:** 7–10 feet.
Exposure: sun or partial shade.
Texture: medium.
Flower effects: deep pink to red.
Fruit effects: red berries.
Fall color: blue-green.
Use: groups, border mass, screen, hedge.

HYDRANGEA, HILLS-OF-SNOW
(Hydrangea arborescens
grandiflora).   **Zones 1–3**
Fast-growing, broad, upright plant that gives a good texture accent. Showy flowers. Requires severe pruning in spring.
Height: 4–8 feet. **Spread:** 5–8 feet.
Exposure: either sun or shade.
Soil: likes moist soil.
Texture: coarse.
Flower effects: white in August.
Fruit effects: dry flower clusters in fall.
Use: border mass, corner, group.

JETBEAD, BLACK (Rhodotypos
scandens).   **Zones 2–3**
Medium rate of growth. Spreading and open growth. Excellent flower and foliage.
Height: 5–6 feet. **Spread:** 4–5 feet.
Exposure: either sun or shade.
Soil: tolerates poor soil.
Texture: medium.

Flower effects: white, late spring through summer.
Fruit effects: black, summer into winter.
Use: border mass, corner, hedge.

JUNIPER, BLUE RUG (Juniperus
horizontalis wiltonii).   **Zones 1–3**
Fast-growing, extremely flat, spreading evergreen with vivid blue foliage the year round. Blight resistant.
Height: 6–8 inches. **Spread:** 6–8 feet.
Exposure: sun or partial shade.
Soil: tolerates dry, sandy soil.
Texture: fine.
Use: corner, doorway, facer, slopes.

JUNIPER, COMPACT PFITZER (Juniperus
chinensis Pfitzer Compact). **Zones 1–3**
Fast to medium growing, dwarf, spreading evergreen with plumelike foliage.
Height: 5 feet. **Spread:** 5 feet.
Exposure: requires sun.
Soil: tolerates sandy soil.
Texture: fine.
Flower effects: not showy.
Fruit effects: gray-white berry in fall.
Use: corner, doorway, facer.

JUNIPER, HENRY SARGENT (Juniperus
chinensis sargenti var. Henry). **Zones 1–3**
Fast to medium rate of growth, flat-spreading evergreen with steel-blue foliage. Excellent, serviceable plant, blight resistant.
Height: 12–18 inches. **Spread:** 8–10 feet.
Exposure: sun or partial shade.
Soil: tolerates dry, sandy soil.
Texture: fine.
Use: corner, doorway, facer, slopes.

JUNIPER, PFITZER (Juniperus
chinensis Pfitzer).   **Zones 1–3**
Fast-growing, large, spreading evergreen with plumelike blue-green foliage.
Height: 8–10 feet. **Spread:** 8–10 feet.
Exposure: requires sun.
Soil: tolerates sandy soil.
Texture: fine.
Flower effects: not showy.
Fruit effects: blue berry in fall.
Use: border mass, corner, group.

Descriptive Outlines of Shrubs

JUNIPER, PROSTRATE (Juniperus communis depressa). **Zones 1–3**
Medium to slow rate of growth, low-spreading habit with ascending branches. Blight resistant.
Height: 3–4 feet. **Spread:** 6–8 feet.
Exposure: sun or partial shade.
Soil: tolerant of dry, sandy soils.
Texture: fine.
Use: corner, doorway, facer, group.

JUNIPER, WAUKEGAN (Juniperus horizontalis var. Waukegan). **Zones 1–3**
Medium rate of growth. Flat, spreading, somewhat trailing evergreens. Blue-green foliage.
Height: ½–1 foot. **Spread:** 5 feet.
Exposure: either sun or partial shade.
Soil: tolerates sandy soil.
Texture: fine.
Flower effects: not showy.
Fruit effects: blue berry in winter.
Use: corner, doorway, facer, slopes.

KERRIA, JAPANESE (Kerria japonica). **Zones 1–3**
Medium growing, broad, loose habit with year-round interest in flowers, foliage, and twigs. Requires annual pruning.
Height: 4–6 feet. **Spread:** 6–8 feet.
Exposure: either sun or shade, best in partial shade.
Texture: fine.
Flower effects: orange-yellow in May.
Fruit effects: not showy.
Fall color: yellow.
Use: border mass, facer, group.

LILAC (Syringa varieties). **Zones 1–3**
Medium rate of growth. Reliable upright round shrub. Handsome, showy flowers in both single and double varieties.
Height: 6–15 feet. **Spread:** 6–12 feet.
Exposure: requires sun.
Texture: medium to coarse.
Flower effects: white to lavender in May.
Fruit effects: not showy.
Use: border mass, group, screen, specimen.

LILAC, PERSIAN (Syringa persica). **Zones 2–3**
Medium rate of growth. Dense and shapely, valued for flowers.
Height: 4–8 feet. **Spread:** 5–10 feet.
Exposure: requires sun, but tolerates light shade.
Texture: fine.
Flower effects: violet to white in May.
Fruit effects: not showy.
Use: border mass, corner, group, screen.

MAGNOLIA, SAUCER (Magnolia soulangeana). **Zones 2–3**
Medium rate of growth. Shrubby tree with showy flowers effective in front of evergreens. Because of fleshy roots, plants should always be moved with a ball of earth. Numerous varieties and flower colors available.
Height: 25 feet. **Spread:** 30 feet.
Exposure: requires sun.
Soil: prefers rich, moist soil.
Texture: coarse.
Flower effects: blue to white before leaves appear.
Fruit effects: rose-pink, conelike.
Fall color: bronze.
Use: specimen.

MAGNOLIA, STAR (Magnolia stellata). **Zones 2–3**
Slow growing; dense, broad, round, treelike. Showy flowers effective in front of evergreens. Will not tolerate competition with other tree roots. Because of fleshy roots, plants should always be moved with a ball of earth.
Height: 8–10 feet. **Spread:** 10–15 feet.
Exposure: requires sun.
Soil: prefers rich, moist, slightly acid soil.
Texture: coarse.
Flower effects: white before leaves appear.
Fruit effects: rosy red in fall.
Fall color: bronze.
Use: specimen.

MAGNOLIA, SWEETBAY (Magnolia virginiana). **Zone 3**
Slow to medium rate of growth, small, irregular tree or large shrub with a loose, open habit. Valued for flowers.
Height: 10–30 feet. **Spread:** 10–15 feet.
Exposure: partial shade, sheltered.
Soil: moist to wet soil.
Texture: medium.
Flower effects: creamy white, fragrant.
Fruit effects: red, conelike.
Use: lawn.

MOCKORANGE (Philadelphus varieties). **Zones 1–3**
Slow growing; varieties compact, rounded, or erect. Valued for flowers, which are usually fragrant.
Height: 4–12 feet. **Spread:** 4–12 feet.
Exposure: either sun or partial shade.
Texture: medium to coarse.
Flower effects: white in May and June.
Fruit effects: not showy.
Use: border mass, group, screen.

NANDINA (Nandina domestica). **Zone 3**
Medium rate of growth. Upright, loose. Valued more for fruit than flowers. Not hardy.
Height: 3–8 feet. **Spread:** 6 feet.
Exposure: either sun or partial shade.
Texture: medium.
Flower effects: white in July.
Fruit effects: red to purple in fall and winter.
Fall color: bright red to scarlet.
Use: border mass, corner, group, specimen.

NINEBARK, COMMON (Physocarpus opulifolius). **Zones 1–3**
Fast-growing, loose, spreading shrub, resembling spirea. Because of coarseness not recommended in refined small gardens.
Height: 10 feet. **Spread:** 10 feet.
Exposure: either sun or shade.
Texture: coarse.
Flower effects: white in June.
Fruit effects: red to brown in fall.
Use: border mass, hedge, woodland gardens.

Descriptive Outlines of Shrubs

NINEBARK, DWARF (Physocarpus monogynus). Zones 1–3

Fast-growing, dense shrub with bright green foliage.

Height: 4 feet. Spread: 3 feet.

Exposure: sun or shade.

Texture: medium.

Use: hedge, facer, corner.

PACHISTIMA, CANBY (Pachistima canbyi). Zones 2–3

Medium rate of growth. Low, dense, rounded. Excellent texture accent when used in mass.

Height: 12 inches. Spread: 6–12 inches.

Exposure: either shade or partial sun.

Soil: prefers acid, moist soil.

Texture: medium fine.

Fall color: bronze.

Use: dwarf hedge, planter box, tub.

PEARLBUSH (Exochorda racemosa). Zones 1–3

Medium rate of growth. Slender-branched, upright shrub with loose, irregular growth, sometimes tree-like. Becomes leggy in old age, requiring facer shrubs. Variety Wilson is heavier flowering variety.

Height: 10–15 feet. Spread: 10–15 feet.

Exposure: sun or partial shade.

Soil: well-drained, not tolerant of lime.

Texture: fine.

Flower effects: pearl-like white flowers.

Fruit effects: not showy.

Use: group, border mass.

PEASHRUB, SIBERIAN (Caragana arborescens). Zones 1–3

Fast growing, oval, erect and thin with age. Useful in sandy areas; good foliage mass.

Height: 15–18 feet. Spread: 12 feet.

Exposure: prefers sun, but can stand partial shade.

Texture: fine in summer, coarse in winter.

Flower effects: yellow in spring, but not showy.

Fruit effects: not showy.

Fall color: yellow.

Use: border mass, screen.

PINE, DWARF MUGHO (Pinus mugho mughus Dwarf). Zones 1–3

Slow-growing, round evergreen. Easily confined to small size by pruning.

Height: 4–8 feet. Spread: 12–20 feet.

Exposure: either sun or partial shade.

Soil: prefers moist soil.

Texture: medium.

Flower effects: yellow, not showy.

Fruit effects: cones, yellow-brown.

Use: corner, doorway, planter box.

PLUM, FLOWERING (Prunus triloba). Zones 2–3

Fast growing, rounded, spreading.

Height: 8–10 feet. Spread: 8 feet.

Exposure: sun or partial shade.

Soil: prefers rich, moist soil.

Texture: medium.

Flower effects: double flowers, pink in April and May.

Fruit effects: not showy.

Fall color: yellow.

Use: border mass, corner, group.

PLUM, THUNDERCLOUD (Prunus var. Thundercloud). Zones 1–3

Fast growing, round.

Height: 15–20 feet. Spread: 10 feet.

Exposure: either sun or partial shade.

Texture: medium.

Flower effects: white to pink in April to May.

Fruit effects: yellow-red in late summer.

Fall color: yellow to red.

Use: group, specimen.

PRIVET, AMUR (Ligustrum amurense). Zones 1–3

Fast growing; dense upright branches with round top. Tolerates pruning.

Height: 10–15 feet. Spread: 6–10 feet.

Exposure: either sun or shade.

Texture: fine to medium.

Flower effects: not showy.

Fruit effects: blue-black in fall.

Use: border mass, hedge, screen.

PRIVET, IBOLIUM (Ligustrum Ibolium). Zones 1–3

Medium growing, broad, spreading. Tolerant to pruning.

Height: 10–12 feet. Spread: 12 feet.

Exposure: either sun or shade.

Texture: fine.

Flower effects: white in early summer.

Fruit effects: blue-black in fall and winter.

Fall color: green to purple.

Use: border mass, hedge, screen.

PRIVET, LODENSE (Ligustrum vulgare var. Lodense). Zones 1–3

Medium rate of growth, low, dense plant with glossy foliage. Tolerates pruning.

Height: 4–5 feet. Spread: 3 feet.

Exposure: sun.

Texture: medium.

Flower effects: white.

Fruit effects: black.

Use: hedge, group, border mass.

PRIVET, REGELS BORDER (Ligustrum obtusifolium regelianum). Zones 1–3

Medium rate of growth. Horizontally branching, dense foliage. Reliable, excellent form.

Height: 6 feet. Spread: 6 feet.

Exposure: either sun or shade.

Texture: medium.

Flower effects: not showy.

Fruit effects: blue-black in fall and winter.

Fall color: russet to purple.

Use: border mass, corner, group.

QUINCE, FLOWERING (Chaenomeles lagenaria). Zones 1–3

Fast-growing, spreading plant. Good foliage, showy flowers, winter color.

Height: 6–8 feet. Spread: 6 feet.

Exposure: requires sun.

Texture: medium to fine.

Flower effects: white, pink, and red in April and May.

Fruit effects: yellow in late summer.

Fall color: bronze.

Use: border mass, group, hedge.

QUINCE, FLOWERING JAPANESE (Chaenomeles japonica). Zones 1–3

Fast growing, spreading; good foliage, showy flowers, winter color.

Height: 3–4 feet. Spread: 4 feet.

Exposure: requires sun.

Texture: medium to fine.

Flower effects: white through deep red in May.

Fruit effects: yellow in late summer.

Fall color: green to bronze.

Use: corner, doorway, facer, hedge.

Descriptive Outlines of Shrubs

REDCEDAR, CANAERT EASTERN (*Juniperus virginiana* Canaert). Zones 1–3

Medium rate of growth. Loose and open yet slender pyramidal form of evergreen.

Height: 20 feet. **Spread:** 8–10 feet.

Exposure: requires sun.

Soil: tolerates sandy soil.

Texture: fine.

Flower effects: not showy.

Fruit effects: blue in fall.

Use: accent, group.

RHODODENDRON, CATAWBA (*Rhododendron catawbiense* hybrids). Zones 1–3

Medium rate of growth, extremely hardy broad evergreen shrub wider than high and rounded in form. Profuse flowers in late spring or early summer. A number of hybrids to choose from.

Height: 6–10 feet. **Spread:** 8 feet or more.

Exposure: shade or partial sun, must be protected.

Soil: rich, well-drained, acid.

Texture: coarse, heavy.

Flower effects: white to purple, depending on hybrid.

Use: border mass, woodland.

RHODODENDRON, P. J. M. HYBRID. Zones 2–3

Medium rate of growth. Broad rounded shrub that flowers heavily every year in early spring. Excellent plant.

Height: 6–8 feet. **Spread:** 6 feet.

Exposure: either sun or shade.

Soil: rich, well-drained, acid.

Texture: coarse.

Flower effects: vivid, lavender pink.

Foliage: broadleaf evergreen, turning rich purple in fall.

Use: specimen, border mass, woodland.

RHODODENDRON, WILSON (*Rhododendron* × *laetevirens*). Zones 1–3

Moderate rate of growth, low-growing shrub with evergreen foliage. Flowers small compared to other Rhododendrons, neat habit of growth.

Height: 4 feet. **Spread:** 4–5 feet.

Exposure: shade or partial sun.

Soil: rich, well-drained, acid.

Texture: medium.

Flower effects: pink to purple.

Use: foundations, facer, border mass.

ROSE, (FLORIBUNDA TYPE) (*Rosa* varieties). Zones 1–3

Medium rate of growth. Rounded, upright, small-growing rose that flowers all season. Many varieties and flower colors from which to select.

Height: 3–5 feet. **Spread:** 3–4 feet.

Exposure: requires sun.

Soil: prefers well-drained soil.

Texture: medium.

Flower effects: white to red all summer.

Fruit effects: red in fall.

Use: facer, group, unclipped hedge.

ROSE, FATHER HUGO (*Rosa hugonis*). Zones 2–3

Fast growing, dense, rounded. Excellent, showy flowers.

Height: 6–10 feet. **Spread:** 10 feet.

Exposure: requires sun.

Soil: requires well-drained soil.

Texture: fine.

Flower effects: yellow in June.

Fruit effects: black in midsummer.

Fall color: yellow.

Use: border mass, specimen.

ROSE OF SHARON (SHRUBALTHEA) (*Hibiscus syriacus* varieties). Zones 2–3

Slow to medium growing; upright, somewhat vase-shaped; tolerates city conditions. Showy flowers in late summer. Young plants are less winter-hardy than older plants.

Height: 10–15 feet. **Spread:** 6–10 feet.

Exposure: requires sun or partial shade.

Texture: medium.

Flower effects: various colors, single or double varieties, August and September.

Fruit effects: not showy.

Use: border mass, group, hedge, screen, specimen.

ST. JOHNSWORT, SUNGOLD (*Hypericum* var. Sungold). Zones 2–3

Medium growth rate, dense, rounded. Showy flowers in summer.

Height: 3–4 feet. **Spread:** 3 feet.

Exposure: either sun or partial shade.

Soil: tolerates sandy, dry soil.

Texture: medium fine.

Flower effects: yellow in July and August.

Fruit effects: not showy.

Use: facer, foundation, group, woodland gardens.

SANDCHERRY, PURPLELEAF (*Prunus cistena*). Zones 1–3

Medium rate of growth. Oval form. Outstanding in fruit and foliage color.

Height: 7 feet. **Spread:** 6–7 feet.

Exposure: requires sun.

Texture: medium.

Flower effects: white in May.

Fruit effects: dark purple in late summer.

Fall color: purple.

Use: group, specimen.

SERVICEBERRY, SHADBLOW (*Amelanchier canadensis*). Zones 1–3

Fast growing, loosely round to oval, treelike. Good combined with broadleafed evergreens.

Height: 25 feet. **Spread:** 12 feet.

Exposure: prefers partial shade, but can stand sun.

Soil: any well-drained soil will do.

Texture: fine.

Flower effects: white in early spring.

Fruit effects: purple berry in early summer.

Fall color: orange to red.

Use: border mass, group, specimen, woodland.

Descriptive Outlines of Shrubs

SPIREA, ANTHONY WATERER (Spiraea bumalda Anthony Waterer). Zones 2–3
Fast growing, low, broad, flat on top. Attractive foliage, tinged pink when it first appears.
Height: 2–3 feet. Spread: 3 feet.
Exposure: requires sun.
Texture: fine.
Flower effects: pink to crimson, spring to fall.
Fruit effects: not showy.
Fall color: reddish.
Use: doorway, facer, unclipped hedge.

SPIREA, BRIDALWREATH (Spiraea prunifolia). Zones 1–3
Fast growing, graceful, upright. Reliable, showy flowers, excellent fall color. Double variety available.
Height: 6 feet. Spread: 6 feet.
Exposure: requires sun.
Soil: prefers moist soil.
Texture: medium to fine.
Flower effects: white in early spring.
Fruit effects: not showy.
Fall color: orange.
Use: border mass, group.

SPIREA, VAN HOUTTE (Spiraea vanhouttei). Zones 1–3
Fast growing, vase-shaped, round top. Showy when in bloom.
Height: 8–10 feet. Spread: 8 feet.
Exposure: requires sun.
Texture: medium.
Flower effects: white in May.
Fruit effects: not showy.
Fall color: orange to yellow.
Use: border mass, screen.

SUMAC, FRAGRANT (Rhus aromatica). Zones 1–3
Medium rate of growth. Round and spreading. Valuable for handsome foliage, flowers, and fall color.
Height: 2–4 feet. Spread: 5–8 feet.
Exposure: either sun or shade.
Texture: medium.
Flower effects: yellow in early spring.
Fruit effects: red berry-like in summer.
Fall color: yellow, scarlet, and crimson.
Use: facer, slopes; leaves hold dust so avoid use in dusty areas.

SUMAC, STAGHORN (Rhus typhina). Zones 1–3
Fast growing, irregular, picturesque. Cutleaf variety available. Interesting fuzzy twigs which hold dust so avoid use in dusty areas.
Height: 20–25 feet. Spread: 20 feet.
Exposure: either sun or shade.
Soil: tolerates sterile soil.
Texture: medium in summer, coarse in winter.
Flower effects: not showy.
Fruit effects: red in fall.
Fall color: orange-red.
Use: clumps, masses, specimen, not suitable for small properties.

VIBURNUM, AMERICAN CRANBERRYBUSH (Viburnum trilobum). Zones 1–3
Fast growing, dense, broad, round. Fruit showy in color and mass.
Height: 6–12 feet. Spread: 8–12 feet.
Exposure: either sun or shade.
Texture: medium.
Flower effects: white in May and June.
Fruit effects: red in August.
Fall color: reddish.
Use: corner, group, screen.

VIBURNUM, ARROWWOOD (Viburnum dentatum). Zones 1–3
Fast growing, upright, dense, with handsome foliage.
Height: 15 feet. Spread: 6–12 feet.
Exposure: either sun or partial shade.
Texture: medium to coarse.
Flower effects: white in May.
Fruit effects: blue in late summer.
Fall color: bronze-red.
Use: border mass, corner, group, and screen.

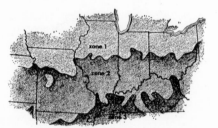

VIBURNUM, BURKWOOD (Viburnum burkwoodi). Zones 2–3
Medium rate of growth, upright, with fragrant flowers and attractive foliage.
Height: 4–8 feet. Spread: 6–8 feet.
Exposure: requires sun.
Soil: tolerates poorer but well-drained soil.
Texture: coarse.
Flower effects: white in April and May.
Fruit effects: red to black in late summer.
Fall color: muted red.
Use: border mass, corner, group, specimen.

VIBURNUM, COMPACT AMERICAN CRANBERRYBUSH (Viburnum trilobum compactum). Zones 1–3
Medium rate of growth, rounded, compact, hardiest of Cranberrybush types. Heavy fruit, usable for preserves. Other varieties include Hahs, Andrews, and Wentworth.
Height: 5–6 feet. Spread: 5 feet.
Exposure: sun or partial shade.
Texture: medium to coarse.
Flower effects: white in May.
Fruit effects: scarlet in fall.
Use: corner, group, border mass.

VIBURNUM, COMPACT EUROPEAN CRANBERRYBUSH (Viburnum opulus compactum). Zones 1–3
Medium rate of growth, upright, rounded. This shrub flowers and fruits well.
Height: 5 feet. Spread: 4–5 feet.
Exposure: sun or shade.
Texture: medium to coarse.
Flower effects: white in May.
Fruit effects: red berries in fall and winter.
Fall color: red.
Use: doorway, corner, group, border mass.

VIBURNUM, DOUBLEFILE (Viburnum tomentosum). Zones 1–3
Medium rate of growth. Broad spreading, interesting horizontal branching. Outstanding in flowers.
Height: 8–10 feet. Spread: 8–10 feet.
Exposure: either sun or shade.

Descriptive Outlines of Shrubs

Texture: coarse.

Flower effects: white in May.

Fruit effects: red to black in late summer.

Fall color: muted red.

Use: corner, group, screen, specimen.

**VIBURNUM, DWARF EUROPEAN
CRANBERRYBUSH (Viburnum
opulus nanum).** **Zones 1–3**

Medium rate of growth. Dense, dwarf irregular, picturesque. Tolerates pruning.

Height: 2 feet. Spread: 2 feet.

Exposure: either sun or shade.

Texture: medium.

Fall color: reddish.

Use: doorway, facer, planter box, under low windows.

**VIBURNUM, EUROPEAN CRANBERRYBUSH
(Viburnum opulus).** **Zones 1–3**

Medium rate of growth. Vase-shaped, with outstanding color and massing of fruit.

Height: 10–12 feet. Spread: 12–15 feet.

Exposure: either sun or shade.

Texture: medium to coarse.

Flower effects: white in May.

Fruit effects: yellow to crimson in fall.

Fall color: yellow-red.

Use: border mass, group, screen.

**VIBURNUM, FRAGRANT SNOWBALL
(CARLCEPHALUM) (Viburnum ×
carlcephalum).** **Zones 1–3**

Medium rate of growth, upright, slightly spreading with handsome glossy foliage and large fragrant flowers.

Height: 9 feet. Spread: 6–8 feet.

Exposure: sun.

Soil: prefers well-drained soils.

Texture: coarse-medium.

Flower effects: small, white in large clusters.

Use: border mass, corner, group, specimen.

**VIBURNUM, KOREANSPICE
(Viburnum carlesi).** **Zones 1–3**

Medium rate of growth. Upright, with fragrant flowers and attractive foliage.

Height: 4–8 feet. Spread: 6–8 feet.

Exposure: requires sun.

Soil: prefers well-drained soils.

Texture: coarse.

Flower effects: pink to white in April and May.

Fruit effects: red to black in late summer.

Fall color: muted red.

Use: border mass, corner, group, specimen.

**VIBURNUM, LEATHERLEAF (Viburnum
rhytidophyllum).** **Zones 2–3**

Medium rate of growth. Upright evergreen, with lustrous, dark-green, puckered foliage.

Height: 9 feet. Spread: 8–9 feet.

Exposure: prefers partial shade.

Soil: requires well-drained soil.

Texture: coarse.

Flower effects: pink in June.

Fruit effects: red to black in fall.

Use: border mass, corner, group, specimen.

**VIBURNUM, MAPLELEAF
(Viburnum acerifolium).** **Zones 1–3**

Slow growing. Outstanding in foliage and fruit color.

Height: 4–6 feet. Spread: 3–4 feet.

Exposure: requires shade or partial shade.

Soil: tolerates dry soil, but prefers moist situation.

Texture: medium.

Flower effects: white in May and June.

Fruit effects: red to black in early fall.

Fall color: yellow-red.

Use: border mass, corner, woodland plantings.

WEIGELA (Weigela varieties). Zones 2–3

Fast growing, round, spreading, with showy flowers. Requires annual pruning because of general die-back of branches. Often suffers winter injury in north. Many varieties available.

Height: 4–6 feet. Spread: 5–6 feet.

Exposure: requires sun.

Texture: coarse.

Flower effects: crimson-red in June.

Fruit effects: not showy.

Use: border mass, corner, group, texture accent.

**WITCHHAZEL, CHINESE
(Hamamelis vernalis).** **Zones 2–3**

Slow-growing, upright to spreading plant, valued for early flowering and dense foliage. Root-prune before transplanting.

Height: 6 feet. Spread: 6–8 feet.

Exposure: requires sun or partial shade.

Soil: prefers moist soil.

Texture: medium to coarse.

Flower effects: yellow in late winter.

Fruit effects: not showy.

Fall color: bright yellow to brown.

Use: border mass, group, or specimen.

**WITCHHAZEL, COMMON
(Hamamelis virginiana).** **Zones 1–3**

Slow growing; loose irregular habit of growth; tolerates city conditions. Root-prune before transplanting. Attractive flower appearing after foliage drops in fall.

Height: 12–20 feet. Spread: 12–20 feet.

Exposure: requires sun or partial shade.

Soil: prefers moist soil.

Texture: coarse.

Flower effects: yellow in October and November.

Fruit effects: not showy.

Fall color: yellow.

Use: border mass, group, specimen.

**YEW, DENSE (Taxus
densiformis).** **Zones 1–3**

Slow-growing, dense, upright evergreen. Deep color. Sexes are separate. Do not plant too deep.

Height: 4–5 feet. Spread: 4 feet.

Exposure: requires shade.

Soil: tolerates most soil, but prefers well-drained situations.

Texture: medium.

Flower effects: not showy.

Fruit effects: red in fall and winter.

Use: doorway, hedge, planter box.

Descriptive Outlines of Shrubs

YEW, DWARF SPREADING JAPANESE
(*Taxus cuspidata nana*). Zones 1–3
Slow-growing, compact, spreading evergreen. Deep color. Sexes separate. Do not plant too deep.
Height: 3–4 feet. **Spread:** 4–5 feet.
Exposure: best in shade, but tolerates sunlight.
Soil: tolerates most soil, but prefers well-drained situations.
Texture: medium.
Flower effects: not showy.
Fruit effects: red in fall and winter.
Use: corner, doorway, facer, group, planter box.

YEW, HATFIELD OR HICKS
(*Taxus media* varieties). Zones 1–3
Slow-growing, dense, slender, conical evergreen. Tolerates pruning. Deep color. Sexes separate. Do not plant too deep.
Height: 8 feet. **Spread:** 4–5 feet.
Exposure: requires shade.
Soil: tolerates most soil, but prefers well-drained situations.
Texture: medium.
Flower effects: not showy.
Fruit effects: red in fall and winter.
Use: accent, corner, hedge, planter box.

YEW, SPREADING JAPANESE
(*Taxus cuspidata*). Zones 1–3
Slow-growing, spreading evergreen. Deep color. Sexes are separate. Do not plant too deep.
Height: 8–10 feet. **Spread:** 8–12 feet.
Exposure: best in shade, but tolerates sunlight.
Soil: tolerates most soil, but prefers well-drained situations.
Texture: medium.
Flower effects: not showy.
Fruit effects: red in fall and winter.
Use: border mass, corner, specimen.

YEW, TAUNTON ANGLOJAP (*Taxus
media* var. *Taunton*). Zones 1–3
Slow-growing, excellent spreading evergreen, neat grower. Displays great resistance to "winterburn." Do not plant too deep.
Height: 6–10 feet. **Spread:** 8–10 feet.
Exposure: prefers shade but tolerates sunlight.
Soil: tolerates most well-drained soils.
Texture: medium.
Fruit effects: red in fall and winter.
Use: doorway, corner, facer, group.

YEW, UPRIGHT JAPANESE (*Taxus
cuspidata capitata*). Zones 1–3
Slow-growing, erect, broad, pyramidal evergreen. Deep color. Sexes separate. Do not plant too deep.
Height: 10–40 feet. **Spread:** 15–20 feet.
Exposure: best in shade, but tolerates sunlight.
Soil: tolerates most soil, but prefers well-drained situations.
Texture: medium.
Flower effects: not showy.
Fruit effects: red in fall and winter.
Use: accent, corner.

YEW, WARDS ANGLOJAP (*Taxus
media* var. *Wards*). Zones 1–3
Slow growing, semi-spreading, dense habit of growth. Dark green evergreen foliage. Do not plant too deep.
Height: 3 feet. **Spread:** 5–8 feet.
Exposure: prefers shade but tolerates sunlight.
Soil: tolerates most well-drained soils.
Texture: medium.
Fruit effects: red in fall and winter.
Use: doorway, corner, facer, group.

YUCCA (ADAMSNEEDLE) (*Yucca
filamentosa*). Zones 1–3
Fast-growing, stiff, upright, dramatic evergreen.
Height: 3 feet. **Spread:** 3–4 feet.
Exposure: requires sun.
Texture: coarse.
Flower effects: yellow to white in July.
Fruit effects: not showy.
Use: specimen; blends well with large rocks.

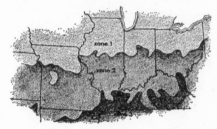

Descriptive Outlines of Ground Covers

BEARBERRY (KINNIKINNICK)
(*Arctostaphylos uva-ursi*). Zones 1–3
Slow-growing, spreading woody evergreen. Handsome foliage and fruit. Difficult to transplant.
Height: 6 inches. **Spacing:** 18–24 inches.
Exposure: either sun or shade.
Soil: tolerates dry sandy soils; requires well-drained soil.
Texture: fine.
Flower effects: pink.
Fruit effects: red.
Use: steep slopes or low cover under broadleafed evergreens.

BUGLE, CARPET (*Ajuga
reptans*). Zones 1–3
Fast-growing, herbaceous, semi-evergreen. Easy to grow.
Height: 6 inches **Spacing:** 8–12 inches.
Exposure: either sun or shade.
Soil: prefers moderately moist soil.
Texture: coarse.
Flower effects: blue.
Fruit effects: not showy.
Use: excellent low cover around trees and rocks and on low banks.

BUGLE, GENEVA (*Ajuga
genevensis*). Zones 1–3
Medium rate of growth. Herbaceous semi-evergreen. Spreads less rapidly than other varieties. Height is a disadvantage.
Height: 14 inches. **Spacing:** 8–12 inches.
Exposure: either sun or shade.
Texture: coarse.
Flower effects: blue.
Fruit effects: not showy.
Use: general.

Descriptive Outlines of Ground Covers

CANDYTUFT, EVERGREEN
(Iberis sempervirens).   **Zones 2–3**
Fast-growing, woody semi-evergreen. Upright; brilliant white flowers.
Height: 12 inches. **Spacing:** 12 inches.
Exposure: prefers sun, tolerates partial shade.
Soil: prefers rich, moist soil.
Texture: medium.
Flower effects: white in spring.
Fruit effects: not showy.
Use: in masses in small planting areas and in rockeries.

COTONEASTER, BEARBERRY (Cotoneaster
dammeri).   **Zones 1(?), 2, 3**
Slow-growing woody evergreen. Glossy dark-green leaves, attractive fruit.
Height: 6–12 inches. **Spacing:** 18–24 inches.
Exposure: sun or semi-shade.
Soil: prefers well-drained but moist soil.
Texture: fine.
Flower effects: white.
Fruit effects: red.
Use: general planting areas, low banks, around large rocks.

COTONEASTER, CREEPING
(Cotoneaster adpressa).   **Zones 1–3**
Slow growing, mounding, woody, deciduous. Hard to transplant. Best to buy potted plants.
Height: 12 inches **Spacing:** 18–24 inches.
Exposure: requires sun.
Soil: prefers well-drained soil.
Texture: fine.
Flower effects: pink.
Fruit effects: red.
Fall color: deep red.
Use: does well on banks; handsome texture contrasts with rock surfacings.

EUONYMUS, BABY WINTERCREEPER
(Euonymus fortunei
minimus).   **Zones 1(?), 2, 3**
Slow-growing woody evergreen. Not a vigorous spreader.
Height: 2–6 inches. **Spacing:** 12 inches.
Exposure: requires partial shade.
Texture: fine.
Use: general, but confined to small planting masses.

EUONYMUS, COMMON WINTERCREEPER
(Euonymus fortunei
radicans).   **Zones 1(?), 2,3**
Slow-growing woody evergreen. Tends to mound into dense growth. Requires pruning to give prostrate effect. Big-leaf wintercreeper (E. fortunei vegetus) can also be used.
Height: 6–24 inches. **Spacing:** 18–24 inches.
Exposure: either sun or shade; may need protection against sun and wind in winter.
Texture: medium.
Flower effects: not showy.
Fruit effects: orange in fall.
Use: general.

EUONYMUS, PURPLELEAF (Euonymus
fortunei coloratus).   **Zones 1(?), 2, 3**
Slow-growing woody evergreen. Vigorous, dense, close growing. Requires pruning of upright shoots to keep ground-cover effect. Larger leaves than others in group.
Height: 6–18 inches. **Spacing:** 15–18 inches.
Exposure: either sun or shade.
Texture: medium fine.
Flower effects: not showy.
Fruit effects: not showy.
Fall color: purplish-red through winter.
Use: general.

GERMANDER, CHAMAEDRYS
(Teucrium chamaedrys).   **Zones 2–3**
Medium to slow growing, dense, woody evergreen. May need winter protection in Zone 2 and northern half of Zone 3.
Height: 10 inches **Spacing:** 8 inches.
Exposure: requires sun.
Soil: prefers well-drained soil.
Texture: medium to fine.
Flower effects: rose-purple.
Fruit effects: not showy.
Use: general; border edging plant.

GOUTWEED, BISHOPS (Aegopodium
podograria).   **Zones 1–3**
Fast growing, herbaceous, deciduous. Can become a weed.
Height: 8 inches. **Spacing:** 18 inches.
Exposure: either sun or shade.
Soil: tolerates poor soils.
Texture: medium.

Flower effects: not showy.
Fruit effects: not showy.
Use: good for difficult situations.

HONEYSUCKLE, HALLS JAPANESE
(Lonicera japonica
halliana).   **Zones 1(?), 2, 3**
Fast-growing extremely vigorous woody deciduous plant with fragrant flowers.
Height: 24 inches. **Spacing:** 3 feet.
Exposure: either sun or shade.
Texture: medium to coarse.
Flower effects: white to yellow in late spring through fall.
Fruit effects: not showy.
Fall color: bronze.
Use: not recommended for small areas; good for long steep banks because of fast growth and rooting along stems.

IVY, BALTIC (Hedera helix
baltica).   **Zones 1(?), 2, 3**
Fast-growing woody evergreen. Hardier than English ivy.
Height: 6 inches. **Spacing:** 6–12 inches.
Exposure: shade or partial sun.
Soil: prefers rich, moist soil.
Texture: medium.
Flower effects: not showy.
Fruit effects: black in fall.
Use: general garden areas, gentle slopes, and areas where grass will not grow.

IVY, BULGARIAN (Hedera helix
Bulgaria).   **Zones 1(?), 2, 3**
Fast-growing woody evergreen. Rich, shining leaves.
Height: 6 inches. **Spacing:** 6–12 inches.
Exposure: either sun or shade.
Soil: prefers rich, moist soil.
Texture: medium.
Flower effects: not showy.
Fruit effects: black in fall.
Use: general garden areas, gentle slopes, and areas where grass will not grow.

JUNIPER, BLUE RUG (Juniperus
horizontalis wiltonii).   **Zones 1–3**
Fast-growing, extremely flat, spreading evergreen with vivid blue foliage the year round. Blight resistant.
Height: 6–8 inches. **Spread:** 6–8 feet.
Exposure: sun or partial shade.

Descriptive Outlines of Ground Covers

Soil: tolerates dry, sandy soil.

Texture: fine.

Use: planting beds, slopes, terraces.

JUNIPER, CREEPING (Juniperus horizontalis).   Zones 1–3

Medium rate of growth. Woody evergreen, low creeping, not too dense.

Height: 6–12 inches. Spacing: 5–8 feet.

Exposure: requires sun.

Soil: tolerates poor soil.

Texture: fine.

Flower effects: not showy.

Fruit effects: blue berry.

Use: general level areas and banks.

JUNIPER, HENRY SARGENT (Juniperus chinensis sargenti var. Henry). Zones 1–3

Fast to medium rate of growth, flat-spreading evergreen with steel-blue foliage. Excellent, serviceable plant, blight resistant.

Height: 12–18 inches. Spread: 8–10 feet.

Exposure: sun or partial shade.

Soil: tolerates dry, sandy soil.

Texture: fine.

Use: planting beds, slopes, terraces.

JUNIPER, JAPANESE (Juniperus chinensis japonica).   Zones 1–3

Slow-growing woody evergreen, low spreading with upright shoots.

Height: 18–36 inches. Spacing: 5 feet.

Exposure: requires sun.

Soil: tolerates poor soil.

Texture: fine.

Flower effects: not showy.

Fruit effects: blue berry.

Use: planting beds, slopes, terraces.

JUNIPER, SARGENT (Juniperus chinensis sargenti).   Zones 1–3

Fast-growing woody evergreen, low spreading often to 8–10 feet. Blue-green foliage turning to bronze in winter.

Height: 6–12 inches. Spacing: 5–8 feet.

Exposure: requires sun.

Soil: tolerates poor soil.

Texture: fine.

Flower effects: not showy.

Fruit effects: blue berry.

Use: general level areas and banks.

JUNIPER, WAUKEGAN CREEPING (Juniperus horizontalis douglasi). Zones 1–3

Medium rate of growth. Woody evergreen. Blue in summer, turning lavender in fall.

Height: 6–12 inches. Spacing: 5 feet.

Exposure: requires sun.

Soil: tolerates poor soil.

Texture: fine.

Flower effects: not showy.

Fruit effects: blue berry.

Fall color: lavender.

Use: good for large areas and banks.

MAHONIA, CREEPING (Mahonia repens).   Zones 2–3

Slow-growing woody evergreen that spreads by underground roots. Fragrant flowers.

Height: 10 inches Spacing: 18–24 inches.

Exposure: prefers shade or partial shade.

Texture: medium to coarse.

Flower effects: yellow in spring.

Fruit effects: purple black, grapelike in midsummer.

Use: general and in rockeries.

PERIWINKLE, COMMON (MYRTLE) (Vinca minor).   Zones 1–3

Medium-slow growing reliable woody evergreen. Glossy, dark-green foliage. Subject to stem canker.

Height: 3–6 inches. Spacing: 12 inches.

Exposure: either sun or shade.

Soil: tolerates poor soil, but prefers moist situation.

Texture: medium.

Flower effects: blue to lavender.

Fruit effects: not showy.

Use: general level areas, short slopes, and underplanting for trees or shrubs.

ROSE, MEMORIAL (Rosa wichuraiana).   Zones 2–3

Slow growing, dense, woody, deciduous.

Height: 12 inches. Spacing: 8 feet.

Exposure: either sun or partial shade.

Texture: fine.

Flower effects: white in midsummer.

Fruit effects: red in late summer.

Use: adapted to banks; good barrier planting.

SPURGE, JAPANESE (PACHYSANDRA) (Pachysandra terminalis).   Zones 2–3

Slow to medium growth. Woody evergreen that gives good texture accent. Subject to stem rot.

Height: 6–8 inches. Spacing: 12 inches.

Exposure: prefers shade or partial shade.

Texture: coarse.

Flower effects: not showy.

Fruit effects: not showy.

Use: general level areas and under trees where grass will not grow. Blends with yellow or yellow-green but not with blue-green.

THYME, MOTHER-OF- (Thymus serpyllum).   Zones 1–3

Reliable fast-growing woody evergreen. Lowest growing of the ground covers.

Height: 1 inch. Spacing: 6–8 inches.

Exposure: either sun or light shade.

Soil: tolerates poor soils.

Texture: fine.

Flower effects: rose to lilac.

Fruit effects: not showy.

Use: a good matting between stones on terraces or walks.

VIRGINIA CREEPER (Parthenocissus quinquefolia).   Zones 1–3

Fast-growing, rank-growing, woody deciduous plant. Will climb any object.

Height: 18 inches. Spacing: 2 feet.

Exposure: either sun or shade.

Texture: medium to coarse.

Flower effects: not showy.

Fruit effects: purple in summer and fall.

Fall color: rich, crimson-red.

Use: in large areas, particularly adapted to banks.

YARROW, WOOLLY (Achillea tomentosa).   Zones 1–3

Medium rate of growth. Herbaceous evergreen. Withstands light traffic, such as between stepping stones.

Height: 6 inches. Spacing: 12 inches.

Exposure: requires sun.

Texture: medium fine.

Flower effects: yellow.

Fruit effects: not showy.

Use: general.

Descriptive Outlines of Vines

AKEBIA, FIVELEAF (Akebia quinata).   **Zones 1–3**

Moderate to slow growing. Gives light shade. Fragrant flowers. Often becomes bare of foliage. Could become a weed if it escapes.

Height: 12–40 feet.

Method of climbing: twining stems.

Soil: prefers well-drained soil.

Texture: medium to fine.

Flower effects: violet to red in spring.

Fruit effects: purple in early summer (not often formed).

Use: fence, trellis, wall.

BITTERSWEET, AMERICAN (Celastrus scandens).   **Zones 1–3**

Medium rate of growth. Handsome and showy foliage and fruit. Must have male and female plants for fruit development. Can kill shrubs or trees used for support.

Height: 30–40 feet.

Method of climbing: twining stems.

Texture: medium to coarse.

Flower effects: not showy.

Fruit effects: yellow-red in fall.

Fall color: yellow.

Use: good vertical screen, bank, fence.

BITTERSWEET, ORIENTAL (Celastrus orbiculata).   **Zones 1–3**

Medium rate of growth. Handsome foliage. Must have male and female plants for fruit development. Can kill shrubs or trees used for support. Vigorous grower.

Height: 30–40 feet.

Method of climbing: twining stems.

Texture: medium to coarse.

Flower effects: not showy.

Fruit effects: yellow and orange in fall.

Fall color: yellow.

Use: good vertical screen, bank, fence.

CLEMATIS, JACKMAN (Clematis jackmani).   **Zones 2–3**

Medium rate of growth. Vigorous; striking appearance, good color accent. Many varieties available. Likes shade around roots. Can be heavily pruned in spring.

Height: 5–12 feet.

Method of climbing: twining stems and petioles.

Soil: prefers moist and alkaline soil.

Texture: medium.

Flower effects: blue through red to purple in summer and fall.

Fruit effects: not showy.

Use: good in flower gardens as accent or specimen.

DUTCHMANSPIPE, COMMON (Aristolochia durior).   **Zones 1–3**

Fast and rank grower. Requires plenty of room. Coarse texture provides accent, but could be out of scale in small gardens.

Height: 15–30 feet.

Method of climbing: twining stems.

Soil: prefers well-drained soil.

Texture: coarse.

Use: fence, trellis.

FLEECEFLOWER, SILVERVINE (Polygonum auberti).   **Zones 1–3**

Fast-growing, perennial climber, valued for quick cover and for fleecy effect in flower late in season.

Height: 25 feet.

Method of climbing: twining stems and tendrils.

Texture: medium (fine when flowering).

Flower effects: white in spring and late summer.

Fruit effects: not showy.

Fall color: red-green.

Use: fence, slope, wall.

GLORYVINE (GRAPE) (Vitis coignetiae).   **Zones 2–3**

Fast growing, handsome large foliage, brilliant autumn color, vigorous, reliable, covers large areas quickly.

Height: 25 feet.

Method of climbing: forked tendrils.

Soil: prefers moist, rich soil.

Texture: coarse.

Flower effects: not showy.

Fruit effects: purple in fall.

Fall color: brilliant scarlet.

Use: fence, slope, wood or wire supports.

HONEYSUCKLE, HALLS JAPANESE (Lonicera japonica halliana). **Zones 1–3**

Slow establishing itself; then fast growing. Popular fragrant vine, good for all purposes.

Height: 15–30 feet.

Method of climbing: twining stems.

Texture: medium to coarse.

Flower effects: white to yellow in spring through fall.

Fruit effects: black in midsummer through fall.

Use: fence, slope, wall.

HONEYSUCKLE, TRUMPET (Lonicera sempervirens).   **Zones 1–3**

Slow-growing semi-evergreen. Showy flowers, attracts hummingbirds.

Height: 10–20 feet.

Method of climbing: twining stems.

Soil: prefers light moist soil.

Texture: medium to coarse.

Flower effects: scarlet and yellow in spring and summer.

Fruit effects: orange-red in summer and early fall.

Fall color: blue-green.

Use: fence, slope, wall.

HYDRANGEA, CLIMBING (Hydrangea petiolaris).   **Zones 1–3**

Slow establishing itself; then fast growing. Rank grower, attractive flowers. Tolerates either sun or shade, but flowers more heavily in sun. Red bark interesting in winter.

Height: 60–80 feet.

Method of climbing: aerial roots.

Soil: prefers rich, moist soil.

Texture: coarse.

Flower effects: white in summer.

Fruit effects: not showy.

Use: fence, slope, wall.

IVY, BOSTON (Parthenocissus tricuspidata).   **Zones 1–3**

Fast growing, handsome, and rank growing. Withstands city conditions.

Height: 60 feet.

Descriptive Outlines of Vines

Method of climbing: tendrils.

Texture: coarse.

Flower effects: not showy.

Fruit effects: blue in fall.

Fall color: rich red purple.

Use: fence, slope, wall.

MONKSHOOD VINE (Ampelopsis aconitifolia). Zones 1–3

Slow growing; delicately shaped leaves give texture variation.

Height: 10–30 feet.

Method of climbing: tendrils.

Texture: fine.

Fruit effects: yellow to orange in fall.

Use: fence, low wall, trellis.

TRUMPET VINE (TRUMPETCREEPER, COMMON) (Campsis radicans). Zones 1–3

Medium rate of growth. Often bare of foliage at base; clings to wood and stone, but often needs support because of weight. Showy flowers. Attractive variety for northern areas is "Madame Galen."

Height: 30–50 feet.

Method of climbing: aerial roots and twining.

Soil: prefers rich, well-drained soil.

Texture: medium.

Flower effects: orange in summer.

Fruit effects: brown pods, autumn through winter.

Use: accent, specimen, on trellis or wall.

VIRGINIA CREEPER (Parthenocissus quinquefolia). Zones 1–3

Fast-growing, rank-growing woody deciduous plant. Will climb any object.

Height: 30–50 feet.

Method of climbing: tendrils and aerial roots.

Texture: medium to coarse.

Flower effects: not showy.

Fruit effects: purple in summer and fall.

Fall color: rich crimson-red.

Use: fence, slope, wall.

VIRGINSBOWER (Clematis virginiana). Zones 1–3

Medium rate of growth. Handsome, flowering, interesting fruit. Often has a thin base. Prefers sun.

Height: 12–20 feet.

Method of climbing: twining stems and petioles.

Soil: prefers moist and alkaline soil.

Texture. medium.

Flower effects: white in summer.

Fruit effects: gray plumes in fall.

Fall color: yellow.

Use: bank, fence, trellis.

WISTARIA, JAPANESE (Wistaria floribunda). Zones 1–3

Slow growing. Handsome flowers and foliage. Good as climber or trained as a standard. Hard to transplant, slow to reestablish. Many varieties available.

Height: 30 feet.

Method of climbing: twining stems form woody trunk or standard.

Soil: prefers rich loam but tolerates sand.

Texture: medium.

Flower effects: violet-blue in late spring.

Fruit effects: not showy.

Fall color: yellow.

Use: trellis, wall.

Descriptive Outlines of Trees

ASH, BLUE (Fraxinus quadrangulata). Zones 1–3

Fast-growing, broad rounded form with handsome foliage. Heavy, corky bark.

Height: 70–80 feet. Spread: 60 feet.

Rooting habit: fibrous, spreading.

Soil: tolerant to limestone.

Texture: medium.

Fall color: yellow to purple.

Use: lawn.

ASH, GREEN (Fraxinus pennsylvanica lanceolata). Zones 1–3

Fast growing, dense, oblong to round form. Subject to breakage and oyster-shell scale.

Height: 60 feet. Spread: 40–50 feet.

Rooting habit: spreading, shallow.

Soil: prefers moderately moist soil.

Texture: medium.

Flower effects: not showy.

Fruit effects: not showy.

Fall color: yellow.

Use: lawn, street.

ASH, MARSHALL SEEDLESS (Fraxinus pennsylvanica lanceolata var. Marshall seedless). Zones 1–3

Fast-growing, seedless tree with a definite uniform pyramidal shape. Rich, dark, glossy green foliage. Dense crown.

Height: 60 feet. Spread: 50 feet.

Rooting habit: spreading, somewhat shallow.

Soil: prefers moderately moist soils.

Texture: medium.

Fall color: yellow.

Use: lawn, street.

ASH, MORAINE (Fraxinus holotricha var. Moraine). Zones 2–3

A fast-growing small tree, low-growing with upright and narrow form. Bears very little seed. Glossy green foliage.

Height: 35 feet. Spread: 20–25 feet.

Rooting habit: fibrous.

Texture: medium.

Fall color: yellow to purple.

Use: lawn, street.

Descriptive Outlines of Trees

BEECH, AMERICAN (Fagus grandifolia).   **Zones 1–3**
Slow growing, oval to pyramidal, stately, horizontal branching extending to the ground. Interesting form, excellent foliage, and attractive winter bark.
Height: 70–80 feet. **Spread:** 50 feet.
Rooting habit: spreading, shallow.
Texture: medium.
Flower effects: not showy.
Fruit effects: not showy.
Fall color: yellow-orange.
Use: lawn, specimen, also effective planted in masses.

BEECH, EUROPEAN (Fagus sylvatica).   **Zones 1–3**
Slow growing, oval to pyramidal, dense, stately, horizontal branching extending to the ground. Available in cutleaf, columnar, and purple-leaf varieties.
Height: 70–80 feet. **Spread:** 50–70 feet.
Rooting habit: spreading, shallow.
Soil: prefers light soil.
Texture: medium.
Flower effects: not showy.
Fruit effects: not showy.
Fall color: red to yellow or brown.
Use: lawn, specimen.

BIRCH, CANOE (Betula papyrifera).   **Zones 1–3**
Medium rate of growth. Graceful, upright, slender; interesting bark.
Height: 60 feet. **Spread:** 30 feet.
Rooting habit: spreading, descending.
Soil: prefers moist soil.
Texture: medium in summer; fine in winter.
Flower effects: yellow catkins in early spring.
Fruit effects: brown conelike in summer.
Fall color: yellow.
Use: group, lawn, specimen.

BIRCH, EUROPEAN WHITE (WEEPING) (Betula pendula).   **Zones 1–3**
Fast growing; oval, pendulous form, graceful and airy; interesting bark color.
Height: 40 feet. **Spread:** 25 feet.
Rooting habit: spreading, descending.
Soil: prefers light, moist soil.
Texture: fine.

Flower effects: pale yellow catkins before leaves.
Fruit effects: brown conelike clusters in late summer and fall.
Fall color: yellow.
Use: accent, lawn, specimen.

BIRCH, GRAY (Betula populifolia).   **Zones 1–3**
Grows quickly into a graceful, slender tree. Bark is white with triangular black markings. Grows in clumps with slender, resilient trunks.
Height: 30 feet. **Spread:** 20–25 feet.
Rooting habit: spreading, descending.
Soil: rocky to wet.
Texture: fine.
Flower effects: yellow catkins.
Fruit effects: brown, cone-like clusters in late summer.
Fall color: yellow.
Use: lawn.

BIRCH, RIVER (Betula nigra). **Zones 1–3**
Fast-growing, open, pyramidal form with paper-thin red-brown, exfoliating bark. Valued for ability to grow in wet places.
Height: 60 feet. **Spread:** 25–30 feet.
Rooting habit: spreading.
Soil: moist to wet.
Texture: medium-fine.
Flower effects: greenish-yellow catkins.
Fruit effects: brown, cone-like.
Fall color: yellow.
Use: naturalistic, low wet areas.

CHERRY, KWANZAN ORIENTAL (Prunus serrulata var. Kwanzan).   **Zones 2–3**
Medium growing rate, generally growing upright with graceful structure. Outstanding double pink flowers, 2½ inches in diameter contrasted with early spring foliage color of reddish-copper. Glossy, colorful bark.
Height: 18–25 feet. **Spread:** 8–10 feet.
Texture: medium-coarse.
Flower effects: double, pink.
Use: specimen, street, lawn.

COFFEETREE, KENTUCKY (Gymnocladus dioicus).   **Zones 1–3**
Medium rate of growth. Oval form, best used in large areas. Tree structure and branches interesting in winter. Fruit can become a nuisance.
Height: 60–80 feet. **Spread:** 40–50 feet.

Rooting habit: descending.
Texture: medium in foliage; coarse in appearance during winter.
Flower effects: not showy.
Fruit effects: brown pod in fall.
Fall color: yellow.
Use: lawn.

CORKTREE, AMUR (Phellodendron amurense).   **Zones 1–3**
Fast growing, handsome round form, striking bark. Tolerates heat and drouth. Heavy feeder. Sexes separate.
Height: 40–60 feet. **Spread:** 30 feet.
Rooting habit: spreading, shallow.
Texture: medium in summer, coarse in winter.
Flower effects: white, not showy.
Fruit effects: black in fall.
Fall color: bronze.
Use: lawn, street.

CRABAPPLE, FLOWERING (Malus sp.).   **Zones 1–3**
Medium rate of growth. Oval, round, spreading, depending on variety. Striking plant in flower and fruit. Wide selection of flower color, form, and size.
Height: 8–45 feet. **Spread:** 12–35 feet.
Rooting habit: spreading, descending.
Texture: medium.
Flower effects: many colors, white through red, in spring.
Fruit effects: red, yellow, or green in summer and fall.
Fall color: yellow to orange to red.
Use: accent, border mass, group, specimen.

CYPRESS, COMMON BALD (Taxodium distichum).   **Zones 1–3**
Medium rate of growth with narrow pyramidal form while young, and broadly rounded at maturity. Foliage appears late, light feathery appearance. Limited use on small property because of huge size.
Height: 100+ feet. **Spread:** 12–20 feet.
Root habit: long, horizontal.
Soil: rich, moist.
Texture: very fine, soft.
Flower effect: not showy.
Fruit effect: not showy.
Fall color: briefly yellow-orange-brown.
Use: lawn tree for large areas only.

Descriptive Outlines of Trees

DOGWOOD, CORNELIANCHERRY (Cornus mas). Zones 1–3
Medium rate of growth. Oval form. Valued for early flowers, which appear before leaves.
Height: 25 feet. **Spread:** 20 feet.
Rooting habit: spreading, descending.
Soil: prefers rich, well-drained soil.
Texture: medium.
Flower effects: yellow in early spring.
Fruit effects: scarlet in summer.
Fall color: red to green.
Use: border mass, group, hedge, lawn, specimen.

DOGWOOD, FLOWERING (Cornus florida). Zones 2–3
Slow growing, flat crowned, picturesque, horizontally branched. Attractive foliage, flower, and brilliant red berries.
Height: 25 feet. **Spread:** 15 feet.
Rooting habit: descending.
Soil: prefers rich, well-drained soil.
Texture: medium.
Flower effects: white in early spring.
Fruit effects: red in early fall.
Fall color: red to violet.
Use: lawn, shrub border, specimen, street. Effective underplanting in woodland gardens.

FRINGETREE, WHITE (Chionanthus virginicus). Zones 1–3
Slow growing. Upright, spreading form; showy, fragrant flowers. Withstands city conditions.
Height: 10–20 feet. **Spread:** 8–20 feet.
Rooting habit: spreading.
Soil: prefers moist soil.
Texture: coarse.
Flower effects: white in late spring.
Fruit effects: blue in late summer.
Fall color: yellow.
Use: border mass, group, lawn, specimen.

GINKGO (Ginkgo biloba). Zones 1–3
Slow growing. Male tree has pyramidal form. Handsome foliage. Excellent for city conditions; free of pests and diseases. Plant male tree only; female fruit has objectionable odor.
Height: 70 feet. **Spread:** 40 feet.
Rooting habit: spreading.
Texture: medium.
Flower effects: not showy.
Fruit effects: drupe (ill smelling).
Fall color: yellow.
Use: lawn, specimen, street.

GOLDRAINTREE, PANICLED (Koelreuteria paniculata). Zones 2–3
Fast-growing, handsome round tree. Tolerates drouth and wind. Prefers sun. Showy in blossom, followed by attractive fruit. Tends to have weak wood.
Height: 30 feet. **Spread:** 20 feet.
Rooting habit: descending.
Soil: tolerates alkaline soil.
Texture: medium.
Flower effects: yellow in midsummer.
Fruit effects: yellow to brown in late summer.
Fall color: brown.
Use: lawn, specimen, street.

HACKBERRY, COMMON (Celtis occidentalis). Zones 2–3
Fast growing. Oblong to vase-shaped, resembling American elm. Reliable; subject to witches' brooms, which do not harm the tree but make it somewhat unsightly in winter.
Height: 90 feet. **Spread:** 50 feet.
Rooting habit: spreading, shallow.
Texture: fine to medium.
Flower effects: not showy.
Fruit effects: purple in early fall.
Fall color: yellow.
Use: lawn, street.

HACKBERRY, SOUTHERN (SUGAR) (Celtis laevigata). Zones 2–3
Fast rate of growth, spreading — sometimes pendulous — branches, rounded form, foliage open and fine.
Height: 70 feet. **Spread:** 50–60 feet.
Rooting habit: spreading, descending.
Texture: fine.

Flower effect: not showy.
Fruit effect: hard, black berry.
Fall color: yellow.
Use: lawn, street.

HAWTHORN, COCKSPUR (Crataegus crus-galli). Zones 1–3
Fast growing, usually round-headed but sometimes flat. Dense, horizontal branches with long thorns. Foliage glossy, lustrous, and dense. Withstands shearing, hence good for hedges. Thornless variety available.
Height: 35 feet. **Spread:** 25–30 feet.
Rooting habit: descending to tap root.
Texture: medium-fine.
Flower effects: white.
Fruit effects: bright red, persistent into winter.
Fall color: orange to scarlet.
Use: lawn, specimen.

HAWTHORN, WASHINGTON (Crataegus phaenopyrum). Zones 1–3
Fast growing, oval to upright, good color and texture. Excellent in flower, foliage, and fruit. Tolerates pruning.
Height: 30 feet. **Spread:** 20–25 feet.
Rooting habit: taproot.
Texture: medium to fine.
Flower effects: white in midspring.
Fruit effects: red in late summer through winter.
Fall color: red to bronze.
Use: border masses, group, hedge, lawn, street.

HONEYLOCUST, THORNLESS (Gleditsia triacanthos inermis). Zones 1–3
Fast growing, round and spreading, somewhat horizontally branched. Provides light shade, withstands city conditions, blends well with contemporary architecture. Patented varieties available that are both thornless and sterile. All types subject to mimosa webworm.
Height: 75 feet. **Spread:** 40–50 feet.
Rooting habit: descending.
Texture: fine.
Flower effects: not showy.
Fruit effects: brown pods in late summer.
Fall color: yellow.
Use: lawn, street.

Descriptive Outlines of Trees

HORNBEAM, AMERICAN (Carpinus caroliniana). **Zones 1–3**
Slow growing, dense, compact. Tolerates pruning. Excellent color.
Height: 30 feet. **Spread:** 15 feet.
Rooting habit: shallow.
Texture: medium.
Flower effects: not showy.
Fruit effects: not showy.
Fall color: yellow, orange to red.
Use: hedge, street (small areas).

HORNBEAM, HOP (Ostrya virginiana). **Zones 1–3**
Slow-growing, pyramidal form with dense foliage. Somewhat difficult to transplant. Free from serious insects and diseases.
Height: 40–60 feet. **Spread:** 20–25 feet.
Soil: tolerates dry situations.
Texture: medium-coarse.
Flower effect: not showy.
Fruit effect: clusters of bladder-like pods.
Fall color: clear yellow.
Use: lawn.

HORSECHESTNUT, COMMON (Aesculus hippocastanum). **Zones 1–3**
Medium rate of growth. Handsome, oval, showy in flower. Casts dense shade.
Height: 40 feet. **Spread:** 30 feet.
Rooting habit: spreading, descending.
Texture: coarse.
Flower effects: white in spring.
Fruit effects: nut in fall.
Fall color: yellow-brown.
Use: lawn.

HORSECHESTNUT, RUBY (Aesculus carnea brioti). **Zones 1–3**
Medium rate of growth. Large, round, ornamental with striking spring color.
Height: 50–75 feet. **Spread:** 30–40 feet.
Rooting habit: spreading, descending.
Texture: coarse.
Flower effects: scarlet in spring.
Fruit effects: nut in fall.
Use: lawn.

LINDEN, AMERICAN (Tilia americana). **Zones 1–3**
Medium rate of growth. Oval to round form; excellent shade. Requires little attention. Some European species are superior.
Height: 70–80 feet. **Spread:** 50–60 feet.
Rooting habit: spreading, descending.
Soil: prefers well-drained soil.
Texture: coarse.
Flower effects: white to yellow in summer; fragrant.
Fruit effects: not showy.
Fall color: yellow-brown.
Use: lawn.

LINDEN, CRIMEAN (Tilia euchlora). **Zones 2–3**
Medium rate of growth. Round, somewhat pendulous. Excellent bright, glossy foliage.
Height: 50 feet. **Spread:** 40–50 feet.
Rooting habit: spreading, descending.
Texture: medium to coarse.
Flower effects: yellow to white; fragrant.
Fruit effects: not showy.
Use: lawn, street.

LINDEN, GREENSPIRE SMALL-LEAFED (Tilia cordata var. Greenspire). **Zones 1–3**
Medium rate of growth. Dense foliage with narrow-oval form. Tolerates city conditions. Patented variety.
Height: 50 feet. **Spread:** 20–25 feet.
Rooting habit: spreading, descending.
Texture: medium.
Flower effects: yellow to white in early summer.
Fruit effects: nutlet in fall.
Fall color: yellow.
Use: street, lawn.

LINDEN, LITTLELEAF (Tilia cordata). **Zones 1–3**
Medium rate of growth. Dense, tight, pyramidal. Tolerates city conditions.
Height: 50 feet. **Spread:** 40 feet.
Rooting habit: spreading, descending.
Texture: medium.
Flower effects: yellow to white in early summer.
Fruit effects: nutlet in fall.
Fall color: yellow.
Use: lawn, street.

MAGNOLIA, SAUCER (Magnolia soulangeana). **Zones 2–3**
Slow growing; rounded form; particularly effective against a background of evergreens.
Height: 25 feet. **Spread:** 30 feet.
Rooting habit: descending.
Soil: prefers rich, moist soil.
Texture: coarse.
Flower effects: white to purple in early spring.
Fruit effects: rose-pink cone in fall.
Fall color: green to bronze.
Use: lawn, specimen.

MAGNOLIA, STAR (Magnolia stellata). **Zones 2–3**
Slow growing, broad to round. Showy flowers, appearing before leaves; particularly effective against a background of evergreens. Will not tolerate dryness, lime, or fresh manure. Difficult to transplant. Prefers sun.
Height: 8–15 feet. **Spread:** 10–15 feet.
Rooting habit: spreading, shallow.
Soil: prefers rich, moist, slightly acid soil.
Texture: coarse.
Flower effects: white in early spring.
Fruit effects: rosy red in fall.
Fall color: green to bronze.
Use: border mass, lawn, specimen.

MAPLE, AMUR (Acer ginnala). **Zones 1–3**
Medium rate of growth. Very hardy, semi-round, dense. Excellent foliage.
Height: 20 feet. **Spread:** 10–20 feet.
Rooting habit: spreading.
Texture: fine to medium.
Flower effects: not showy.
Fruit effects: red in late summer.
Fall color: scarlet.
Use: lawn, screen, specimen, street.

MAPLE, FASSEN BLACK (Acer platanoides var. Fassen). **Zones 1–3**
Medium rate of growth, broad oval shape, extremely dense. Holds red leaf color throughout summer months. Difficult to grow grass underneath. Withstands city conditions.
Height: 50–60 feet. **Spread:** 30–50 feet.

Descriptive Outlines of Trees

Rooting habit: spreading, feeding roots close to surface.

Soil: prefers moist but well-drained soil.

Texture: coarse.

Flower effects: yellow.

Fruit effects: not showy.

Fall color: red.

Use: lawn.

MAPLE, NORWAY (Acer platanoides). Zones 1–3

Medium to fast growing, broad oval shape, extremely dense. Difficult to grow grass underneath. Withstands city conditions. Showy in blossom.

Height: 50–60 feet. Spread: 30–50 feet.

Rooting habit: spreading, feeding roots close to surface.

Soil: prefers moist but well-drained soil.

Texture: coarse.

Flower effects: yellow in spring.

Fruit effects: not showy.

Fall color: yellow.

Use: lawn, street.

MAPLE, OCTOBER RED AND AUTUMN GLORY (Acer rubrum var. October Red and var. Autumn Glory). Zones 1–3

Medium rate of growth. Very hardy, oval, dense. Excellent foliage, brilliant crimson-red in fall. Leaves persist for longer time than on the Red Maple.

Height: 50–60 feet. Spread: 30–40 feet.

Rooting habit: spreading.

Texture: medium.

Flower effects: red, before leaves.

Fruit effects: red.

Fall color: crimson-red.

Use: lawn, street.

MAPLE, RED (Acer rubrum). Zones 1–3

Fast growing; excellent oval, dense, spreading habit. Good color in all seasons. Showy flowers, brilliant fall color.

Height: 60 feet. Spread: 30–40 feet.

Rooting habit: spreading (seeks water).

Texture: medium.

Flower effects: red before leaves.

Fruit effects: red.

Fall color: crimson.

Use: lawn, street.

MAPLE, SCHWEDLER (Acer platanoides schwedleri). Zones 1–3

Medium rate of growth. Oblong to oval, dense. Withstands city conditions. Interesting foliage, color changes from red in spring to a muted purple-green in summer.

Height: 60 feet. Spread: 30 feet.

Rooting habit: deep, widespreading.

Texture: coarse.

Flower effects: not showy.

Fruit effects: not showy.

Fall color: red.

Use: lawn, street.

MAPLE, SUGAR (Acer saccharum). Zones 1–3

Slow growing, oval, dense, excellent foliage and fall color, reliable. One of our finest native trees.

Height: 80–120 feet. Spread: 50–80 feet.

Rooting habit: spreading, descending.

Texture: medium.

Flower effects: not showy.

Fruit effects: not showy.

Fall color: orange to yellow to red.

Use: lawn, street.

MOUNTAINASH, EUROPEAN (Sorbus aucuparia). Zones 1–3

Fast-growing, oval tree, dramatic when in fruit. Attracts birds. Prefers sunny location.

Height: 35 feet. Spread: 25 feet.

Rooting habit: spreading, shallow.

Texture: medium to fine.

Flower effects: white in spring.

Fruit effects: orange in midsummer.

Fall color: yellow-orange.

Use: lawn and street.

MULBERRY, WHITE (Morus alba). Zones 1–3

Fast growing, broad, rounded. Excellent color, texture, and form. Fruit attracts insects. Use sterile variety if available.

Height: 30 feet. Spread: 25–35 feet.

Rooting habit: spreading, shallow.

Texture: medium.

Flower effects: not showy.

Fruit effects: pale red in late summer.

Fall color: yellow.

Use: group, lawn.

OAK, ENGLISH (Quercus robur). Zones 2–3

Medium rate of growth. Broad, rounded form; strong and massive. Some insect problems.

Height: 75–125 feet. Spread: 80–120 feet.

Rooting habit: taproot.

Texture: medium to coarse.

Flower effects: not showy.

Fruit effects: acorn in second fall.

Fall color: bronze (not as intense as others).

Use: lawn.

OAK, NORTHERN RED (Quercus borealis maxima). Zones 1–3

Medium rate of growth, but faster than most oaks. Broad and round. Excellent shade. Transplants easily.

Height: 70 feet. Spread: 60–75 feet.

Rooting habit: taproot.

Soil: prefers well-drained soil.

Texture: medium to coarse.

Flower effects: not showy.

Fruit effects: brown acorn in fall.

Fall color: red-bronze.

Use: lawn, street.

OAK, PIN (Quercus palustris). Zones 1–3

Fast growing, pyramidal, becoming round in old age. Well-defined horizontal branching; excellent foliage. Blends well with contemporary architecture. Avoid soils with high pH and compacted soils; they can result in iron deficiencies.

Height: 40–70 feet. Spread: 40–50 feet.

Rooting habit: spreading.

Soil: prefers rich, moist soil.

Texture: medium.

Flower effects: not showy.

Fruit effects: brown acorn in fall.

Fall color: bronze-scarlet.

Use: lawn, narrow street, specimen.

Descriptive Outlines of Trees

OAK, WHITE (Quercus alba).   **Zones 1–3**
Slow growing; sturdy, majestic, broad, rounded form. Difficult to transplant.
Height: 80–100 feet. **Spread:** 50–90 feet.
Rooting habit: taproot.
Soil: prefers well-drained soil.
Texture: coarse to medium.
Flower effects: not showy.
Fruit effects: acorn in fall.
Fall color: red to wine.
Use: lawn.

PAGODATREE, JAPANESE (Sophora japonica).   **Zones 1–3**
Fast-growing, reliable, broad oval tree. Withstands city conditions. Showy flowers in late season.
Height: 45–70 feet. **Spread:** 30 feet.
Rooting habit: spreading, shallow.
Soil: tolerates poor, dry soil.
Texture: fine.
Flower effects: yellow in late summer.
Fruit effects: not showy.
Fall color: yellow.
Use: lawn, street.

PEAR, BRADFORD (Pyrus calleryana var. Bradford).   **Zones 1–3**
Medium rate of growth, upright while young to broad oval in maturity. Outstanding in fall color. Pest-free.
Height: 40–50 feet. **Spread:** 30 feet.
Rooting habit: spreading, descending.
Texture: medium.
Flower effects: white.
Fruit effects: small, russet, bears infrequently.
Fall color: yellow, bronze red to dark purple.
Use: street, lawn.

PLANETREE, LONDON (Platanus acerifolia).   **Zones 2–3**
Fast growing; rounded form; interesting flaking bark, exposing underbark of lighter color. Tolerates city conditions. Subject to anthracnose disease.
Height: 80 feet. **Spread:** 50–70 feet.
Rooting habit: spreading.
Soil: prefers moist soil.
Texture: coarse.
Flower effects: not showy.
Fruit effects: not showy.
Fall color: brown to yellow.
Use: lawn, street.

REDBUD (Cercis canadensis). Zones 1–3
Medium rate of growth. Round; excellent foliage; attractive in bloom. Tolerates partial shade.
Height: 20 feet. **Spread:** 12 feet.
Rooting habit: shallow.
Soil: prefers rich, moist soil.
Texture: coarse to medium.
Flower effects: red in early spring.
Fruit effects: not showy.
Fall color: bronze to yellow.
Use: specimen, shrub border, street.

SASSAFRAS, COMMON (Sassafras albidum).   **Zones 1–3**
Medium to slow growing; oval form; fragrant flowers; excellent fall color. Sexes may be separate.
Height: 30–60 feet. **Spread:** 25–40 feet.
Rooting habit: deep descending.
Soil: prefers well-drained soil.
Texture: coarse.
Flower effects: yellow in early spring.
Fruit effects: blue in late summer.
Fall color: orange-red.
Use: border mass, group, lawn, naturalistic plantings.

SERVICEBERRY (Amelanchier laevis).   **Zones 1–3**
Slow growing, irregular but graceful and airy. Interesting bark. Tolerates shade.
Height: 35 feet. **Spread:** 15 feet.
Rooting habit: spreading, shallow.
Texture: fine.

Flower effects: white in midspring.
Fruit effects: purple in late spring.
Fall color: red-bronze.
Use: border mass, group, lawn, specimen.

SILVERBELL, CAROLINA (Halesia carolina).   **Zones 2–3**
Medium rate of growth. Low ascending narrow head; showy in flower. Should be in sheltered location.
Height: 30 feet. **Spread:** 20 feet.
Rooting habit: descending.
Soil: prefers well-drained soil.
Texture: medium.
Flower effects: white in midspring.
Fruit effects: not showy.
Fall color: yellow.
Use: lawn, shrub border, street; most effective when used in front of an evergreen background.

SMOKETREE (Cotinus coggygria).   **Zones 2–3**
Medium rate of growth. Dense, oval form, picturesque. Especially valued for smoky effect from flowers appearing in summer.
Height: 15 feet. **Spread:** 15–20 feet.
Rooting habit: spreading.
Soil: prefers well-drained, poor soil.
Texture: medium.
Flower effects: yellow to lavender (smoky) in midsummer.
Fruit effects: range of colors in late summer.
Fall color: yellow-orange.
Use: border mass, group, lawn, specimen.

SWEETGUM (Liquidambar styraciflua).   **Zones 1–3**
Medium rate of growth. Handsome, pyramidal form; rich foliage color all seasons. Difficult to transplant.
Height: 60 feet. **Spread:** 40 feet.
Rooting habit: taproot.
Soil: prefers moist soil.
Texture: medium.
Flower effects: not showy.
Fruit effects: brown balls in late summer.
Fall color: red-orange to yellow.
Use: lawn, specimen, street.

Descriptive Outlines of Trees

TULIPTREE (*Liriodendron tulipifera*).   **Zones 1–3**

Medium rate of growth. Oblong to spreading form. Showy flowers appear after ten to twelve years. Handsome foliage.

Height: 80 feet.   **Spread:** 30–40 feet.

Rooting habit: spreading, descending.

Soil: prefers well-drained soil.

Texture: coarse.

Flower effects: green and orange in midspring.

Fruit effects: not showy.

Fall color: yellow.

Use: lawn, street.

TUPELO (BLACK GUM) (*Nyssa sylvatica*).   **Zones 1–3**

Medium rate of growth. Picturesque, pyramidal, irregular form. Outstanding fall color, and excellent winter form. Sexes separate. Lustrous foliage.

Height: 70–90 feet.   **Spread:** 30–50 feet.

Rooting habit: descending to tap.

Soil: likes moist or wet soil.

Texture: medium.

Flower effects: not showy.

Fruit effects: blue in midsummer.

Fall color: orange, red, scarlet.

Use: border mass, group, lawn, specimen.

YELLOW-WOOD, AMERICAN (*Cladrastis lutea*).   **Zones 1–3**

Medium rate of growth. Broad oval form, graceful, excellent foliage; subject to scale.

Height: 35–40 feet.   **Spread:** 40 feet.

Rooting habit: spreading, shallow.

Soil: prefers rich, moist soil; does well in alkaline soil.

Texture: medium.

Flower effects: white in late spring (fragrant).

Fruit effects: green in late summer.

Fall color: yellow.

Use: border mass, lawn, specimen.

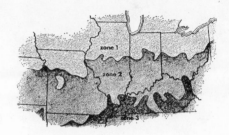

ZELKOVA, JAPANESE (*Zelkova serrata*).   **Zones 2–3**

Fast growing, graceful, vase-shaped. Excellent shade, similar to American elm.

Height: 50–90 feet.   **Spread:** 40–80 feet.

Rooting habit: spreading, shallow.

Soil: prefers moist soil.

Texture: fine to medium.

Flower effects: not showy.

Fruit effects: not showy.

Fall color: yellow to russet.

Use: lawn, street.